Trends and Issues in Business Education

National Business Education Association Yearbook, No. 50

2012

Editor
Wanda L. Stitt-Gohdes
University of Georgia
Athens, Georgia

Published by

NBEA

National Business Education Association
1914 Association Drive
Reston, VA 20191-1596
(703) 860-8300 • Fax: (703) 620-4483
www.nbea.org

Trends and Issues in Business Education

Copyright © 2012 by the National Business Education Association

National Business Education Association
1914 Association Drive
Reston, VA 20191-1596

ISBN 0-933964-76-5

The Web addresses listed were accurate when this book was written but may have changed since publication.

TABLE OF CONTENTS

Major Trends and Issues Affecting Business Education Curriculum Development

Judith Lambrecht
University of Minnesota
Minneapolis, MN

Cyril Kesten
University of Regina
Regina, Saskatchewan

Integrating Business Ethics in Business Courses

O. C. Ferrell
Linda Ferrell
University of New Mexico
Albuquerque, NM

Integration of Soft Skills into Business Classes

Susan L. Miertschin
Sharon Lund O'Neil
Jamison Kovach
David S. Ding
University of Houston
Houston, TX

Betty S. Johnson
Stephen F. Austin State University
Nacogdoches, TX

Stacey McCroskey
Strayer University–Northwest Houston
Houston, TX

PREFACE

The *2012 NBEA Yearbook* is developed in five units, which provide the framework for a review of current trends and issues in business education. This organizational structure provides common places for important discussions on a number of factors affecting business education today and into the future.

Unit One, "Issues and Trends Impacting Education for Business," begins with chapter 1 and a thought-provoking discussion of a collection of factors deemed key elements in business education for the future. The second chapter on ethics and sustainability provides foundational information easily used in many business education classes. The third chapter on integration of soft skills into business classes offers a wealth of information on exactly what soft skills are and how they may be included in everyday instruction.

Unit Two, "Critical Issues in the Core Content Areas," includes three chapters. The first addresses the changing accounting curriculum at both secondary and post-secondary levels. A discussion of the Pilot and Bridge Project, hopefully leading to the advanced placement accounting course, is also included. Chapter 5 discusses issues in economic education and personal finance, a topic that is especially timely. Then, chapter 6 reviews current issues relevant to entrepreneurship and related basic business skills.

Unit Three, "The Impact of Technology," includes two chapters. Chapter 7 reviews a variety of the ever-present technological trends affecting business education—some here on *terra firma* and some in the "Cloud"! Chapter 8 discusses a wide variety of social media tools and how they may enhance classroom instruction.

Unit Four, "Business Programs at Various Levels," includes three chapters, which describe current trends and issues at, respectively, the middle/high school, postsecondary, and college/university levels. The fourth chapter presents a review of model business education programs.

Unit Five, "Professionalism," is an appropriate topic on which to conclude this yearbook. The three chapters in this unit address professional association membership, research in business education, and business teacher preparation and certification.

As is always the case, this *2012 NBEA Yearbook* provides a wealth of information and insight into those trends and issues directly affecting business education from a variety of perspectives. As editor, I am extremely grateful to all those authors who answered the call to develop a chapter for this yearbook. Writing such a piece is demanding work—work that is ultimately reviewed and used by one's peers. What has emerged from this hard work is a valuable resource for business education professionals at every level. I am privileged to have had the opportunity to work with these talented writers.

Wanda L. Stitt-Gohdes
Editor, *2012 NBEA Yearbook*
University of Georgia
Athens, Georgia

ACKNOWLEDGMENTS

The Editorial Review Board provided exemplary feedback throughout this project. In addition to critically evaluating the chapter manuscripts, they contributed to the development of the table of contents and thesis statements that served as the basis for the chapter manuscripts. Each chapter was blind reviewed by three reviewers through separate review cycles. Their time and effort is greatly appreciated.

Faridah Awang
Eastern Kentucky University

Rose Marie Kuceyeski
Owens Community College

Marsha Bayless
Stephen F. Austin State University

Judith Lambrecht
University of Minnesota

Herbert F. Brown
Appalachian State University

Nancy Noe
Linn-Benton Community College

Tamra Davis
Illinois State University

Kimberly Schultz
Kirkwood Community College

Rita Davis
Eastern Kentucky University

Barbara Tietsort
University of Cincinnati

Roger Fulk
Wright State University–Lake Campus

Lila Waldman
University of Wisconsin–Whitewater

Barbara Hagler
Southern Illinois University Carbondale

Ivan Wallace
East Carolina University

Ronda Henderson
Middle Tennessee State University

Lynn Wells
Zane State College

Cyril Kesten
University of Regina

Major Trends and Issues Affecting Business Education Curriculum Development

Judith Lambrecht
University of Minnesota
Minneapolis, MN

Cyril Kesten
University of Regina
Regina, Saskatchewan

As part of the broad field of education, business historically has been one of the most popular elective areas at the secondary level and frequently the largest major field of study for students at the collegiate level (Davis, 2007; "Top 10 College Majors," 2011). Business knowledge is viewed as essential for everyone to be able to function as citizens in the full range of social engagements touched by economics—as household members, consumer decisionmakers, employees, employers, and entrepreneurs, and as leaders in a range of institutions who must deal with budgets and financial decisions. Key questions related to this needed business knowledge include the following: Where does one learn how to participate economically? Where in our education system should formal engagement in business instruction be located? Who should teach this content? Should such content be required of all students? What is the nature of the outcomes sought?

These questions are not unique to business education. However, current social forces —economic, technological, and cultural—are changing the answers to these questions. Business education must also be aware of and respond to these changing factors.

THE COMMONPLACES

Schwab (1973) pointed out that curriculum making relies on knowledge and understanding of what he calls "commonplaces": the learner, the teacher, the milieu, and the subject matter. These commonplaces have become a common lens through which educational environments are investigated and analyzed (Craig, 2008; Clandinin, Pushor, & Murray Orr, 2007; Gowin, 1981; Novak & Gowin, 1984; Sack, 2008). By suggesting questions for each of the areas, Schwab's commonplaces allow us to investigate and understand any educational context:

Learners: Who are the students? Why are they in that context? What are their skills? What motivates them? What kind of learners are they? What assumptions are being made about learning?

Teachers: Who are the teachers? Why are they in that context? What skills do they bring? What motivates them? What is their purpose in teaching? What skills do they need? What is the role of the teacher in relation to the students, the subject matter, and the milieu?

Milieu: What is the social context of the classroom? Of the school? Of the jurisdiction? Of the community? How do students relate to each other, to the teacher, to the curriculum? What are the cultures of the school? Who decides who can teach? Who decides how to assess educational outcomes? Who decides who pays for education?

Subject matter: What subject matter is pertinent? What is the structure of the subject matter? What is the nature of the content? What skills are necessary to master this type of content? What skills are necessary to teach this type of content?

These commonplaces are used in this chapter to understand the trends and issues facing business educators that were identified in a recent Delphi study.

DELPHI STUDY ABOUT THE FUTURE OF BUSINESS EDUCATION

This Delphi Study (Lambrecht & Kesten, 2005; Lambrecht, 2007; Kesten & Lambrecht, 2009; Kesten & Lambrecht, 2010) consisted of three stages during which data were collected, analyzed, and synthesized in order to focus business educators on the issues facing them now and for some time in the future.

The third stage culminated in responses to 20 statements that described issues and trends facing business educators. For this chapter we reorganized these responses to explore these issues and trends through the lens provided by Schwab's commonplaces.

IDENTIFYING TRENDS THROUGH THE COMMONPLACES

Ten of the statements were associated with the subject matter of business education. This is not surprising, because as Ravitch observed, "Reform efforts begin with what students should know and be able to do (the curriculum) and then proceed to other parts of the educational system to support the goals of learning" (Ravitch, 2010, p. 32). Three of the statements related to the milieu of education. Six were concerned with teaching and one statement dealt specifically with student characteristics. Space does not permit discussion of each of the Delphi statements, so the broad issues and trends within each cluster will be discussed. First, subject matter trends and issues identified in the final stage of the Delphi study will be addressed.

Subject Matter Trends and Issues

The subject matter of business education will be examined from the following perspectives: the overall purposes of the field, focus on career pathways, integration of academic content and preparation of students to critique the field, implications of teaching "soft" skills, and implications of technology as business content.

Purposes of business education. Business teachers have consistently confirmed the employment-preparation purposes of business education, employment that may begin after high school or college. They feel less strongly that business education represents general education for all students. There was even less agreement that economics was foundational to the field; some teachers thought accounting, communication, or technology was more foundational. The place of economics within the business education curriculum needs continued attention by the field, especially as economics is the one business content area regularly identified as part of a common core curriculum for educational programs as a whole (Common Core, 2009; Partnership for 21st Century Skills, 2006a and 2006b). If business educators are to provide leadership for and participation in common core curriculum development, then the field needs to continue to provide visible, dynamic leadership in the development and teaching of economics. The Delphi study also showed concerns about the breadth of technology preparation for which business education is responsible; personal use applications, business applications, and career preparation in areas including networking, Web design, and programming. These findings prompt us to believe that key questions about the uniqueness of business education and breadth of the field ought to be explored.

Business education is not unique regarding the purpose of education as employment related. In fact, all of the major statements about education in general in the past 30 years have used economic arguments to justify its importance (Grubb & Lazerson, 2004). Education is viewed as necessary for citizens to be able to compete in a global economy. Furthermore, the education of most value in competing for the best jobs, especially the best-paying jobs, is a four-year degree (Carnevale, Smith, & Strohl, 2010).

Ultimately, the argument is made that the best employment-related education is an academic education that prepares students for college (Carnevale & Desrochers, 2003; Partnership for 21st Century Skills, 2004). Using current language, the goals of secondary education are to prepare students who are "college- and career-ready" (Achieve, 2009; "Race to the Top," 2009), but these goals merge into "college ready" when the majority of jobs are judged to require at least a two-year degree (Carnevale, Smith, & Strohl, 2010).

The value of academic preparation for eventual postsecondary school success is such that federal and state testing mandates focus on teaching and testing basic academic skills. Elective courses in high schools have shrunk in number as schools focus limited and shrinking resources on school reform and on assisting students to meet required standards (Fouts, Baker, Brown, & Riley, 2006; Giles, 2006; Ravitch, 2010). When the primary aim of education is believed to be employment preparation, whether for education in general or for business education specifically, and the best preparation for employment is judged to be academic college prep, the result is a narrowing of the curriculum. A focus on college prep with fewer options means reduction in the breadth of curriculum and lack of responsiveness to a wide range of student needs and interests. And business education, as it is historically construed, will be part of the reduction.

In a high school environment where the primary goal is preparation for college, the business program may be encouraged to offer advanced placement courses, such as in economics, or to participate in other dual enrollment programs, which allow students to obtain postsecondary course credits while in high school. Dual enrollment options can include taking courses on actual college campuses while still a high school student or taking courses that offer college-level credit in the high school building where students are enrolled. The cost savings for parents and students can be considerable if a semester or even a year of college credits can be accumulated while a student is in high school. Business programs that can participate in these dual-purpose offerings may be seen as more attractive electives (Karp, Calcagno, Hughes, Jeong, & Bailey, 2007). If such courses can be organized into Career Pathways (Brand, 2008; States' Career Clusters Initiative, 2011), potential exists for planning articulated programs among secondary and postsecondary institutions.

Career pathways. Of 16 career cluster or career pathways (States' Career Clusters Initiative, 2011), five are related to business: business management and administration, finance, hospitality and tourism, information technology, and marketing, sales, and service. Each of these main areas encompasses four to seven separate career fields, and all of these areas assume more fundamental prior preparation such as career exploration, the legal environment of business, personal finance, personal-use technology, business communication, and business math. Business education is a broad field, and within the context of the professional organizations that focus on strategic planning for the future, professionals need to consider whether such breadth can reasonably be encompassed in a single teaching license. Can bachelor-level preparation, even with the expectation of business work experience, provide sufficient depth of preparation for teaching courses ranging from economics to Web development?

Academic integration and critique of the field. The data from the Delphi study showed that business educators were in relatively high agreement that students should be prepared to critique business practices and business employment settings. To engage in such critique, indeed, to prepare students who can look at business practices from different perspectives, business teachers need depth of subject-matter preparation. The Delphi data also showed that, although business teachers agreed that academic content (language and numeracy) should be integrated into business courses, the business content was primary. Again, the charge of integrating rigorous academic content into business courses while focusing on challenging business content requires in-depth content knowledge and business experience. Such expertise requires continued reconceptualization of what business teacher preparation includes—a topic to be addressed further when the "commonplace" of teaching is discussed below.

Teaching "soft" skills. Reports such as those from the Partnership for 21st Century Skills (2004) argue that the best preparation for employment is the same as the academic preparation for college, but differences of opinion exist about this similarity. The demands of the workplace are not necessarily the same as those of academia (Barton, 2006). Over the years, surveys of employers have documented different sets of skills that lead to successful employment or that lack of these skills leads to employment termination. Attaining these skills in high school is of particular importance for students who do not choose to continue to postsecondary education. For students who do pursue further education immediately after high school, the cost of higher education may require that they work while in school. Success in employment matters, and this success depends on the educational opportunities available in the K–12 system.

The nature of the distinctive employment skills that affect hiring and termination decisions can generally be characterized as the "soft" skills, the type of skills identified by the 1991 Secretary's Commission on Achieving Necessary Skills (SCANS) study. The importance of "soft skills" was reiterated by labor economists Murnane and Levy (Murnane & Levy, 1996; Levy & Murnane, 2004) and is the focus of a monograph for teaching these "soft" skills (Wilhelm, Logan, Smith, & Szul, 2002). When employers such as the National Association of Manufacturers have been asked why workers have been rejected for employment, the basic competency at the top of the list has been "inadequate basic employability skills" (Barton, 2006). These "soft" employability skills are of an ambiguous nature, as their application is context dependent. Using the SCANS language, they contain such capabilities as the following:

- Reading, writing, arithmetic/mathematics, listening, and speaking

- Thinking skills of creative thinking, decisionmaking, problem solving, seeing things in the mind's eye, knowing how to learn, and reasoning

- Personal qualities of responsibility, self-esteem, sociability, self-management, and integrity/honesty

When presented with such a list, a teacher will think of examples contextualized within the subject matter taught. The Delphi study asked business teachers, if "soft" skills were the core of business education, whether the field would be indistinguishable from other subject areas that also teach those skills. The answer was "no"; the context in which these skills are taught is so compelling and important that business cannot avoid teaching this content. The need for these skills was considered to be so great that it was appropriate that "soft" skills be integrated into many parts of the curriculum.

There is a link between teaching "soft" skills and integrating academic content in a visible and rigorous way; business content allows such skills and capabilities to come to life. If these skills are to be developed by students in a way that leads to meaningful involvement in employment, then the employment context matters; such employment-related skills are not likely to transfer from more general education areas. The challenge for business teachers is to use this evidence to retain visible business content in the secondary curriculum.

Technology as business content. Technology as a business content area was included in several of the final 20 Delphi statements, and dealing with this area means looking at the overlap in the commonplaces among content, teaching, and the milieu in which teaching occurs. At least two important issues and trends stem from the breadth of the technology area and the interest on the part of several teaching fields and even individual teachers, in addition to business, for teaching technology skills.

Regarding the first issue related to the breadth of the technology area, respondents to the Delphi study viewed the higher-end, technology career-preparation areas to be part of business education along with personal-use applications and career-related desktop applications. Respondents also acknowledged that teaching in higher-end career areas depended on special teacher expertise. The technology areas of Web development, programming, game and video development, and network management are considered "higher end" because of their complexity and because they generally require prior technology coursework. Desktop computer applications are needed by all students and should be required for all students before high school graduation. In contrast, the higher-end career areas are different; these areas are not intended as general education for all students, and career preparation needs to be coupled with business content. Ultimately, application software use needs to be integrated into business subject-matter courses, not taught solely as stand-alone software courses. Furthermore, many career areas require postsecondary education, so secondary-level offerings are necessarily career exploration and preparation for more advanced coursework.

A key question to ask is whether secondary-level teachers in their licensing programs get adequate preparation to teach the breadth of the technology areas as well as preparation for other core areas of business. Given the scope of the business field as a whole, is it reasonable that adequate preparation be part of an initial teacher license?

The second trend and potential issue affecting business teachers is that teachers in other subject areas teach technology-related content, not just business teachers. The higher-end career areas of Web programming, game and video development, and network administration are often taught by teachers who possess special interest and expertise in these high-tech areas. This expertise is likely to have been gained through employment experiences and self-learning, as well as formal education. Although special expertise is needed to teach higher-end career applications of technology, personal-use computer applications can be taught in ways that draw on common, every day, and school-related problems. This means that many teachers, in addition to business teachers, want to teach applications software (word processers, spreadsheets, presentation software, databases, and the Internet). In some states, all teachers, including business teachers, can teach personal-use computer applications through state licensing endorsements. Student interest in technology makes it attractive content by itself as well as a teaching tool for teachers across all content fields. Staff configurations in a school and reputations for teaching expertise determine which subject-matter fields/departments among the several licensed to teach computing skills are actually assigned to teach such technical content. The issue for business teachers is whether priority needs to be given to career-related courses for which business content is conspicuously necessary, or in contrast, whether secondary-level technology courses, particularly desktop applications, should be viewed as personal use and open to any qualified teacher. And what should business teachers do when licensing allows teachers from several fields to teach personal-use content? A related question, of course, can be raised for other business content. Business teachers have shared economics, law, and consumer and personal finance courses with other licensing fields. How can business teachers present themselves as the most highly qualified to teach these courses?

Educational Milieu

Several trends and issues affecting business education come from forces outside the educational system itself, forces that control who can teach certain subjects (alluded to above regarding teaching technology-related courses), how programs are to be funded, and how decisions will be made about student success or about accountability, as well as demographic and economic forces that demand certain types of content and approaches to teaching. In the Delphi study used as the basis for this chapter, two potential sources of funding were considered problematic: dedicated federal and state funds for career and technical education (CTE) and the potential of funding from non-public sources such as business and industry and foundations. Regarding accountability, external testing and certifications are available in business areas and teachers need to decide how these will affect what they teach. The Delphi study also asked business teachers about the importance of preparing students for outside credential assessments. Both funding and external assessments are addressed next.

Funding of business programs. Federal CTE funds have been important for business education since the passage of the 1963 Vocational Education Act and continuing through the current Perkins IV funding. Such funds have supported the purchase of up-to-date equipment, provided staff development, and mandated such aspects of teaching as the provision of vocational student organizations and specialized teacher licensing rules. As important as this funding has been, it presents two key problems: it separates business programs receiving these funds from the rest of the general education programs in a school, and it makes such programs vulnerable when these funds shrink, which they have done at the secondary level in many states for the past decade (Lynch, 2000; National Association of State Directors of Career and Technical Education, 2010).

Relying on business or other externally sourced funding would be equally precarious. External sources of funds often also come with the "strings" of expecting certain types of programs and outcomes, reducing the control of professional educators over their work. Again, business educators need to clarify the purposes to be served by business programs at different educational levels and to become part of the larger debate about educational funding.

External assessment and certification. Regarding educational accountability mandates from outside of local school programs, business programs as part of CTE programs have been asked to offer programs for which external certifications are available, such as Microsoft Office Specialist certification (Austin, 2010; Collins, 2010). Secondary-level advanced placement offerings, such as in the business subjects of economics and potentially accounting, are also examples of external assessment. The respondents to the Delphi survey agreed that, although such credentials can be attractive to students, they carry the risk of narrowing the curriculum to focus on standardized tests. Such tests necessarily focus on more easily tested objective content or software procedures rather than open-ended problem solving. Business teachers need to consider ways to incorporate both external confirmations of students' accomplishments as well as potentially more complex performance-based assessments. Business teachers have a long history of creating and using performance-based tests to assure that students possess in-depth understanding directed toward solving realistic business problems. It is time to affirm and continue this legacy.

Teachers and Teaching

Trends and issues related to teaching have already been raised on the interest in teaching technology-related content as well as other business content on the part of many teachers and other subject areas. The Delphi study supporting this discussion asked teachers whether business content could reasonably be taught by other groups of teachers or whether there were specialized methodological practices unique to business. Part of these specialized teaching practices includes a focus on procedural skills; questions need to be raised about whether there is an overemphasis on procedural teaching by business teachers. Procedural teaching is most prominent in courses teaching computing skills using some of the most popular textbooks. These textbooks have a high concentration of step-by-step presentations of computer operations, thus encouraging attention to explicit procedures in contrast to discovery of different options for accomplishing a software goal. A teacher may need to trade comprehensive coverage of software features with the assignment of end-of-chapter activities that ask for open-ended problem solving without extensive prompting of software steps.

Questions were also raised about whether online or alternative routes to teacher licensing were adequate to prepare high-quality business teachers. Related to the topic of teacher preparation, the Delphi respondents were also asked about the role of professional organizations in ongoing professional development. Issues related to specialized teaching methodology, alternative and online teacher licensing, teaching procedural skills, and the role of professional organizations are discussed next.

Specialized teaching methodology. The question about the existence of specialized business teaching methodology drew the highest degree of disagreement of the 20 Delphi questions; respondents thought business was unique as a teaching field because of its focus on skills and the need for teaching procedural understandings. Without specialized courses in business teaching pedagogy, these unique teaching skills would not automatically be part of a teacher's repertoire. The absence of specialized courses would also lead to a lack of awareness of how to integrate student vocational organizations into the curriculum or how to develop and manage cooperative/internship programs.

Alternative and online teacher preparation. However, Delphi respondents agreed that the specialized methodologies that are part of business education could likely be conveyed by high-quality alternative licensing programs, including online instruction. Alternative licensing programs aimed at career changers were to be encouraged, as long as the alternative pathways focused on quality preparation, not just expedited progress. Online programs were also seen as promising—given quality development and ongoing assessment of student progress. Continued attention needs to be given to those aspects of teaching that benefit from face-to-face engagement as well as ways to use a variety of media to bring teachers and students together to learn in a mobile and decentralized way.

Teaching procedural skills. Teaching procedural skills has a long history in the field. So does teaching critical thinking and problem solving, both of which accompany the procedural skills of using software. Business teachers need special expertise in teaching complex learning and problem solving (van Merriënboer & Kirschner, 2007). If an issue exists, it may be whether the field provides appropriate balance in teaching how software works in contrast to using software for open-ended problem solving that focuses on business needs. Furthermore, does the field offer an opportunity to critique the use of software, that is, how it is used to support learning or to support given business practices?

Moving beyond procedural teaching on any business topic takes time and is unpredictable. Giving students more latitude to develop solutions to problems of a variety of kinds—software, personal finance, marketing, business planning, or management—means more teacher preparation, more instructional time, and more grading time than assigning well-structured tasks. Students learn when they question, and they question when answers are not self-evident and when solutions break down. Do business teachers know how to work in such indeterminate settings? Or, do large classes and a set curriculum compromise their instructional choices?

Role of professional organizations. Professional organizations were seen by the Delphi respondents as important vehicles for providing ongoing professional development as well as providing leadership for legislative issues, such as funding, licensing, and accountability. As the number of specialized business teacher education programs has shrunk, business teachers need to make greater use of professional organizations and other organizational media tools to communicate and focus their collective efforts. The identity of the field historically has been reflected through professional organizations, and such gatherings will continue to be ways for business teachers to overcome the isolation of being the sole representative of business in a local school. Leadership through professional organizations will continue to be important as a way to retain the vitality of the field.

The Learner Roles

The final stage of the Delphi study, the 20 statements on which this chapter has focused, did not ask directly about teachers' assumptions about student learning. But we can infer some things about the nature of the business education learner. Such questions were part of the first stage of Delphi questions, and unanimity of opinion meant that none of these became part of the next Delphi stages. This does not mean that assumptions about learning and how teachers should respond to students' needs have all been settled.

Two of the statements in the third stage of the Delphi study asked teachers to think about globalization and the need for and place of cross-cultural education within business education. Our respondents generally agreed that cross-cultural studies should be a significant part of a student's business education. The World Trade Organization (2007) reports that "The volume of world trade since 1950 has increased twenty-seven fold from $296 billion to more than $8 trillion in 2005" (p. xxxii). The American economy is a global economy. Therefore, the focus on integrating cross-cultural issues into the business education classroom will become even more important.

Participants in the third stage of the Delphi study also agreed that, given the globalization of our economy and the diversity among the students in our schools, business education should distinguish itself as a content area in which students with differing backgrounds and mother tongues other than English can thrive and in which business teachers have special preparation for integrating all students into business courses. The primary trend coming out of this issue is dealing with students for whom English is not their first language. According to the U.S. Census Bureau's *Statistical Abstract of the United States* (2011), net immigration to the United States between 2000 and 2009 totaled in excess of 7.7 million people. Of these, it is likely that a very large segment were children who were unable to speak or understand English. In 2008, according to the same report, more than 55 million people reported that the language spoken at home was something other than English.

These children will appear in our classrooms and will benefit from business education preparation. They will likely retain another language besides English and thus will have an advantage in coping with the increasing globalization of business and industry. In the past, students needing extra support while learning English have been enrolled in keyboarding. This will likely continue to be the case. Beyond keyboarding instruction, business teachers need to become skilled in integrating English language learners into all business courses.

As all teachers are asked to be responsive to a diversity of student backgrounds and student needs, are business teachers prepared to respond intelligently to the students they meet in their classes? As all teachers are asked to be accountable to pre-set outcomes, do business teachers have the freedom to notice that a variety of outcomes may be more appropriate for different students? Business teachers generally teach elective courses that give them more freedom to choose both the desired student outcomes and their teaching practices. Elective courses can free both teachers and students to think about important problems in business. Business courses, thus, offer teachers the luxury of being able to respond more flexibly than other teachers to students' interests and learning needs. This means business teachers have a special opportunity to engage students in business topics that will affect students' lives as economic citizens.

SUMMARY
Of the "commonplaces" of education articulated by Schwab (1973)—content, milieu, teachers, and learners—the primary issues and trends affecting business education have come from the need to define the content domain. Over the years, business educators have maintained a strong commitment to the dual purposes of the field—"for and about business." However, the "about" business purposes include sharing the teaching of several content areas with other licensing fields—economics, consumer and financial literacy, law, personal-use technology, math, and communications. Even the "for" business area is shared with other fields for the career-focused technology areas. The irony of this technology overlap is that business education as a field is dominated by interest in teaching technology-related topics. A key question for business teachers is this one: How should the field address the breadth of technology-related content in a way that is distinctive to business?

The specialized career areas in marketing, including entrepreneurship education, may still be largely in the business domain, although marketing as a field still likes to consider itself to be separate from "business," especially when membership in professional organizations is concerned. The keyboarding area has migrated to the elementary- and middle-school levels, although business teachers still participate in the teaching of this course and identify keenly with this skill as part of technology (Lambrecht,

Kyle, & Cherry, 2008; Rader and Meggison, 2007). Does this leave accounting as the primary business course taught by business teachers without involvement of other fields? Is accounting an example of career preparation, college preparation, or personal use, a key way for many students to enter into conversation about the big ideas related to business? If accounting is not the key exemplar of uniquely business content at the secondary level, what is? Furthermore, if career preparation is the unique hallmark for business purposes, how does shrinkage in state and federal career funding (and the shrinkage of elective courses in general in schools) affect these offerings? Can creating curricula that respond to external assessment demands, such as advanced placement offerings and other career credentials, enhance the attractiveness of business electives? Furthermore, can increased articulation with postsecondary business programs build bridges for students and career opportunities for business teachers? The "milieu" in which business education operates has become more complex, as external forces both narrow the curriculum focus and increase external accountability for educational accomplishments.

Business educators need to continue to clarify the distinctive features of the business curriculum for which they assume responsibility. This decision will drive decisions about the licensing preparation appropriate for business teachers, preparation that in the future will be provided by several alternative routes. Both the commonplaces of content and milieu work together to tailor workplace demands and preparation opportunities available for business teachers. Thus the commonplace of the teacher's role is a by-product of external demands as well.

Beyond the need to clarify the nature of the field and to deal with the serendipity of school funding and accountability demands, other social pressures on the field are shared in common with all subject areas—the need to recognize the global economy and society and to offer courses supportive of students' diverse learning needs. The commonplace of the learners has changed in the past several decades to include students with more diverse needs and interests than were recognized throughout most of the 20th century. All teachers face the need for eventually developing individualized learning plans for all students as they now do for those with recognizably distinct learning needs. These special learning needs range from including English language learners as active learners as well as responding to the learning needs of immigrant students and students with a myriad of special health and daily-living needs. Teaching in the business field has become more complex and demanding, but the teaching task becomes more focused and satisfying when the domain of the business education field is established and supported by both sound teacher preparation and professional development support.

REFERENCES

Achieve. (2009, December). *Race to the top: Accelerating college and career readiness in states.* Retrieved from http://www.achieve.org/RTTT-Sustainability

Austin, J. T. (2010). *Certificates and certifications: Credential clarification is critical!* Columbus: Ohio State University, Center on Education and Training for Employment. Retrieved from http://www.cete.org/_documents/Certificates%20and%20 Certifications.pdf

Barton, P. E. (2006). *High school reform and work: Facing labor market realities.* Policy Information Report. Princeton, NJ: Educational Testing Service. Retrieved from http://www.eric.ed.gov/ERICWebPortal/search/detailmini.jsp?_nfpb=true&_& ERICExtSearch_SearchValue_0=ED492034&ERICExtSearch_SearchType_0=no& accno=ED492034

Brand, B. (2008). *Supporting high quality career and technical education through federal and state policy.* Washington, DC: American Youth Policy Forum. Retrieved from http://www.aypf.org/documents/SupportingHighQualityCTE.pdf

Carnevale, A. P., & Desrochers, D. M. (2003). *Standards for what? The economic roots of K–16 reform.* Princeton, NJ: Educational Testing Service. Retrieved from http:// www.learndoearn.org/For-Educators/Standards-for-What.pdf

Carnevale, A. P., Smith, N., & Strohl, J. (2010). *Help wanted: Projections of jobs and education requirements through 2018.* Washington, D. C.: Georgetown University, Center on Education and the Workforce. Retrieved from http://www9.georgetown. edu/grad/gppi/hpi/cew/pdfs/FullReport.pdf

Clandinin, D. J., Pushor, D., & Murray Orr, A. (2007, January/February). Navigating sites for narrative inquiry. *Journal of Teacher Education, 58*(1), 21–35.

Collins, D. A. (2010, July). *Industry assessments for CTE students: IC3®, Microsoft® Office and Adobe® certifications.* PowerPoint presentation at Georgia CTE 2010 Summer Conference, Atlanta, GA.

Common Core. (2009). *Why we are behind: What top nations teach their students but we don't.* Retrieved from http://www.commoncore.org/_docs/CCreport_ whybehind.pdf

Craig, C. J. (2008). Joseph Schwab, Self-study of teaching and teacher education practices proponent? A personal perspective. *Teaching and Teacher Education: An International Journal of Research and Studies, 24*(8), 1993–2001.

Davis, H. (2007, January 2). Most popular majors. *The Most Popular Journal.* Retrieved from http://most-popular.net/majors-college

Fouts, J. T., Baker, D. B., Brown, C. J., & Riley, S. C. (2006). *Leading the conversion process: Lessons learned and recommendations for converting to small learning communities.* Tucson, AZ: Fouts & Associates.

Giles, C. (2006). Sustaining secondary school visions over time: Resistance, resilience and educational reform. *Journal of Educational Change, 7*(3), 179–208.

Gowin, D. B. (1981). *Educating.* Ithaca, NY: Cornell University Press.

Grubb, W. N., & Lazerson, M. (2004). *The education gospel: The economic power of schooling.* Cambridge, MA: Harvard University Press.

Karp, M. M., Calcagno, J. C., Hughes, K. L., Jeong, D. W., & Bailey, T. R. (2007). *The postsecondary achievement of participants in dual enrollment: An analysis of student outcomes in two states.* St. Paul, MN: University of Minnesota, National Research Center for Career and Technical Education.

Kesten, C. A., & Lambrecht, J. J. (2009). *Future directions for business education: A Delphi study.* Final report. Little Rock, AR: Delta Pi Epsilon Foundation.

Kesten, C. A., & Lambrecht, J. J. (2010). Future directions for business education: A Delphi study. *The Delta Pi Epsilon Journal, 52*(2), 57–76.

Lambrecht, J. J. (2007). Business education Delphi study of future directions for the field: TAG responses. *The Delta Pi Epsilon Journal, 49*(1), 15–25.

Lambrecht, J. J., & Kesten, C. A. (2005). Business educators' assessments of trends, assumptions, and actions affecting practice in the field. *Business Education Forum, 60*(1), 44–48.

Lambrecht, J. J., Kyle, J., & Cherry, J. (2009, April). *Survey of Minnesota Business Education Programs.* Presentation at NABTE Research Conference, NBEA, Chicago, IL.

Levy, F., & Murnane, R. F. (2004). *The new division of labor: How computers are creating the next job market.* Princeton, NJ: Princeton University Press.

Lynch, R. L. (2000). *New directions for high school career and technical education in the 21st century* (Information Series No. 384). Columbus, OH: ERIC Clearinghouse on Adult, Career, and Vocational Education.

Murnane, R. J., & Levy, F. (1996). *Teaching the new basic skills: Principles for teaching children to thrive in a changing economy.* New York, NY: Free Press.

National Association of State Directors of Career and Technical Education Consortium. (2010, November). *A look inside: A synopsis of CTE trends.* Silver Spring, MD: Author.

Novak, J. D., & Gowin, D. B. (1984). *Learning how to learn.* New York, NY: Cambridge University Press.

Partnership for 21st Century Skills. (2004). *Learning for the 21st century.* Retrieved from http://www.p21.org/storage/documents/P21_Report.pdf

Partnership for 21st Century Skills (2006a). *Are they really ready to work? Employers' perspectives on the basic knowledge and applied skills of new entrants to the 21st century U.S. workforce.* Retrieved from http://www.p21.org/documents/FINAL_REPORT_PDF09-29-06.pdf

Partnership for 21st Century Skills. (2006b). *Results that matter: 21st century skills and high school reform.* Retrieved from http://www.p21.org/documents/RTM2006.pdf

"Race to the top: Promising approaches to achieving college- and career-ready goals (goal 1)." (2009, March). *ECS* [Education Commission of the States] *Briefing Memo, Promising Practices.* Retrieved from http://www.ecs.org/clearinghouse/79/97/7997.pdf

Rader, M., & Meggison, P. (2007). The business education curriculum. *The Delta Pi Epsilon Journal, 49*(1), 26–31.

Ravitch, D. (2010). *The death and life of the great American school system: How testing and choice are undermining education.* New York, NY: Basic Books.

Sack, J. J. (2008) Commonplace intersections within a high school mathematics leadership institute. *Journal of Teacher Education, 59*(2), 189–199.

Secretary's Commission on Achieving Necessary Skills. (1991). *What work requires of schools: A SCANS report for America 2000.* Washington, DC: U.S. Department of Labor.

Schwab, J. (1973). The practical 3: Translation into curriculum. *The School Review, 81*(4), 501–522.

States' Career Clusters Initiative. (2011). *Career clusters: Pathways to college and career readiness.* National Career Technical Education Foundation. Retrieved from http://www.careertech.org/career-clusters/glance

"Top 10 college majors." (2011). *The Princeton Review.* Retrieved from http://www.princetonreview.com/college/top-ten-majors.aspx

U.S. Census Bureau. (2011). *Statistical abstract of the United States.* Washington, DC: Government Printing Office.

Van Merriënboer, J. J. G., & Kirschner, P. A. (2007). *Ten steps to complex learning: A systematic approach to four-component instructional design.* New York, NY: Lawrence Erlbaum Associates.

Wilhelm, W. J., Logan, J., Smith, S. M., & Szul, L. F. (2002). *Meeting the demand: Teaching "soft" skills.* Little Rock, AR: Delta Pi Epsilon.

World Trade Organization. (2007). *World trade report 2007, Six decades of multilateral trade cooperation: What have we learnt?* Retrieved from http://www.wto.org/english/res_e/booksp_e/anrep_e/world_trade_report07_e.pdf

Integrating Business Ethics in Business Courses

O. C. Ferrell

Linda Ferrell

University of New Mexico

Albuquerque, NM

Teaching business ethics requires an understanding of the organizational dimensions of ethical decisionmaking. Although most people believe that employees learn to be ethical at home and school and through life experiences, the work environment creates challenges for even the most ethical person. For example, employees cannot always make independent ethical decisions due to a corporate culture that has many types of managers and employees using their own concepts of right and wrong. Managers sometimes pressure employees into questionable activities. However, business ethics becomes more transparent once an organization establishes codes of ethics, as well as compliance requirements and ethical leadership. The objective of this chapter is to provide some essential strategies for integrating business ethics into business courses. The authors examine the role of stakeholders, implications of the global financial crisis, and important issues in teaching business ethics, as well as providing resources to integrate business ethics successfully into a course.

THE IMPORTANCE OF BUSINESS ETHICS

Business courses provide an essential and dynamic foundation for students developing their business careers. Although it is important to teach many traditional concepts such as human resources and marketing, emphasizing emerging topics that are reshaping the changing world of business today, including business ethics, is crucial. Trust—or the lack of it—in business has become a major issue in our society. In fact, only 46%

of consumers in the United States trust business to do what is right, according to the 2011 Edelman Trust Barometer. Trust of business is a global issue too, as only 48% of French consumers and 44% of U.K. consumers trust business to do what is right (Edelman, 2011). There is no doubt that the recent financial crisis has destroyed trust in business due to a decline in housing values and to high unemployment and government bailouts. Even governments are facing difficulties in meeting their financial obligations, as can be seen by Standard & Poor's downgrade of the U.S. debt from a AAA to AA+ rating ("Looking for someone to blame," 2011). Questionable ethical decisionmaking in the financial industry has probably contributed to an overall drop in trust of business. Addressing business ethics is important in providing a foundation for understanding how to succeed in business. Many educators have limited experience in addressing business ethics, and providing a framework to teach this important topic can be helpful (Sims & Sims, 1991).

Incorporating business ethics into coursework as early as possible is important so that students may begin to explore their own morality juxtaposed with how an organization might view ethics and ethical behavior. This first requires that they understand their own values and ethical principles and how they can use their personal moral compass to assist them in an organization. Students may find that, while working in an organization, their personal ethics do not always coincide with the values and codes of conduct of that organization (Lewis, 2002). Individuals experience ethical conflict when they think their own personal values do not align with their organization (Navran, 2002). In such cases, students and newly hired employees lack the knowledge and experience needed to deal with complex business ethics issues (Elango, Paul, Kundu, & Paudel, 2010). Telling students to just do the right thing fails to consider the "gray areas" associated with most organizational ethical issues. The nature of an ethical decision is to examine alternatives and select the right one based on more than one person's opinion. Therefore, the first step in understanding ethical issues is recognizing what constitutes individual and organizational interests and concerns.

A key concept that students must learn is that they may have problems making the correct ethical decisions based on the many conflicts that can exist. According to Tseng and Fan (2011), an organizational ethical climate influences employee attitudes toward ethics as well as how they participate in activities. The first step is to know more about one's personal ethical perspective and the second is to understand the organization's ethical perspective. Ethical leadership by top managers clarifies roles, generates approaches to ethical decisionmaking, and establishes fairness. Research indicates that having conscientious, agreeable leaders is positively related to ethical leadership (Kalshoven, Den Hartog, & De Hoogh, 2011). Instructors can explain this ethical decisionmaking environment to help students assess their own ethics and explore the ethical dilemmas in the workplace. One way to discuss balancing interests in ethical decisionmaking is to introduce the stakeholder perspective.

STAKEHOLDERS AND ETHICAL DECISIONMAKING

Stakeholders are individuals, groups, and communities who can directly or indirectly affect a firm's activities. Although most corporations emphasize shareholders as the most important stakeholder group, failure to consider all significant stakeholders can lead to ethical lapses. Stakeholders include employees, investors, regulators, suppliers, communities, clients, and shareholders (Maignan, Gonzalez-Padron, Hult, & Ferrell, 2011). Some executives believe that if their companies adopt a market orientation and focus only on customers and shareholders, everything else will take care of itself. Unfortunately, failing to recognize the needs and potential impact of various stakeholders can lead to regrettable consequences.

A strategy to ascertain the needs of stakeholders is to recognize the relationship among ethics, social responsibility, and quality management (Tarí, 2011). Research has shown that a culture that focuses on all stakeholders and values a team orientation and openness in internal communications leads to improved financial performance (Maignan, et al., 2011). Therefore, those stakeholders with interests or concerns must be identified, and the organization needs to gather information and respond to these important stakeholders in a positive manner.

Hence, business ethics programs must identify and prioritize stakeholders and their concerns about organizational activities as well as gather information to respond to significant individuals, groups, and communities. For example, at one time Walmart focused mainly on customers and on the lowest prices possible. This approach likely contributed to the abuse that led to an employee class-action lawsuit against Walmart filed in 2001, in which Walmart managers were alleged to have denied employees meal and restroom breaks and forced them to work off the clock ("Wal-Mart to Face," 2005). Today, Walmart recognizes the importance of employees and community issues such as sustainability. Stakeholder groups apply their own ethical values and principles to their perception of many diverse issues. They supply resources—for example, capital, labor, expertise, infrastructure, sales, etc.—that are critical to a firm's long-term survival, and their ability to withdraw these resources is power.

One approach to stakeholders is to deal proactively with their concerns and ethical issues and stimulate a sense of bonding within the firm. When an organization listens to stakeholder concerns and tries to resolve issues, the result is tangible benefits that can translate into customer loyalty, employee commitment, supplier partnerships, and improved corporate reputation. This requires going beyond basic regulatory requirements and making a difference by genuinely listening to stakeholders and addressing their concerns. Firms that do this demonstrate a fundamental interconnectedness of all entities in the market system (Mish & Scammon, 2010).

In the financial industry many ethical issues are related to transparency and truthfulness about complex intangible products such as derivatives. When firms look only at the financial incentives for employee performance, they lose sight of important stakeholder responsibilities, such as providing relevant product information. To achieve expected results, employees may bend the rules and their firm can limit transparency to manipulate decisions or use legal loopholes. These firms fail to recognize today's changed societal context of business, which necessitates addressing multiple stakeholders. According to Smith, Drumwright, and Gentile (2011), businesses must (a) identify stakeholders, (b) determine stakeholder salience, (c) research stakeholder issues and expectations and measure impact, and (d) engage with stakeholders and embed a stakeholder orientation in all of the firm's activities.

LEGISLATION RELATED TO BUSINESS ETHICS

The beginning of the 21st century was marked by a number of corporate scandals that prompted the need for major legislation. It started with the accounting scandals discovered at Enron and Arthur Andersen in 2001. The scandal caused thousands of employees to lose their jobs and their retirement savings, as well as the demise of the firms. The next year saw even more incidents of fraud at WorldCom (2002) and Tyco (2002). While Tyco was able to recover, WorldCom filed for bankruptcy. These scandals prompted the government to pass the 2002 Sarbanes-Oxley Act (referred to as SOX), which mandated a new way of doing business. This corporate reform legislation responded to growing concerns over the financial reporting of firms. SOX was designed to help assure distrustful stakeholders that corporations would now be subject to greater oversight in order to restore key stakeholder confidence. At the time the legislation passed, a poll by the *Wall Street Journal* and NBC found that 57% of the general public believed that "standards and values of corporate leaders and executives had dropped in the last 20 years" (Hellweg, 2002). SOX improved financial disclosures, offered whistle-blower protection, and encouraged ethical standards and expectations of financial officers.

Unfortunately, SOX did not deter the disastrous corporate misconduct that occurred less than a decade later. Perhaps no event highlights the importance of ethical business conduct in recent years as much as the global financial crisis beginning in 2008. Subprime mortgages (loans provided to people who would not normally qualify for a loan) and the use of complex financial instruments were major contributors to the crisis. Although a variety of different factors led to the crisis, most originated from the willingness of businesses to sacrifice ethics and long-term sustainability for short-term gains (Crotty, 2009). Many companies had an incentive system that rewarded executives and employees for bringing in profits without monitoring how these profits were generated. This lack of accountability led employees to engage in questionable conduct to obtain desired incentives (Crotty, 2009). For instance, Countrywide Financial was the biggest provider of "liar loans"—loans provided to homeowners without proof of assets or income. Today, we are still trying to unravel the financial crisis, but it all started through risky investments and liar loans to encourage those without enough resources to obtain home loans.

The financial crisis caused the government to create a new law aimed at widespread financial reform. The Dodd-Frank Wall Street Reform and Consumer Protection Act was passed in 2010 to increase "accountability and transparency" in the financial industry, protect stakeholders from deceptive financial practices (Falaschetti, 2011), and establish a new Consumer Financial Protection Bureau to protect consumers from unsafe financial products (Reddy, 2010). Part of the responsibility of this bureau is to make financial products and services easier to understand, curtail unfair lending and credit card practices, and ensure the safety of financial products before their launch into the market (Liberto & Ellis, 2010).

However, not all laws that affect the ethical decisionmaking of business occurred after major misconduct disasters. For the past 20 years, the Federal Sentencing Guidelines for Organizations have provided incentives for organizations to develop organizational ethics and compliance programs (Johnson, 2004). The 2004 and 2008 amendments to the guidelines require organizations' boards of directors to be well informed about their organizations' ethics programs regarding content, implementation, and effectiveness. In fact, the board is required to budget adequate resources and provide authority for developing and maintaining ethics programs. There must be confidential mechanisms or hotlines so that employees and agents may report or seek guidance on ethical issues without any fear of retribution. Furthermore, the board must identify ethical issues and design and implement an effective program to deal with organizational risks, modifying the program as needed over time to maximize overall performance.

How does all this legislation relate to teaching business ethics? Students should learn that some aspects of business ethics have been institutionalized through legally mandated directives. This means that requirements for responsible ethical conduct have been mandated through requirements for legal compliance.

New Business Ethics Priorities and Performance Results

Business ethics is now, it is hoped, a high priority for top corporate executives and boards of directors. Although some aspects of business ethics are being legislated by the Sarbanes-Oxley Act, Federal Sentencing Guidelines for Organizations, and the Dodd-Frank act, companies are ultimately responsible for improving business ethics in all of their business decisions. The legislation has helped institutionalize business ethics, and today, ethics programs are a core requirement to avoid misconduct and a tool to develop ethical organizational cultures. For example, a code of ethics should address risk for a firm's senior financial officers in their decisions, as well as the immediate disclosure "of any change in or waiver of" the code of ethics. Such transparency should reduce opportunities and temptations to "cook the books." Indeed, the New York Stock Exchange now requires listed companies to create written ethics codes for their employees and board members (Stern, 2002). Business ethics, when properly implemented and infused into strategic planning, provides an opportunity to craft a corporate culture that does not have to be overly concerned about the presence of regulatory oversight in order to do the right thing. *Ethisphere* (2010), a leading business ethics magazine, developed an index of the world's most ethical companies. Proof exists in the 2010 ranking that it pays to be ethical in business. When comparing the stock performance of the world's most ethical companies with the Financial Times Stock Exchange 100 and the Standard & Poor's 500, the World's Most Ethical (WME) Index performs significantly better. This answers an important question about the impact of business ethics in financial performance.

Business educators can demonstrate the importance of ethical decisionmaking through a class discussion that focuses on WME companies. Many students or educators may believe that unethical companies make more profits. The data related to Ethisphere's WME companies indicate that a responsible corporate reputation translates into profits. Students could form teams and discuss some of the WME companies and compare them with companies not on this list that have been involved in serious misconduct.

What the Global Financial Crisis Taught Us about Business Ethics
Students need to know that business ethics can be a difficult area to manage, especially in areas such as accounting and finance in which very complex products affect many stakeholders. The global financial crisis provides the perfect opportunity to discuss how the complexity of financial instruments such as derivatives and collateral debt obligations are often seen through the narrow scope of a broker or sales agent assigned to provide these products to customers. The same is true in any organization in which employees do not take a holistic view of how their decisions fit into the total organizational outcome. Challenging students to deal with these complex decisions in the classroom will provide them the opportunity to see the need for more than just one individual's perspective about the right thing to do in business ethics.

The failure to understand and manage ethical risks played a significant role in the financial crisis and the ensuing Great Recession. Although there is a difference between bad business decisions and business misconduct, there is also a thin line between the ethics of using only financial incentives to gauge performance and the use of holistic measures that include ethics, transparency, and responsibility to stakeholders. From chief executive officers (CEOs) to traders and brokers, lucrative financial incentives had existed for performance in the financial industry before the crisis (Crotty, 2009). These incentives still exist today, but the consequences of misconduct should help individuals and organizations see the benefits of the responsible use of incentives. A major part of the financial crisis was the financial industry's culture of focusing on the bottom line. Wall Street is a highly interconnected system rife with opaque decisionmaking, lack of accountability, and unreliable accounting methods. CEOs received sometimes hundreds of millions of dollars in compensation, even for poor performance or when misconduct occurred during their watch. Lower-level traders received huge commissions for transactions, regardless of the firm's economic outcome. Ethical concerns were isolated within a silo, and codes of conduct became mere window dressing. Combine this with rampant leveraging and the widespread use of complex computer models that few understood and the financial system became a volatile house of cards. It did not take much to bring the system to its knees.

Many who should have known were ignorant of the risks because of risk "compartmentalization," wherein strategic business units within corporations are unaware of the big picture in terms of the consequences of their actions. A good example is Google's $500 million settlement with the Justice Department. The Justice Department charged Google with deliberately accepting hundreds of millions of dollars from Canadian online pharmacies for posting advertisements that resulted in illegal sales of prescription drugs in the United States. Google's sales department for online advertisements either failed to see the consequences of this misconduct or intentionally engaged in misconduct (Catan, 2011). Although most companies endeavor to comply with the legal system, they often look for loopholes and unregulated means of maximizing profits and financial rewards. The regulatory system needed remaking to better govern safety, conduct, and systematic risk to stakeholders. Many companies are trying to do what is ethical; however, because of the complex nature of the global economy, individuals—far too concerned with their own interests—do not always avoid misconduct.

WHY TEACH BUSINESS ETHICS?

The first decade of the 21st century, with its highly visible corporate misconduct, has called our attention to the often underaddressed area of business ethics in business courses. Instructors arm students with tools, techniques, and frameworks to succeed in business. But how much have they done to enlighten students about the risks of misconduct, the importance of standards of appropriate conduct, and an understanding of the complex ethical issues that students will likely face in their careers?

Of course, personal values are extremely important to succeeding in business. Many managers believe that the key to managing organizational ethics is hiring "good" people with strong personal moral development. However, it is often difficult for employees to stand up to superiors or question their authority. No one at Enron questioned their managers until the federal investigations began. They seem to have assumed that if people above them knew what was going on, the burden of responsibility was lifted from their shoulders. Enron's lawyers and accountants were also telling top management that they were operating legally. Many operations were so complex that few employees understood how they all fit together in the organization (Ferrell & Ferrell, 2011). To improve business ethics, organizational systems must support, reinforce, and educate what behaviors are expected of employees. The good news is that research has found that in supervisor–subordinate relationships, attempts to deceive subordinates will negatively impact desired outcomes. In other words, deceptive managers will destroy relationships and even their own promotability (Carlson, Carlson, & Ferguson, 2011).

Can Ethics Be Taught?

All this discussion begs the question, "can ethics be taught?" Looking at the available evidence that psychologists have provided (Velasquez, Andre, Shanks, & Meyer, 1987), the answer is "yes." Still, many believe ethics cannot be taught because it is developed at an early age and cannot be changed (Churchill, 1982). As a reply, Velasquez, et al. (1987) wrote the following:

> The issue is an old one. Almost 2,500 years ago, the philosopher Socrates debated the question with his fellow Athenians. Socrates's position was clear: Ethics consists of knowing what we ought to do, and such knowledge can be taught.

Velasquez, et al. (1987) agreed with Socrates's conclusions and cited support from contemporary psychologists. They went on to summarize the studies of psychologist James Rest, whose findings are described as follows:

- Dramatic changes occur in young adults in their 20s and 30s in terms of the basic problem-solving strategies they use to deal with ethical issues.

- These changes are linked to fundamental changes in how a person perceives society and his or her role in society.

- The extent to which change occurs is associated with the number of years of formal education (college or professional school).

- Deliberate educational attempts (formal curriculum) to influence awareness of moral problems and to influence the reasoning or judgment process have been demonstrated to be effective.

- Studies indicate that a person's behavior is influenced by his or her moral perception and moral judgments (Velasquez, et al., 1987).

Traditional students sit in business ethics classes and say ethics is common sense, black and white. They sometimes look at ethical issues in business and fail to see the gray. However, this seems to happen less to those students coming back to school after gaining several years of work experience. Teachers of business ethics never forget the phone calls or e-mail from former students who are thankful for the class as their careers are developing or who ask for advice about a specific ethics issue they face. When discussing business ethics in class, students usually have personal experiences and want to provide their perspectives.

A Teaching Business Ethics Perspective

One approach to teaching business ethics is focusing on the different moral philosophies and looking at personal approaches to making ethical decisions. Instructors who want to take this approach should examine Forsyth's Taxonomy of Ethical Ideologies. These four distinct ethical perspectives include the following:

> (a) situationism, which advocates a contextual analysis of morally questionable actions; (b) absolutism, which uses inviolate, universal moral principles to for-

mulate moral judgments; (c) subjectivism, which argues that moral judgments should depend primarily on one's own personal values; and (d) exceptionism, which admits that exceptions must sometimes be made to moral absolutes. (Forsyth, 1980, p. 175)

This taxonomy can be reduced to the philosophy of relativism versus idealism, in which idealism is associated with universal moral rules (Forsyth, 1980). Learning about these different ethical perspectives can help students in developing individual critical thinking skills and assist them in understanding how values and principles can be part of ethical decisionmaking. Students learn to use their own moral compass to access ethical decisions. It is almost impossible to change these personal ethical perspectives in an organizational context. Firms encourage cultural diversity, which will result in employees with different ethical perspectives or what is sometimes called ethical diversity. There is no agreement on universal moral principles, and many people believe that exceptions must be made to moral absolutes. Therefore, students need to understand how to navigate ethical conflicts and know when to refuse to participate in unethical or illegal conduct in the workplace.

Approaching business ethics from a descriptive, as opposed to normative, approach is not without controversy, of course. A descriptive approach describes how things are being done, whereas a normative approach describes a more idealistic view of what ought to be. Many business leaders believe that personal moral development and character is all that is needed to have effective business ethics.

Hiring ethical employees with good character can provide the foundation for limiting unethical behavior when combined with a strong ethical culture (Treviño, Brown, & Wall, 2004). Business educators often believe that ethical values and business knowledge are two different worlds. One world involves values such as truthfulness, honesty, and transparency, and the other world involves the unique business dilemmas that are faced on a daily basis. The two worlds need to be integrated so that values can be understood in the context of the employee's competence to make business decisions. In other words, there are many gray areas, and it is not always obvious what is honest, truthful, or transparent.

However, for most organizations, ethical leadership can help employees from diverse backgrounds with different personal ethical values gain a shared understanding of what is defined as ethical behavior, thus creating an ethical organizational culture. To help students understand these dynamics in business ethics, changes are needed in both the way business ethics courses are taught and in societal approaches to the development and implementation of business ethics in corporate America. For example, case studies are very useful when discussing different sides of ethical dilemmas. Debate on ethical business issues that encourages students to voice their positions is also helpful. A later section in this chapter provides resources for these teaching tools.

ORGANIZATIONAL AND INDIVIDUAL DIMENSIONS OF BUSINESS ETHICS

Ethics has been called the study and philosophy of human conduct, with an emphasis on the determination of right and wrong. For managers, ethics at work refers to principles, rules, or standards governing the conduct of organizational members. Business ethics can be defined as the principles and standards that determine acceptable conduct in business organizations.

Business ethics in the context of an organization should address ethical risks facing the firm and industry. Besides codes of ethics, training, and compliance requirements, organizations rely on a legal foundation for appropriate adherence to laws and regulations. Laws and regulations can be quite complex and unique depending on the industry. However, strong codes of ethics and training programs can act as a good buffer for avoiding legal entanglements.

Businesses that demonstrate good ethical leadership provide role models for developing an effective ethical organizational culture. For instance, Waste Management CEO David Steiner is leading the company in a new organizational direction. Although Waste Management is the nation's largest waste handler, it is also the largest recycler. Waste Management is investing in ways to capture and reuse the energy and materials that are found in waste, including recycling common products such as compact fluorescent light bulbs. Waste Management is promoting an ethical organizational culture that adopts a long-term perspective to sustainability (Gunther, 2010; "Waste Management named," 2010).

The fundamental difference between an ordinary organizational decision and an ethical decision is the added concern about the decision being right or wrong. Whether a certain behavior is judged right or wrong—ethical or unethical—is often determined by the stakeholders involved, including the mass media, interest groups, customers, the legal system, and/or public opinion. Although these groups are not necessarily "right," their judgments influence society's acceptance or rejection of an organization and its activities. Consequently, their values, judgments, and outcomes all play a critical role in ethical decisionmaking. Society may institutionalize these processes through legislation and social sanctions or approval.

In reality, ethical decisions are often difficult, and in some cases, it is not easy to say that a business decision is either ethical or unethical. For example, although derivatives are not necessarily unethical, the 2008 financial crisis resulted from the use of derivatives in ways that almost caused our entire financial system to collapse (Eisinger, 2008). Business decisions sometimes result in unintended consequences that no one can predict. Decisions have to be reviewed and sometimes reversed after more information from stakeholders is available.

Ethical Challenges from an Individual Perspective

Most people would agree that high ethical standards require both organizations and individuals to conform to sound moral principles. However, a couple of special factors must be considered when applying ethics to business organizations. First, to survive, businesses must obviously make a profit. Second, businesses must balance their desire for profits against the needs and desires of society. Maintaining this balance often requires compromises or tradeoffs. To address these unique aspects of business ethics, society has developed rules—both explicit or legal, and implicit—to guide owners, managers, and employees in their efforts to earn profits in ways that do not harm individuals or society as a whole. Organizational practices and policies often create pressures, opportunities, and incentives that may sway employees to make unethical decisions. News articles often describe some "decent, hard-working family person" who had a highly ethical personal life engaging in illegal or unethical activities in business. The *Wall Street Journal* reported that Betty Vinson, a mid-level accountant for WorldCom, was asked by her superiors to make false accounting entries. She balked at least seven times but ultimately caved in to management and made illegal entries to bolster WorldCom's profits. At the end of 18 months, she had helped falsify at least $3.7 billion in profits (Pulliam, 2003). When an employee's livelihood is on the line, it is tough to say no to a powerful boss.

The integrity standards we learn in our personal lives may not always prepare us for ethical pressures at work. It is encouraging that after recent scandals and widespread observation of misconduct in the workplace, more employees appear to be reporting ethical misconduct in their organizations (Ethics Resource Center, 2009). But if employees still perceive misconduct, clearly ethical problems and issues remain.

Organizational Responsibilities in Business Ethics

Understanding organizational ethics is important in developing ethical leadership. An individual's personal values and moral philosophy are only one factor in the decisionmaking process that can raise potential legal issues. It is true that moral rules can be related to a variety of situations in life and some people do not distinguish everyday ethical issues from those that occur on the job. Students must understand the application of rules and principles in a work environment. They cannot succeed just by using their own perspectives about what is ethical or unethical, as most people judge their own behavior based on intentions and judge others based on their behavior. This means that individuals often hold others to a high standard and rationalize or fail to see their own ethical lapses (Bazerman & Tenbrunsel, 2011).

Just considering yourself to be an ethical person may not be sufficient to handle the ethical issues that arise in the workplace. Students are often told to do the right thing and be ethical. Without both legal and ethical training, how can they define what is "the right thing"? Recognizing the relationship between legal and ethical decisions is important. Although abstract virtues such as honesty, fairness, and openness are often assumed to be self-evident and accepted by all employees, a high level of personal moral development may not prevent an individual from violating the law in an organizational context, where even experienced lawyers debate the exact meaning of the law. Because organizations are ethically diverse, a collective agreement on workplace ethics is as vital as other managerial decisions. For example, would an organization expect to achieve its mission without communicating goals to employees? Would a company expect to implement an information technology initiative without educating every employee on their responsibilities in the process? Workplace ethics needs to be treated similarly: with clear expectations on what comprises ethical conduct.

The 2010 Dodd-Frank act provides financial consumer protection through specific requirements for consumer information. The 2002 SOX created rules and principles for accounting ethics. What are the acceptable ethical practices associated with decisions related to hiring, firing, diversity, and discrimination? What does the Better Business Bureau do to resolve marketplace ethical disputes fairly with the use of self-regulation and consumer education? It is impossible for your students to navigate this complex ethical and legal world of business without a foundation in understanding organizational ethics. Business decisionmaking is based on knowledge, critical thinking, and experience. Making the appropriate ethical decision relies on all of these factors, and good decisionmaking is enhanced through an organization that provides an ethical work environment.

Even experienced managers need to have formal training about workplace ethics to help them identify both legal and ethical issues. Changing regulatory requirements and ethical concerns, such as workplace and consumer privacy issues, make the ethical decisionmaking process very dynamic. With the establishment of values and training, a manager will be in a better position to assist employees and customers and provide ethical leadership.

Ethical Decisionmaking and Ethical Climate
An individual's personal values and experiences along with organizational factors influence whether he or she will make an unethical decision (Ferrell & Gresham, 1985). Although it is impossible to describe precisely how or why an individual or a work group might make unethical decisions, average or typical behavior patterns exist within organizations: research indicates that managers and coworkers have the most influence on the decisionmaking process. With this knowledge, managers can use their influence to help guide and control the ethical decisionmaking of employees in the business environment (Ferrell & Gresham, 1985).

Students need to recognize the risks associated with organizational pressure in ethical decisionmaking. Certain personality traits are associated with ethical behavior. For example, Boddy (2011) reports "strong, positive, and significant correlations between the ethical issues of bullying and unfair supervision in the workplace and the presence of Corporate Psychopaths" (p. 367). Furthermore, Boddy's study estimates "that about 26% of bullying is accounted for by 1% of the employee population, those who are Corporate Psychopaths" (p. 367).

Perhaps most important, students need to recognize that acquiring knowledge and experience in business ethics is just as necessary as in other areas of business, such as marketing, accounting, management, and finance. Success in business ethics requires lifelong learning about this important topic.

As a component of corporate culture, the ethical climate comprises the character and decision processes used to determine whether a firm's responses to issues are right or wrong. The ethical climate includes key values that determine the rationales for the selection of issues and the choices that relate to the firm and its stakeholders; thus, it indicates whether organizations have an ethical conscience and defines behavioral expectations when addressing ethical issues. The ethical climate encompasses the values, traditions, and pressures exerted in the workplace to make legal and ethical decisions. It involves formal values and compliance requirements as well as an understanding of how interpersonal relationships affect the informal interpretation of ethics. In an ethical work climate, employees are able to identify ethical issues as they arise and are aware of the company resources available to help them act ethically and according to organizational policy and culture. An ethical climate characterizes businesses that are committed to business ethics and social responsibility.

Students often believe that they will do the right thing in any organizational culture. Organizing a debate around the topic of individual ethics compared with the influence of the organization will promote different viewpoints and discussion.

RESOURCES FOR TEACHING BUSINESS ETHICS

As part of a grant for expanding business ethics education, the authors have developed a Web site (http://danielsethics.mgt.unm.edu) with numerous resources for teaching the subject. The Web site contains cases, debate issues, podcasts, and videos for use in the classroom to teach business ethics. The grant was provided by the Daniels Fund, supported by Bill Daniels, a leader and pioneer in the cable industry. Bill Daniels recognized the importance of business ethics to business success, and after he passed away in 2000, he left more than $1 billion to the Daniels Fund. In addition to the Web site, you can register for free business ethics abstracts through the *Wall Street Journal* (go to http://www.professorjournal.com). Leaders in each subject area summarize three articles each week for classroom discussion. The abstracts also provide questions for classroom discussion and links to the full text articles. These articles and abstracts are searchable by keyword and allow the integration of current examples into the lecture or to create classroom exercises.

SUMMARY

This chapter attempts to defend the perspective that business ethics can and should be taught. In addition, it defines business ethics from an organizational perspective, describes the basic processes of ethical decisionmaking in order to assist in developing an effective approach to teaching ethics in business courses, and provides a link to resources to assist in improving instruction in the area.

Integrating ethics into business courses is crucial to providing an essential foundation for career development. Understanding how stakeholders influence and evaluate the ethical decisions of an organization is the first step in developing a firm's ethical perspective. Understanding how ethical business decisions are made in the context of an organization and the role of individual values in the decisionmaking process is important.

Reviewing some of the ethical issues related to the financial crisis provides a good overview of how ethical decisionmaking interfaces with business success or, in some cases, business failure. An understanding of the legal and regulatory systems is also vital to an understanding of the complexity and inherent incentives for managing ethical risks and engaging in ethical behavior.

REFERENCES

Bazerman, M. H., & Tenbrunsel, A. E. (2011). *Blind spots*. Princeton, NJ: Princeton University Press.

Boddy, C. R. (2011). Corporate psychopaths, bullying and unfair supervision in the workplace. *Journal of Business Ethics, 100*(3), 367–379.

Carlson, J. R., Carlson, D. S., & Ferguson M. (2011). Deceptive impression management: Does deception pay in established workplace relationships? *Journal of Business Ethics, 100*(3), 497–514.

Catan, T. (2011, August 24). Google settles pharmacy ad probe for $500 million. *The Wall Street Journal*. Retrieved from http://online.wsj.com/article/SB10001424053111 904787404576528332418595052.html

Churchill, L. R. (1982, May–June). The teaching of ethics and moral values in teaching: Some contemporary confusions. *The Journal of Higher Education, 53*(3), 296–306.

Crotty, J. (2009). Structural causes of the global financial crisis: A critical assessment of the "new financial architecture." *Cambridge Journal of Economics, 33*(4), 563–580.

Dodd-Frank Wall Street Reform and Consumer Protection Act, PL 111-203, 124 Stat. 1376 (2010). Retrieved from http://www.govtrack.us/congress/bill.xpd?bill=h111-4173

Edelman. (2011). *2011 Edelman trust barometer*. Retrieved from http://www.edelman. com/trust/2011

Eisinger, J. (2008, October 15). The $58 trillion elephant in the room. *Portfolio.com*. Retrieved from http://www.portfolio.com/views/columns/wall-street/2008/10/15/ Credit-Derivatives-Role-in-Crash

Elango, B., Paul, K., Kundu, S. K., & Paudel, S. K. (2010). Organizational ethics, individual ethics, and ethical intentions in international decision making. *Journal of Business Ethics, 97*, 543–561.

Ethics Resource Center. (2009). *2009 National Business Ethics Survey: Ethics in the recession.* Retrieved from http://www.ethics.org/nbes/files/nbes-final.pdf

Ethisphere. (2010). *2010 world's most ethical companies.* Retrieved from http://ethisphere.com/wme2010

Falaschetti, D. (2011, Winter). Dodd-Frank financial reform: Non-market risks and strategies. *Economists ink: A brief analysis of policy and litigation.* Retrieved from http://www.ei.com/vieweconink.php?id=259

Ferrell, O. C., & Ferrell, L. (2011). The responsibility and accountability of CEOs: The last interview with Ken Lay. *Journal of Business Ethics, 100*(2), 209–219.

Ferrell, O. C., & Gresham, L. G. (1985). A contingency framework for understanding ethical decision making in marketing. *Journal of Marketing, 49*, 87–96.

Forsyth, D. R. (1980). A taxonomy of ethical ideologies. *Journal of Personality and Social Psychology, 39*(1), 175–184.

Gunther, M. (2010, December 6). Waste Management's new direction. *Fortune,* 103–108.

Hellweg, E. (2002, April 15). Mopping up after Merrill Lynch. *CNN money.* Retrieved from http://money.cnn.com/2002/04/15/technology/techinvestor/hellweg/index.htm

Johnson, K. W. (2004, December 31). Federal sentencing guidelines: Key points and profound changes. *Ethics resource center.* Retrieved from http://www.ethics.org/resource/fsgo-series-part-1

Kalshoven, K., Den Hartog, D. N., & De Hoogh, A. H. B. (2011). Ethical leader behavior and big five factors of personality. *Journal of Business Ethics, 100*(2), 349–366.

Kohli, A. K., & Jaworski, B. J. (1990). Market orientation: The construct, research propositions, and managerial implications. *Journal of Marketing, 54*(April), 1–18.

Lewis, B. (2002, March 11). The moral compass: Corporations aren't moral agents, creating interesting dilemmas for business leaders. *InfoWorld 24*(10), 54.

Liberto, J., & Ellis D. (2010, June 30). Wall Street reform: What's in the bill. *CNNMoney.* Retrieved from http://money.cnn.com/2010/06/25/news/economy/whats_in_the_reform_bill/index.htm

"Looking for someone to blame." (2011, August 13). *The Economist,* 25.

Maignan, I., Gonzalez-Padron, T. L., Hult, G. T. M., & Ferrell, O. C. (2011, July). Stakeholder orientation: Development and testing of a framework for socially responsible marketing. *Journal of Strategic Marketing, 19*(4), 313–338.

Mish, J., & Scammon, D. L. (2010). Principle-based stakeholder marketing: Insights from private triple-bottom-line firms. *Journal of Public Policy & Marketing, 29*(1), 12–26.

Navran, F. (2002, December 31). Ethical conflicts in ethical companies. *Ethics Resource Center.* Retrieved from http://www.ethics.org/resource/ethical-conflicts-ethical-companies

Pulliam, Susan. (2003, October 3). How following orders can harm your career. *CFO.* Retrieved from http://www.cfo.com/article.cfm/3010537/1/c_3036075

Reddy, S. (2010, September 17). Elizabeth Warren's early words on a consumer financial protection bureau. *The Wall Street Journal*. Retrieved from http://blogs. wsj.com/economics/2010/09/17/elizabeth-warrens-early-words-on-a-consumer-financial-protection-bureau

Sarbanes-Oxley Act, PL 107-204, 116 Stat 745 (2002). Retrieved from http://www. govtrack.us/congress/bill.xpd?bill=h107-3763

Sims, R. R., & Sims, S. J. (1991, March 3). Increasing applied business ethics courses in business school curricula. *Journal of Business Ethics, 10*(3), 211–219.

Smith, N. C., Drumwright, M. E., & Gentile, M. C. (2010). The new marketing myopia. *Journal of Public Policy & Marketing, 29*(1), 4–11.

Stern, L. (2002, September 23). Is your boss honest?" *Newsweek,* 73.

Tarí, J. J. (2011). Research into quality management and social responsibility. *Journal of Business Ethics, 102*(4), 623–638.

Treviño, L. K., Brown, M. E., & Wall, S. J. (2004, May). Managing to be ethical: Debunking five business ethics myths. *The Academy of Management Executive (1993–2005), 18*(2), 69–83.

Tseng, F-C., and Fan Y-J. (2011). Exploring the influence of organizational ethical climate on knowledge management. *Journal of Business Ethics, 101*(2), 325–342.

Velasquez, M., Andre, C., Shanks, T., & Meyer, M. J. (1987, Fall). *Can ethics be taught?* Markkula Center for Ethics, Santa Clara University. Retrieved from http://www.scu. edu/ethics/practicing/decision/canethicsbetaught.html

"Wal-Mart to face employee suit in Missouri." (2005, November 2). *USA Today*. Retrieved from http://www.usatoday.com/money/companies/management/2005-11-02-walmart-employees_x.htm

"Waste Management named one of the world's most ethical companies by Ethisphere Institute." (2010, March 22). Press release. Retrieved from http://www.wm.com/about/press-room/pr2010/20100322_WM_Named_One_of_the_Worlds_Most_Ethical_Companies_By_Ethisphere_Institute.pdf

Integration of Soft Skills into Business Classes

Susan L. Miertschin
Sharon Lund O'Neil
Jamison Kovach
David S. Ding
University of Houston
Houston, TX

Betty S. Johnson
Stephen F. Austin State University
Nacogdoches, TX

Stacey McCroskey
Strayer University–Northwest Houston
Houston, TX

Soft skills are crucial for success at every level in the workplace and in daily life. This chapter defines and describes soft skills in six sections: communication (the "core" soft skill), human relations, positive attitude and motivation, leadership, critical thinking and motivation, and teams and team building. The six sections lay the foundation for business educators to build students' understanding of the importance of soft skills for workplace and life success. The last section of this chapter on developing soft skills in business education classrooms suggests strategies for teaching soft skills to business students, together with examples, which include online studios, technology-based activities, and experiential exercises.

SOFT SKILLS: GOOD FOR WORKERS AND BUSINESSES

Soft skills impact a person's ability to express ideas clearly, work well with others, and manage social and workplace interactions (O'Neil & Chapman, 2008). The areas

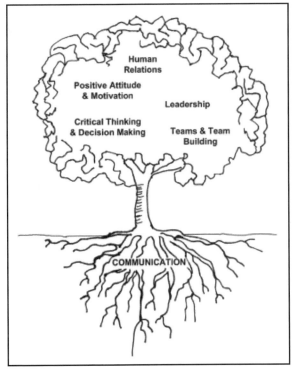

Figure 1. Soft Skills Rooted in Communication

of communication, human relations, positive attitude and motivation, leadership, critical thinking and decisionmaking, and teams and team building contribute knowledge about developing soft skills. As illustrated in figure 1, soft skills are deeply rooted in effective communication; thus, communication is often considered the "core" of all soft skills.

Good communication skills are necessary for development of the other soft skills. Unfortunately, business educators and employers have found substantial evidence that many students lack essential communication skills and other soft skills, which impacts their readiness for the workplace (Erickson, 2001; Rubin & Dierdorff, 2009).

Impact on Work Readiness

New graduates need to understand how crucial soft skills are for hiring and promotion within an organization. An in-depth study of 461 business leaders found that while fundamental reading, writing, and arithmetic skills are still essential, employers view soft skills as even more important to work readiness. The same study found, specifically, that younger workers often lack professionalism, work ethic, communication skills, teamwork skills, and critical thinking skills (Casner-Lotto & Barrington, 2006).

Research also shows that workers themselves often realize they miss out on promotion opportunities due to a lack of understanding about unwritten rules of business. These unwritten rules relate to the soft skills that decisionmakers use to gain an intuitive sense of whether a worker will succeed at a more senior level (Beeson, 2009). For many workers, these unwritten rules are elusive because they do not pertain to technical ability, industry experience, or business knowledge. Wellington (2005) suggested that those who succeed in business have solid technical *and* soft skills. Although technical skills are part of many excellent educational programs, soft skills may need additional emphasis. He noted that a student who learns the importance of soft skills and works to cultivate them will have a "leg up" as they begin a career.

Soft Skills and Business Success

Research has identified the soft skills of (a) effective communication, (b) human relations, (c) positive attitude, (d) leadership, (e) critical thinking, and (f) teamwork ability, as drivers of meaning and connectedness among workers, which help build social identity within the group. Building social identity strengthens bonds among employees, which increases job satisfaction and reduces turnover (O'Reilly, Chatman, & Caldwell, 1991). For the past few decades, organizations have recognized the intrinsic value of satisfied employees who choose not to leave; reduced turnover provides competitive advantage (Heskett, Jones, Loveman, Sasser Jr., & Schlesinger, 1994).

THE SIX SOFT SKILLS

There are many soft skills identified in popular and research literature. Six are chosen and elaborated here. The underlying organizing concept is that these skills are both important to employers and are required in addition to solid technical and functional skills.

1. Communication: The "Core" Soft Skill

The foundation for all soft skills is grounded in the ability to communicate effectively. Brewer and McGlone (2009) suggested students usually perceive their ability to communicate as acceptable; therefore, they do not see the need to strive to improve their skills. However, recruiters often recommend additional training in both written and spoken communication for new graduates (Stevens, 2005).

Effective communication does not happen automatically. Many barriers prevent the communicator's intended message from being heard in the exact way it was intended. In addition to a thorough understanding of the communication process, the communicator should also consider how the receiver will react to the message (Johnson & Bayless, 2005). A communicator must select words carefully and phrase the message to create the appropriate tone. Determining the appropriate psychological approach requires a thorough understanding of the context of the communication event as well as the ability to think critically. Appropriate use of business vocabulary is also considered essential for success.

Written and oral communication. Critical written and oral communication competencies are increasingly valuable as technology intensifies the significance of messages in the workplace. Workers need to communicate quickly and effectively in messages sent by e-mail and instant messaging modes, delivered in meetings and dyadic encounters, and conveyed through letters, memoranda, and reports. In addition, knowing when to speak and when to remain silent is an example of communication competence, as is the ability to speak coherently in impromptu situations.

Nonverbal communication. An additional component of communication exchanges is that of nonverbal communication. Even when no words are exchanged, a strong message is conveyed by the nonverbal signals associated with the sender and the receiver. However, these messages may have different meanings for different people and may vary between and within cultures. For example, in the time-conscious North American culture, tardiness sends a negative nonverbal message. Communicators, therefore, must evaluate nonverbal messages as they relate to or contradict spoken or written messages and be aware of the nonverbal messages they are transmitting. To do so requires active engagement in the communication process.

Listening. The ability to listen is extremely important to interpreting nonverbal cues and writing and speaking. Lehman and DuFrene (2011) indicated that listening commonly consumes more time than reading, writing, and speaking combined. Good listeners are valued by others because they satisfy the basic human need of being heard. Furthermore, the ability to listen effectively is rated consistently as one of the most important skills necessary for success in the workplace. Armed with the ability to write competently, speak convincingly, interpret nonverbal cues correctly, and listen effectively, employees are likely to excel not only in communications but also in other soft skills. And although no single aspect of the communication core should be overlooked, the other soft skills are unique and merit separate consideration.

2. Human Relations

Human relations skills are critical for job success. Human relations constitute a "skill set" that students need to be successful in both career and life (O'Neil & Chapman, 2008). The multidimensional set of human relations skills is critical to success because it reflects respect for others. Human relations skills include being social, exercising courtesy, and being adaptable. These skills enable a person to handle difficult problems better, work well under pressure and demanding conditions, and manage inevitable conflict effectively. Human relations skills also help one to build and maintain long-term relationships.

Human relations skills for work success. Management courses often cover the work of Katz (1955) who categorized skills required for effective management as technical, human, and conceptual. More recent research identified additional managerial competencies, among which persists the competency domain for human relations skills (Rainsbury, Hodges, Burchell, & Lay, 2002). A study by Weber, Finley, Crawford, and Rivera (2009) found that working pleasantly with employees and customers, setting a positive example, and displaying commitment are important human relations skills for managers.

People who create positive interactions with diverse coworkers can navigate effectively among various cultures and hierarchical levels within the organization. These individuals benefit from this skill through increased productivity, which can lead to added responsibilities and promotions. In fact, the reason most often cited for hiring or promoting and also for firing or bypassing a candidate is the quality of his or her human relations skills (Beeson, 2009). Research also shows that managers at all levels with poor human relation skills often fail (DuBrin, 2009).

When employees build social bonds with one another, the organization also benefits. Because contemporary business environments undergo rapid change, businesses need to be collaborative, flexible, and interconnected. Within an organizational structure built to foster these qualities, soft skills are critically important to business success (Horwitz, 2010).

Emotional intelligence. Possessing human relations skills implies understanding and practicing emotional intelligence (EI). Emerging in the early 1990s, the EI concept encompasses the ability to be self-aware, self-managed, socially aware, and able to maintain and nurture interpersonal relationships (Goleman, McKee, & Boyatzis, 2002).

EI has gained popularity in education, where it is hypothesized that teaching students EI skills will help them to be more successful in school. The contemporary workplace routinely has emotional stressors including work overload, organizational tension, and career limitations. These stressors are handled best by emotionally mature employees (Goleman, 2008). Thus, business teachers may serve the business community well by spending some class time working with students to help them become more emotionally mature and capable.

3. Positive Attitude and Motivation

Attitude and motivation are closely connected to emotional intelligence. Attitude is a mindset that causes a person to respond in positive, constructive ways or in more negative, defeatist ways to stimuli that stress the status quo. Attitude is a motivator that spurs some individuals to take action and others to not take action. Attitude is partly the way an individual perceives a situation: some individuals see a problem as a challenge or opportunity and others see the same problem as insurmountable. Attitude is a soft *skill* because research shows that attitude is within the individual's control; hence, it can be developed, practiced, and projected as the individual chooses. Because one's attitude is extremely powerful in influencing action, it makes sense to keep one's attitude as positive as possible.

Continuous improvement and attitude. Individuals can use continuous improvement methods to monitor, maintain, and improve their own attitudes. Frequent self-assessments serve to monitor the state of one's attitude. If found faltering, the individual then takes steps to strengthen his or her attitude with positive thoughts about the way they approach work and problems. People often find that when they project a positive attitude to and around others, their positive attitude is "catching" (O'Neil & Chapman, 2008). That is, being positive and proactive, learning from mistakes and correcting, and viewing problems as opportunities for improvement are smart ways that individuals can improve their attitude and start reaping the benefits from projecting it.

Motivators contribute to attitude. Each individual needs to understand how important motivators are in contributing to a positive attitude so these can be called on as trying situations, career plateaus, and mundane day-to-day activities take a toll on one's positive attitude. Motivators are personal, so each individual must use introspection to assess what these are. Once a person understands them, he or she can mobilize key motivators as needed to stimulate more enjoyment and satisfaction at home, in leisure activities, and at work or school (O'Neil, 2003).

4. Leadership

Good human relations skills, driven by a positive attitude and motivation, can significantly contribute to one's leadership ability. Leadership is influence; it is the use of power to achieve group goals (Maxwell, 1998). Leadership should not be viewed as exclusively reserved for top-level management. Leadership skills are important for every level of work. Leadership skills also contribute to success at home, in leisure activities, and at school.

Interconnectivity of human relations and leadership. A strong connection exists among human relations, emotional intelligence, and leadership. A leader must be able to get the best out of the people led, which depends on how well the leader can make emotional connections with them. Emotional connections require emotional intelligence in the leader. Research has shown that chief executive officers who fail do not do so because they lack the intelligence or drive to succeed, rather they are not able to get along with subordinates and governing board members (Goleman, 2008).

A myriad of leadership skills. A list of leadership skills is nearly inexhaustible. Some of the most important attributes of good leadership are the personal values of honesty, integrity, trust, and respect. Effective leaders are generally creative, innovative, and good decisionmakers. They understand the importance of using communication to influence others and create a shared vision.

Most leaders operate within a certain "style." For example, some leaders may be quite autocratic in their approach to getting things done, whereas others are very analytical, and still others are participative. Some adopt a style that delegates and then supports others as they complete the delegated work with limited intervention. Others adopt a free-rein style that simply delegates and waits for results with very little intervention. All styles can be effective.

Regardless of leadership style, formal leadership usually is a result of influential power derived from either position or role, expertise or knowledge, or personality or charisma (Chapman & O'Neil, 2000). Informal leaders, those without a specific leadership title, can be very effective with their support of organizational goals, management, and fellow workers. They can be equally detrimental with lack of support for the same.

Management-related competencies and models. Leadership in the form of management competence requires skills for planning, organizing, and controlling everyday challenges with structure, process, and procedure to attain high productivity. Leaders also find good negotiating, bartering, and conflict-resolution skills useful in dealing with chaos and rapid change (Abrahamson, 2004; Kotter & Cohen, 2002). From a theory of constraints perspective, leadership is an important limiting constraint that must be considered when contemplating change. Does management have leadership skills adequate to implementing the change successfully? (Goldratt, Cox, & Whitford, 2004).

Leadership models are abundant and include such skills as visioning, decisive decisionmaking, effective communicating, empowering followers, influencing, and exuding a positive attitude (Chapman & O'Neil, 2000). In addition, leaders are expected to create value (Northouse, 2007), develop talent (Adair, 2003), promote relevance, and provide deserved recognition (Wong, 2007). Additionally, Maxwell (1998) suggested that two irrefutable laws of leadership—knowing how to chart a course and knowing when to take the right action—determine a leader's level of effectiveness. Critical thinking and decisionmaking skills are important skills when trying to determine the right action.

5. Critical Thinking and Decisionmaking

Successful businesses value employees who are capable thinkers. Good reasoning based in fact, knowledge, and experience helps people achieve goals. Educators are engaged in multidisciplinary efforts to develop students' thinking skills. Attempts to understand thinking by categorizing types of thinking and ordering types of thinking based on the amount of mental effort required are long-standing (Dominowski & Bourne Jr., 1994). As early as 1956, the historic educational taxonomy by Bloom identified six levels of cognitive activity, with simple recall at the lowest level and evaluating, judging, and assessing at the highest level (Nentl & Zietlow, 2006). Recently, critical thinking has become a particular target of curriculum design.

Thinking critically. Critical thinking is a type of higher-order thinking defined as "reasonably reflective thinking that is focused on deciding what to believe or do" (Ennis, 1993, p. 180). Braun (2004) identified methods employed in business classrooms for the purpose of developing students' critical thinking skills, such as analyzing case studies and problem solving in groups. Additional research emphasizes an attitudinal component of critical thinking that is key. Hence, they argue that business students must be encouraged to develop a habit of routine skepticism, inquiry, and critical appraisal directed at conventional views and accepted assumptions (Smith, 2003).

Decisionmaking processes. To support critical thinking tasks, business students need domain-specific declarative and procedural knowledge, including knowledge about how to make good decisions. Numerous models for decisionmaking are available, all of which recognize that effective decisionmaking processes, whether formal or informal, encompass the subprocesses of (1) clearly stating a problem, (2) identifying decisionmakers, (3) collecting information, (4) postulating alternatives (including maintaining the status quo), (5) considering alternatives, (6) determining the "best" solution(s), (7) implementing solution(s), and (8) evaluating the results. These subprocesses are subject to group, organizational, and societal influences as well as individual cognitive, motivational, and emotional influences (Mintzberg, Raisinghani, & Théorêt, 1976).

6. Teams and Team Building

A group of people linked by a common purpose with complementary skills who generate synergy through a coordinated effort comprise a team. As one of the most frequently used organizational development interventions, teamwork relies heavily on good communication within the team and harmony among members (Wong, 2007).

Team types and purposes. The four major types of teams, although not mutually exclusive, are problem-solving teams, self-managed teams, cross-functional teams, and/or virtual teams. Problem-solving teams generally consist of employees from the same department who meet to find ways to improve quality, efficiency, and/or the work environment. Self-managed teams select their own team members and evaluate each other's performance while collectively controlling work processes and determining work assignments. Cross-functional teams consist of people at the same level in a business hierarchy, but from different functional areas, who come together to develop new ideas, solve problems, and coordinate complex projects. Virtual teams use computer technology to collaborate online (Carney, 2003).

Team-building elements. Team building consists of four major components: goal setting, human relations, problem solving, and role clarification. Goal setting emphasizes communicating objectives to the entire team and developing individual and team goals. Human relations foster true teamwork through mutual supportiveness, careful and courteous communication, and shared feelings. Problem solving emphasizes recognizing major problems among team members and ameliorating them. Role clarification focuses on increasing communication among team members to make sure each team member understands his or her own role as well as the role of the other members within the team (Beer, 1980). To foster collaborative synergy, team building should start with a clear goal statement and mutual agreement on objectives and role clarifications, which can serve as guidelines for identifying major problems and required skill sets in the team (Hackman, 2002).

Managing conflict resolution. Because team members contribute to the team's work through both social inputs and task inputs, conflicts occur at both relationship and task levels. Conflict interferes with team performance, reduces team member satisfaction, produces tension and antagonism, and distracts team members from the assigned task. Negative effects of conflict are minimized through an open environment characterized by collaboration. Task conflicts can have positive effects on interpersonal relations and group performance when team members perceive cooperative, rather than competitive, goal interdependence; when they cultivate an environment that is open and tolerant of diverse viewpoints; and when they use more collaborative communication and less contentious communication when expressing disagreements (De Dreu & Weingart 2003).

DEVELOPING SOFT SKILLS IN BUSINESS EDUCATION CLASSROOMS

Research has shown that competencies desired for top managers are not the same as those typically taught in business schools (Rubin & Dierdorff, 2009). Skills rated most desired for managers include making decisions, managing human capital, motivating others, fostering teamwork, and exhibiting leadership. However, business schools rank these skills lower than technical skills and content knowledge as priorities for student learning. Many business educators recognize the high demand for these soft skills and are working to close the gaps.

Thus, to prepare students for tomorrow's workforce, soft skills must be taught in the business education classroom. A study by Wats and Wats (2009) found that the leading ways soft skills are taught in the classroom are experiential learning, role playing, teamwork methods, case studies, and extracurricular activities.

A Balance of Skills in the Curriculum

Developing listening, communication, teamwork, conflict management skills, as well as other soft skills are important, yet technical skills cannot be de-emphasized to make room in the curriculum for more topics. Examining emerging curricular-content elements is one way to expand soft skills instruction. For example, Jonassen, Carr, and Yueh (1998) identified project management as an activity that requires critical thinking skills. In other research, authors note that managing projects requires human relations skills in conflict management, interpersonal communication, and teamwork (Loo, 2002). In addition, the project management body of knowledge includes skills related to leadership and decisionmaking (Richardson, 2010). Thus, teaching project management as a topic and through hands-on projects is a structured way to incorporate more teaching of soft skills into the curriculum.

Group work around course topics is one way that is frequently used in education to foster soft skills while maintaining a full complement of business topics (Thomas & de Villiers, 2001). As students work in groups to complete an on-topic assignment, they are applying and practicing teamwork and team-building processes.

Another effective method for fostering soft skills development is teaching by example. A business educator must constantly monitor and improve his or her own communication, human relations, leadership, critical thinking, and team-building skills so that students experience firsthand the benefits of excellent soft skills through the instructor's modeling.

Strategies to Develop Students' Soft Skills

Each of the strategies for developing students' soft skills presented below have been practiced and assessed in the authors' classrooms.

Strategy Example 1: Using Online Studios to Enhance Students' Writing Skills

An online writing studio is a student-led writing group that works online to produce an expository deliverable. The objective of the online studio is to create an environment for students to (a) become active participants in their own writing process, (b) develop an understanding of and ability to provide useful feedback to peers about written content, and (c) obtain ideas on how to revise their own writing based on feedback received from others. As part of regular course assignments, students are required to post drafts of their written work to group discussion boards hosted in the course management system. Students within each group critique each other's work and provide feedback to one another through discussion board posts. A writing consultant (if available) can be used to facilitate interactions among students in the online studios and to provide feedback to students for writing improvement.

This approach used in a quality improvement methods course (Kovach, Miley, & Ramos, n.d.) was adaptable to almost any topic. Evaluation of the activity suggested that the use of online writing studios was associated with improved student performance. Specifically, students' final written assignments for the course improved by one level in the grading rubric overall, compared with the previous semester when online writing studios were not used. This finding suggests the possibility that use of online writing studios in intensive nonwriting courses may help to improve students' ability to articulate course concepts in written assignments or may even increase students' conceptual understanding of course content.

Strategy Example 2: Using Technology to Teach Teamwork

Technology, such as podcasts and video productions, can be incorporated within academic project-related activities to enhance students' learning experiences. Because the production process involves brainstorming, drafting, revising, recording, and editing the final product, a team effort is required. Students learn to approach the project by breaking down large project tasks into smaller work packages, which they assign to team members. Projects incorporating technology might also include situations requiring human relation skills, such as interviews with experts and oral communication skills, for example, recording project presentations or demonstrating a real-world business practice.

A technology-rich project in a production and service operations course required students to create videos illustrating principles of project management, quality control, supply chain management, and scheduling (Kovach, Ding, & O'Neil, 2010). Feedback from students about the project was extremely positive and provided evidence that projects involving technology can provide valuable soft skills learning. Students overwhelmingly indicated that the project helped to develop their ability to work as team members. One student commented that "I learned how to communicate more effectively and think on my toes while coordinating with my team members in order to produce a successful end result."

Strategy Example 3: Using Experiential Exercises

Experiential exercises are tasks designed with specific circumstances to generate participant behavior that can be observed, discussed, and evaluated against human relations theory (Hannon, McBride, & Burns, 2004). They can be used for student practice in soft skills. Experiential exercises are widely available, including exercises for attitude and emotional intelligence development, relationship building, decisionmaking, team building, different aspects of communication improvement, and in general, career building—to name a few (O'Neil & Chapman, 2008).

An exercise used in a team leadership course allows students to have fun and learn soft skills related to teamwork. To begin the exercise, form two groups from the students in the class. In an open space, place two pieces of fabric on the floor about two feet apart. The cloth squares should be of sufficient size for all the students to just fit when standing on them. Ask each group of students to stand on one of the two pieces of fabric. Task the teams to turn the fabric under their feet over (from face-down to face up or vice versa) without allowing any team member to touch the bare floor in any way. Although there are various solutions to completing the task, an ideal solution is for both groups to work together to put everyone on one cloth and then turn the vacated cloth over. The teams then repeat the process for the second cloth. Once the activity has been completed or abandoned for lack of a solution or for failure to follow rules, the teacher engages students in discussions about developing leadership and team-building skills, accommodating creative thinking along with problem-solving challenges, maintaining motivation to complete the task, dealing with frustration, seeing the merits of cooperation, organizing to make the most of the team, following directions, and especially, communicating effectively.

SUMMARY

Possessing well-developed soft skills and continuing to hone them on a daily basis determines a person's ability to communicate with others, employ emotional intelligence to develop mutually beneficial relationships, work in teams, employ leadership to further the goals of the organization, and turn change-driven challenges into opportunities for learning. These abilities contribute significantly to job performance; hence, soft skills are commodities that add value to individual employees. Employees with solid soft skills are a commodity that adds value to the organization as a whole by possessing increased levels of job satisfaction. Therefore, developing a wide range of soft skills to their highest potential should not be neglected at any level of business education.

Personal responsibility for behavior is critical to every aspect of life; therefore, business students should be encouraged to practice positive work-related behaviors daily. Business educators who guide students to look for and find the positive aspects of a situation and to determine ways to match personal attributes to the needs of a situation will enhance students' chances of successful outcomes. In addition, by frequently reminding students that their attitude toward work, commitment to a task or project, and ultimate satisfaction in a job well done are influenced by how well they get along with other people, business educators are helping to prepare the workers needed for today's businesses.

REFERENCES

Abrahamson, E. (2004). *Change without pain: How managers can overcome initiative overload, organizational chaos, and employee burnout*. Boston, MA: Harvard Business School Press.

Adair, J. E. (2003). *The inspirational leader*. Sterling, VA: Kogan Page.

Beer, M. (1980). *Organization change and development: A systems view*. Glenview, IL: Scott Foresman.

Beeson, J. (2009, June). Why you didn't get that promotion. *Harvard Business Review, 87*(6) 101–105.

Braun, N. M. (2004). Critical thinking in the business curriculum. *Journal of Education for Business, 79*(4), 232–236.

Brewer, P., & McGlone, T. (2009). Students' perceptions of their oral and written communication skills. *Business Education Forum, 64*(1), 38–41.

Carney, S. H. (2003). *The teamwork chronicles: A startling look inside the workplace for those who want better teamwork*. Austin, TX: Greenleaf Book Group.

Casner-Lotto, J., & Barrington, L. (2006). *Are they really ready to work? Employer's perspectives on the basic knowledge and applied skills of new entrants to the 21st century U.S. workforce*. Conference Board, Corporate Voices for Working Families, the Partnership for 21st Century Skills, and the Society for Human Resource Management. Retrieved from http://www.p21.org/storage/documents/FINAL_REPORT_PDF09-29-06.pdf

Chapman, E. N., & O'Neil, S. L. (2000). *Leadership: Essential steps every manager needs to know* (3rd ed.). Upper Saddle River, NJ: Prentice Hall.

De Dreu, C. K. W., & Weingart, L. R. (2003). Task versus relationship conflict, team performance, and team member satisfaction: A meta-analysis. *Journal of Applied Psychology, 88*(4), 741–749.

Dominowski, R. L., & Bourne Jr., L. E. (1994). History of research on thinking and problem solving. In R. J. Sternberg (Ed.), *Thinking and problem solving: Handbook of perception and cognition* (2nd ed.) (pp. 1–36). San Diego, CA: Academic Press.

DuBrin, A. J. (2009). *Essentials of management* (8th ed.). Mason, OH: South-Western Cengage Learning.

Ennis, R. H. (1993). Critical thinking assessment. *Theory into Practice, 32*(3), 179–186.

Erickson, B. H. (2001). Good networks and good jobs: The value of social capital to employers and employees. In N. Lin, K. Cook, & R. S. Burt (Eds.), *Social capital: Theory and research* (p. 333). New Brunswick, NJ: Transaction Publishers.

Goldratt, E. M., Cox, J., & Whitford, D. (2004). *The goal: A process of ongoing improvement*. Great Barrington, MA: North River Press.

Goleman, D. (2008). The secret to success. *Education Digest, 74*(4), 8–9.

Goleman, D., McKee, A., & Boyatzis, R. (2002). *Primal leadership: Realizing the power of emotional intelligence*. Boston, MA: Harvard Business School Press.

Hackman, J. R. (2002). *Leading teams: Setting the stage for great performances*. Boston, MA.: Harvard Business School Press.

Hannon, S., McBride, H., & Burns, B. (2004). Developing creative and critical thinking abilities in business graduates: The value of experiential learning techniques. *Industry & Higher Education, 18*(2), 95–100.

Heskett, J. L., Jones, T. O., Loveman, G. W., Sasser Jr., W. E., & Schlesinger, L. A. (1994, March/April). Putting the service-profit chain to work. *Harvard Business Review, 72*(2), 164–172.

Horwitz, F. (2010). Transforming the business school. *BizEd, 9*(3), 34–39.

Johnson, B. S., & Bayless, M. L. (2005). *Business communication* (4th ed.). Mason, OH: Thomson Custom Publishing.

Jonassen, D., Carr, C., & Yueh, H.-P. (1998). Computers as mindtools for engaging learners in critical thinking. *TechTrends, 43*(2), 24–32.

Katz, R. L. (1955). Skills of an effective administrator. *Harvard Business Review, 33*(1), 33–42.

Kotter, J. P., & Cohen, D. S. (2002). *The heart of change: Real-life stories of how people change their organizations*. Boston, MA: Harvard Business School Press.

Kovach, J., Ding, D. X., & O'Neil, S. L. (2010). Using podcasting and video productions to create valuable student learning experiences. *Quality Approaches in Higher Education, 1*(1), 10–17.

Kovach, J., Miley, M., & Ramos, M. (n.d.). The use of online writing studio groups to improve writing competency: A case study in a quality improvement methods course. Unpublished working paper. University of Houston, Houston, TX.

Lehman, C. M., & DuFrene, D. D. (2011). *BCOM2*. Mason, OH: South-Western Cengage Learning.

Loo, R. (2002). Journaling: A learning tool for project management training and team-building. *Project Management Journal, 33*(4), 61–66.

Maxwell, J. C. (1998). *The 21 Irrefutable laws of leadership: Follow them and people will follow you*. Nashville, TN: Thomas Nelson Publishers.

Mintzberg, H., Raisinghani, D., & Théorêt, A. (1976). The structure of "unstructured" decision processes. *Administrative Science Quarterly, 21*(2), 246–275.

Nentl, N. J., & Zietlow, R. (2006). Marketing educators should use secondary research methods to teach critical thinking (reasoning) skills as outlined in Bloom's taxonomy. In J. Cherry (Ed.), *Marketing Management Association 2006 Educators' Conference Proceedings* (pp. 49–50).

Northouse, P. G. (2007). *Leadership: Theory and practice* (4th ed.). Thousand Oaks, CA: SAGE Publications.

O'Neil, S. L. (2003). *Motivation: An ATM card for success.* Upper Saddle River, NJ: Prentice Hall.

O'Neil, S. L., & Chapman, E. N. (2008). *Your attitude is showing: A primer on human relations* (12th ed.). Upper Saddle River, NJ: Prentice Hall.

O'Reilly, C. A., Chatman, J., & Caldwell, D. F. (1991). People and organizational culture: A profile comparison approach to assessing person-organization fit. *Academy of Management Journal, 34*(3), 487–516.

Rainsbury, E., Hodges, D., Burchell, N., & Lay, M. (2002). Ranking workplace competencies: Student and graduate perceptions. *Asia-Pacific Journal of Cooperative Education, 3*(2), 8–18.

Richardson, G. L. (2010). *Project management theory and practice.* Boca Raton, FL: CRC Press.

Rubin, R. S., & Dierdorff, E. C. (2009). How relevant is the MBA? Assessing the alignment of required curricula and required managerial competencies. *Academy of Management Learning & Education, 8*(2), 208–224.

Smith, G. F. (2003). Beyond critical thinking and decision making: Teaching business students how to think. *Journal of Management Education, 27*(1), 24.

Stevens, B. (2005). Essential soft skills for success in the twenty-first century workforce as perceived by business educators. *Journal of Employment Counseling, 42*(1), 2–9.

Thomas, T., & de Villiers, C. (2001). Teaching IS soft skills to a diverse student population: Case studies using JAD and co-operative learning techniques. *Journal of Informatics Education Research, 3*(2), 39–52.

Wats, M., & Wats, R. K. (2009). Developing soft skills in students. *International Journal of Learning, 15*(12), 1–10.

Weber, M. R., Finley, D. A., Crawford, A., & Rivera, D. (2009). An exploratory study identifying soft skill competencies in entry-level managers. *Tourism & Hospitality Research, 9*(4), 353–361.

Wellington, J. K. (2005). The "soft skills" of success. *Vital Speeches of the Day, 71*(20), 628–634.

Wong, Z. (2007). *Human factors in project management: Concepts, tools, and techniques for inspiring teamwork and motivation* (1st ed.). San Francisco: Jossey-Bass.

The Changing Accounting Curriculum at the Secondary and Postsecondary Levels

Kate Mooney
Steven P. Mooney
St. Cloud State University
St. Cloud, MN

Susan V. Crosson
Santa Fe College
Gainesville, FL

Who or what causes changes to accounting education? Precisely what changes to curricula, teaching methods, and/or teaching materials provide for effective educational change? Is proactive or reactive change in accounting education more effective? These questions are important for exploring the topic of the changing accounting curriculum. This chapter will, first, identify the professional organizations that affect accounting education and how those entities focus their efforts. Professional organizations have a legitimate stake in the product of accounting education—the new professionals; in an effort to watch out for the future of the accounting profession, these entities subtly influence the educational process. Second, the chapter explores the way regulators pressure for change in accounting education. Regulatory agencies are overt in the ways they affect change through laws and licensing requirements. Next, the chapter looks at how changes in society force change in accounting education; shifts in American society pressure educational institutions to adapt to new attitudes and values. Fourth, the chapter explores some of the broad macro shifts on our planet that are slowly causing change in accounting education. These themes are related to changes in the United States as well as pressures that result from globalization.

PROFESSIONAL ORGANIZATIONS AS A FORCE FOR CHANGE IN ACCOUNTING EDUCATION

Professional organizations for accountants take an active role in monitoring and suggesting the appropriate education for entry-level accountants. The American Institute of Certified Public Accountants (AICPA), the Institute of Internal Auditors (IIA), the Institute of Management Accountants (IMA) all have structures to interact with education. These structures can take the form of committees, suggested curricula, or suggested outcomes. But the effect is the same: to implement change in accounting education that benefits the profession.

American Institute of Certified Public Accountants

The AICPA is the largest accounting professional association in the world (AICPA, n.d.-a) and influences accounting education in three ways. First, the AICPA promotes change through the development and grading of the certified public accountant (CPA) exam. Although educators adamantly resist "teaching to the test," the institution's pass rate—the number of students who successfully pass all parts of the CPA exam on the first sitting—is a relevant statistic in many quarters. Recruiters use it to target schools for interviewing and new hires. Accounting departments brag about high rates in their newsletters. To achieve that success, the curriculum must address the content and structure of the CPA exam. That means, whether educators like it or not, the curriculum is influenced by the AICPA through the CPA exam.

A second way that the AICPA influences accounting education is through publication of the Core Competency Framework (AICPA, n.d.-b). The framework is not content specific, but rather addresses skills, abilities, and attitudes needed by professional accountants beginning their careers. The competencies are mapped to the CPA exam, indicating where and how those competencies are tested. So, successful students need to acquire not only content but also skills, abilities, and attitudes. To prepare students for success, the accounting curriculum must incorporate activities that build student skills and abilities and train their attitudes. Again, that means the curriculum is influenced by the AICPA through the Core Competency Framework.

The third pressure for change associated with the AICPA is through its committee structure. Through several task forces and committees, the AICPA influences accounting education, academic research, and teaching methods. The Pre-Certification Education Executive Committee takes an active role in shaping accounting education, charged with assisting universities in preparing students for entry into the profession by "recommending continuous improvements in curricula, instructional materials, and pedagogy" (AICPA, n.d.-c). Several task forces of the AICPA make awards for teaching innovation and research contributions. The awards are considered a great honor among the academic community and come with cash awards. The presentations of the awards are made publicly at the annual meeting of the American Accounting Association, the academic accountants' professional association. All present there are informed of both the names and the substance of the innovation or research that won awards. Ambitious faculty will likely imitate the winners, and so through the award process the AICPA exerts subtle influence on accounting education.

Clearly, the AICPA has significant influence and promotes change in accounting education. That is not a negative thing; rather, an external voice committed to the public interest can provide a needed perspective in educational institutions dominated by academics with little or no real-world experience.

Institute of Internal Auditors

The AICPA is not the only professional organization that influences accounting education. The IIA also promotes educational change through the Internal Audit Educational Partnership (IAEP) program and through a certification exam. Schools receive resources and career opportunities for their students by establishing coursework and programs that reflect the IIA model curriculum. "IAEP schools work closely with the IIA to develop meaningful internal audit curricula" (Institute of Internal Auditors, n.d.-b) and the model curriculum even provides sample syllabi for various courses (Institute of Internal Auditors, n.d.-a). Although the partnership signals a cooperative effort between the organization and the school, the IIA does influence accounting education for internal auditors.

The IIA also develops and scores the certified internal auditor exam. Like the AICPA, the IIA administers a certification exam for the designation as a certified internal auditor (CIA). Similar to the effect of the content of the CPA exam as a driver of course content, the existence of the CIA exam links with content in accounting courses. However, the IIA goes further by publishing materials for internal audit education for use in college courses and for exam preparation.

The IIA is a force for change in accounting education. The organization has developed a formalized linkage with schools, the Internal Audit Educational Partnership, which promotes good internal audit education. It also develops and administers a certification exam. Like the AICPA, the IIA influences the content and methods used in accounting education.

Institute of Management Accountants

The IMA also has mechanisms for influencing accounting education. Similar to the AICPA and the IIA, the IMA provides certified management accountant (CMA) certification through an exam. The organization publishes content specification for the exam (IMA, n.d.-a) on its Web site. Although instructors of college courses claim academic freedom when designing their syllabi, certification exams do provide some guidance on important topics and the depth of those topics. High pass rates are perceived to reflect the quality of the accounting program, so instructors will take direction from the exam content when planning their courses. Instructors want their students to succeed.

The IMA connects to faculty, which influences accounting education in three ways. First, the IMA meets face to face with faculty. It invites attendees (who are mainly faculty) at the American Accounting Association's annual meeting to breakfast. Second, the IMA supports development of new teaching materials by publishing the *IMA Educational Case Journal*. Through this publication, the IMA is able to influence teaching to include active learning materials with a managerial focus. Third, the IMA supports applied research through the Foundation for Applied Research. The grants awarded by the foundation require academics and practitioners to partner on research projects. These partnerships provide incentives for research on real-world problems with topics that can move to the classroom, thereby influencing accounting education.

Common Threads from Professional Organizations

Fortunately, the influence of professional organizations is consistent in one significant way: all three organizations emphasize an ethics component in their published materials. The AICPA promotes professional demeanor as one of the personal competencies for professional accountants, identifying ethical behavior as a component of that competency. The IIA proposes an entire course on ethics in its model curriculum, also including the topic in two other recommended courses. The IMA developed learning outcomes based on its Statement of Ethical Professional Practice (IMA, n.d.-b).

Topical coverage is also consistent: all three organizations include risk analysis as an important component of their accounting education. The AICPA includes it as a functional competency. The IIA model curriculum places the topic in the foundation course. The IMA lists risk assessment learning objectives in the section on internal controls.

In addition to complete consistency on the items above, two of the three organizations propose some suggestions for effective accounting education. The AICPA and the IIA both list communication skills as important to accounting professionals. Because this comparison of influence on accounting education is limited to analysis of the AICPA competencies, the IIA model curriculum, and the IMA learning outcome statements, omission of communication skills from the IMA documents does not mean that management accountants do not need to be good communicators.

The AICPA and IMA cooperate in an effort to change accounting education. Both organizations are supporters of the Accounting Pilot and Bridge Project, which is seeking to establish an advanced placement (AP) accounting course. The AICPA and IMA view the project as a way to increase the quality and quantity of people entering the accounting profession. Students make career decisions very early, even in high school, and students perceive high school accounting as a vocational track. That perception causes college-bound high achievers to avoid high-school accounting courses and to think negatively about a career in accounting (AICPA, 2000). The Accounting Pilot and Bridge Project is intended to change that negative perception of accounting courses and careers in two significant ways. First, the high-school accounting course curriculum is transformed from a remedial bookkeeping course to an innovative course with challenge and fulfillment that reflects a professional accounting career. Second, universities and high schools are partnering to establish college credit for the first accounting course with the goal of an advanced placement accounting course (Deines, 2011). Through the cooperation of these two professional bodies, plus high schools and universities, the high school accounting course has been changed.

In short, AICPA, IMA, and IIA comprise a significant force for change in accounting education. They are all concerned with the education of future accountants and take various steps to ensure the quality of that education. All three provide guidance on content, skills, abilities, and attitudes that are useful for entry-level accountants. All three develop and score certification exams based on published topics. In an effort to help students succeed in certification exams and to increase employment opportunities, accounting programs are wise to consider that guidance when designing courses.

REGULATORY AGENCIES AS FORCES FOR CHANGE

The accounting profession is regulated by several entities. Direct regulation through licensing and prelicensing education is accomplished at the state level through the State Board of Accountancy. Other organizations, while actively regulating accountants, have less influence on accounting education, focusing instead on practices and procedures for auditing publicly traded companies.

The National Association of State Boards of Accountancy

The National Association of State Boards of Accountancy (NASBA) is the organization that promotes the effectiveness of such state boards. Although individual states set the rules for prelicensing education requirements, NASBA tries to present uniform educational standards for the boards to adopt, making it easier for accountants to obtain licenses in several states. These proposed standards have a direct impact on accounting education.

The NASBA Education Committee has been active in designing a uniform curriculum for prelicensing education. In May 2008, model education rules were approved that call for all states to adopt an accounting ethics course worth three semester credit-hours as an education requirement to be eligible to take the CPA exam (NASBA, 2008). In addition, those rules also propose that students must have completed all credit-hour requirements for licensing before taking the exam. Currently, many states allow candidates to complete the required hours after taking the exam. These two proposals will certainly change accounting education. Although many schools have ethics course requirements, few have separate accounting ethics courses. That means many schools will need to develop and staff courses in accounting ethics if state boards adopt the model education rules. The NASBA-suggested education requirements for licensing through the Uniform Accountancy Act (NASBA, n.d.) will change accounting education.

Other Regulators

The Securities and Exchange Commission (SEC) and the Public Companies Accounting Oversight Board have the authority to regulate the accounting profession, but their influence on education is indirect. Both rely on audits performed by CPAs, individuals who have achieved certification by passing the CPA exam. By restricting who can perform certain services for public companies only to CPAs, these regulators implicitly approve of the education requirements to become a CPA.

Interestingly, a call for a group to study change in accounting education came from the United States Treasury Department, an entity that does not directly regulate accountants. In response to financial reporting scandals in the early 21st century, the Treasury Department commissioned the Advisory Committee on the Auditing Profession. Part of that committee, the Subcommittee on Human Capital, "focused time and effort on the adequate preparation of the accounting student and noted the need to increase the pace of curricular changes in college and university accounting programs to match more effectively the increasing pace of market developments" (Advisory Committee on the Auditing Profession, 2008, p. II-3). The section of the report focusing on human capital makes five recommendations to the profession, the first of which directly calls for changes in accounting education.

This first recommendation of the Subcommittee on Human Capital directs regulators, educators, institutions, and accrediting bodies to update accounting curricula to reflect current content and methods (Advisory Committee on the Auditing Profession, 2008, p. VI:2). The subcommittee noted that "curricula are characteristically slow to change" (p. VI: 4) and regulators can speed the change by developing certification exams that test the most current topics and skills. The subcommittee instructed educators to update teaching materials regularly to mirror the dynamic changes in the business environment (p. VI: 6). The subcommittee also charged accrediting agencies to act as catalysts for curriculum change by giving attention to the responsiveness of an institution's curriculum to recent business developments (p. VI:7).

Federal legislation influences accounting education through laws such as the Sarbanes-Oxley Act of 2002. Various sections of the act require specialized knowledge and courses in financial auditing, internal auditing, and corporate governance; SEC reporting at both the undergraduate and graduate levels struggles to incorporate relevant materials (Bisoux, 2005). For example, sections 302 and 404 of the act emphasize internal control and management's responsibility for adequate internal control. Although auditing courses have always included internal control considera-tions, textbooks and teaching materials stress internal control aspects of the audit process even more after the Sarbanes-Oxley Act.

A second force for change, regulators, exerts pressure for modification and compliance through license requirements pertaining to education. NASBA and State

Boards of Accountancy prescribe specific education requirements, detailing credit hours and broad topics. For students to be successful in the accounting profession, they need the education necessary for the license. Schools will adjust curricula to enable students to qualify for the license, resulting in licensing rules influencing accounting education. In addition to direct regulation, other entities, such as the SEC and Public Company Accounting Oversight Board, support education compliance by restricting auditing activities only to CPAs.

SOCIETAL SHIFTS AS A FORCE FOR CHANGE IN ACCOUNTING EDUCATION

Although it is easy to see the direct pressure for specified change from entities such as professional organizations and regulators, it is not so easy to identify how changing student characteristics will affect accounting education. The Millennials, a generation of people born roughly between 1980 and 2000, are a force for change in the same way Baby Boomers have been and continue to be. Baby Boomers have affected every aspect of society through sheer numbers (Ranier & Ranier, 2011). Millennials will do the same because there are even more people born between 1980 and 2000 than were born in 1946–64, the Boomer generation (Ranier & Ranier, 2011, p. 7).

New Kind of Student

When the old timers on the faculty grumble that students are not like they were 20 years ago, they are absolutely right. Students are different, and different students mean educational change is necessary. The Millennial generation is now in high school and college and beginning their careers. This generation has very distinct characteristics as documented by Ron Alsop (2008) in *The Trophy Kids Grow Up: How the Millennial Generation Is Shaking Up the Workplace.* Alsop identifies unique characteristics of this generation that make for difficulties in traditional universities and workplaces. Some of those characteristics include the following:

- Although concerned for social and environmental issues, Millennials have an "all about me" attitude (p. 6). Many high schools have already changed to student-centered learning, but the traditional university lecture is ineffective with many Millennials.

- Because they have been sheltered by doting parents, they need excessive guidance and constant feedback. The feedback needs to be positive because they are unable to take harsh criticism. Current educational structures, particularly at the university level, do not allow re-doing of assignments for a better grade or flexible due dates to accommodate the student's busy schedule. University instructors want to prepare students for the real world and expect best effort on the first submission and adherence to deadlines as practice for the accounting profession.

- Millennials love attention and are very social. Group work is preferred to solitary projects.

- This generation has always had lots of technology, cell phones, Internet, tablets, etc. They have mastered multitasking skills better than any other generation, but that may result in shorter attention spans. Complex accounting topics may require attention spans that tax the Millennials.

- Millennials focus on achievement, particularly good grades, and are willing to cheat to get them. This generation feels pressured to achieve. With so many other students their age competing for the same spots in college and same entry-level jobs, students feel good grades are vital. Many haggle with instructors over minor points and do not focus on the learning.

- They have a strong sense of entitlement and expect success, work/life balance, and rapid advancement. When challenged with difficult material resulting in less than the desired grade, Millennials will place blame on the instructor.

- Family is important to them, and parents are intimately involved with Millennials, even in college and in their first job. The doting parental involvement that smooths out the bumps and makes things work has limited the Millennials' ability to deal with ambiguity and their capabilities of independent thought. Twenty-first-century business careers require the ability to deal with ambiguity, making this an important aspect of a Millennial's education.

Education Adapted to the Millennial Generation

When Alsop (2008) asked Millennials to identify their dream job, major accounting firms made the list, which is good news for accounting education. This means accounting education must change to effectively educate students with these unique characteristics. A comparison of curricula from 1980 with those of today reveals almost identical topics. If the same topics are necessary, then Alsop declares, "We have no choice but to change our approach as our audience changes" (p. 141), meaning the teaching strategies, methods, and techniques will have to change.

What strategies will effectively educate the Millennial Generation? Wilson and Gerber (2008) make four recommendations for college instructors. The recommendations generate more effective teaching by using the distinctive characteristics of Millennials to enhance learning or by making up for a deficiency associated with a characteristic.

The first recommendation is to be very clear about course structure, assignments, and grading. Millennials have a low tolerance for ambiguity because parents have hovered, reminded, and structured much of their lives. The transition to independence is slow and difficult. College instructors can help by providing a syllabus that has definite due dates, provides reasonable guidance for assignments and projects, and presents specific grading criteria and expectations. Millennials have been told how special they are and often confuse effort with excellence. Providing examples of truly excellent work can clarify this for students.

A second recommendation for change to education to accommodate the Millennial student is to allow participation in course design. This can be accomplished by providing alternatives, such as one of two topics for a paper, or two spreadsheet projects replacing one short research paper. This approach must be crafted carefully to make sure that students pick assignments that include all the skill sets. Millennials, who have no patience for busy work, will feel more invested in the project if they choose it. Instructors are wise to offer them many alternatives that involve technology.

The third recommendation made by Wilson and Gerber (2008) to improve teaching for students of the Millennial generation is to work on ways to reduce the stress for them. They recommend reducing content, but emphasizing analysis and thoughtful processing of material. In accounting, that is best accomplished at the program level, rather than the course level because subsequent courses often depend on previous courses for prerequisite knowledge. Another way to reduce stress is to use modules, flexible deadlines, and reminders. A third suggestion for reducing stress for students is to provide ongoing grade information. Online learning platforms make this easy. Reducing stress for the achievement-oriented Millennials can be accomplished by reducing content when ethically possible, using reminders, and providing grade information throughout the term.

The fourth recommendation deals with a negative aspect of the Millennials' nature. Millennials are driven by achievement and are obsessed with good grades rather than learning. They will cheat to get those good grades. David Callahan (2004) in *The Cheating Culture: Why More Americans Are Doing Wrong to Get Ahead* cites that, in 2002, 74% of students admitted to cheating on an exam at least once in the past year (p. 203). To counteract that, instructors will have to use multiple versions of exams, vigilant proctoring, and plagiarism software to detect cheating. Then, cheaters must be punished to deter others.

In short, societal shifts, particularly changes in student attitudes and characteristics, are a force for change in accounting education. The generation in college at the time of this writing, known as the Millennials, has been studied extensively and has distinct attitudes and characteristics that make old educational methods ineffective. For schools to educate the next generation of accountants effectively, the methods must be appropriate, taking into account the strengths and weaknesses of the Millennial generation.

MACRO FORCES FOR CHANGE

Macro forces are significant structural changes in the way societies and businesses operate. These broad, worldwide themes are drivers of change in business and, therefore, also influence educational change. The themes we will explore are technology, economic recession, and globalization. Technology has transformed many aspects of life. We will explore how technology has changed education and business, making location of worker or student almost irrelevant. Another macro force in the United States—the prolonged economic recession—has reduced resources available for education at a time when the college-aged population is increasing. Furthermore, global competition and the intertwining of economies worldwide are challenging the American education system and the capital markets.

Technology

Technology is driving change in accounting education in two ways. First, the availability of low-cost Internet access has transformed the market for education. With the location of both student or school irrelevant, educational institutions face stiffer competition for students. The school is no longer just competing with other schools within an easy drive of the student's home; instead, the competition is coming from all over the country, if not the world. This increased competition can force change to meet market demands. Unfortunately, however, rapid changes can come at the expense of quality instruction if institutions do not propose quality standards for developing, delivering, and administering courses online (Santovec, 2004).

The second way technology influences accounting education is through the generational gap in technology skills between some instructors and students. Older instructors began their careers with little technology beyond spreadsheet, word processing, and statistical software. On the other hand, the Millennials embrace all technology because it has always been a part of their lives (McBride & Nief, 2011). "To hold the attention of easily distracted Millennials, schools and colleges are making learning a multimedia experience by incorporating podcasts, videos, computer games, and other interactive technologies" (Alsop, 2011, p. 160). Education must adjust from the "sage on the stage" model to interactive multimedia techniques that actively engage students in the learning. This change is a big hurdle for older instructors who are unfamiliar with learning platforms, electronic media, and social networking. Schools must provide training and encouragement to help them move incrementally toward teaching methods based on technology to build on Millennials' love of technology.

Economic Issues and Education Change

The second global trend affecting accounting education is the Great Recession. Stress on public schools and higher education related to economic problems comes from several interrelated pressures. State and local financial support for schools is declining, and educational institutions face the general problems of trying to do more with less. In May 2010, U.S. Secretary of Education Arne Duncan indicated that for the 2010–2011 academic year, layoffs in K–12 schools were estimated at between 100,000 and 300,000 teachers (Anderson, 2010). Layoffs of classroom teachers would not be a problem if enrollments were decreasing, but the economic downturn has forced many students attending private schools to switch to public schools because their parents can no longer afford the private school tuition (Toppo, 2010). The result is that public schools are educating more students with fewer teachers. With more pupils per teacher, education must change.

In addition to decreasing funds resulting in teacher layoffs, legislators and the public are demanding more accountability for education expenditures. At the federal level, the No Child Left Behind Act of 2001 (2002) ties economic incentives to achievement as measured by standardized tests and punishes struggling public schools that do not meet the achievement goals. The pressure to meet the goals is so severe that 82 teachers and principals in Atlanta confessed to "fixing" answers on standardized tests to meet achievement standards (Jonsson, 2011). In that environment, education will change to focus on what is tested. In addition to federal laws affecting public schools, state legislators want documented value for higher education funding, too. In Texas, funding formulas incorporate institutional measures of student success such as total number of bachelor's degrees awarded, total number of bachelor's degrees in critical fields awarded, total number of bachelor's degrees awarded to students from underrepresented ethnic groups, and the six-year graduation rate (Texas Higher Education Coordinating Board, 2011. Minnesota is also focusing on similar measures of degree completion plus retention rates from one year to the next (Minnesota Office of Higher Education, 2009). Accountability and assessment are not unreasonable demands, but measuring and reporting all the information necessary to meet the accountability requirements takes even more of the limited resources away from instruction, estimated at $125–$174 per pupil, or $6.1–$8.5 billion total per year throughout the nation. That is about 1.7%–1.9% of total public education expenditures (Harris & Taylor, 2008). In addition to using resources to achieve compliance, optimal course design may be sacrificed to achieve easy measures of effectiveness. Although accountability and assessment are necessary, the task is complicated in an environment with severe resource constraints.

Globalization as a Force for Change in Accounting Education

Globalization, the increasing interdependence of economies all over the world—affects accounting education in two ways. The first is through the skills students need to be successful in a business with international operations. The second is through technical knowledge required because business activities occur in different countries with different reporting standards and laws.

Accounting education strives to prepare students for successful careers. Those careers are in businesses that may have employees working in India, customers in Minneapolis, and suppliers in China. To be successful, businesses must be culturally sensitive to foreign laws, traditions, and norms (Mooney & Karantonis, 1987). Education can accomplish this through increasing diversity in the institution and through encouraging international experiences for students. The first-hand experience of working on project teams in school with students coming from diverse backgrounds prepares students for the realities of globalization. Students taking classes in a foreign country learn how to adjust to unfamiliar ways of doing things, giving them practice at understanding global business.

Globalization also forces change in the technical content of accounting education. Accounting textbooks will have to integrate International Financial Reporting Standards (IFRS) into textbooks and teaching materials. American textbooks must also include significant coverage of legal issues associated with doing business in foreign countries. Curricula must include topics associated with taxes and reporting of foreign currency.

The SEC has identified convergence of generally accepted accounting principles and international accounting standards as a goal to be achieved by 2015 (Securities and Exchange Commission, 2010). To be adequately prepared for the conversion to new standards, accountants will need additional education, which requires curriculum change. In a 2008 survey of accounting professors, 62% indicated that they had not done much to include coverage of IFRS in their programs (Shinn, 2009). Large accounting firms need new employees with IFRS knowledge and have made nearly $1 million in grants to universities to accomplish the necessary curriculum change (Weiss, 2011). The globalization of accounting standards has forced change in accounting curricula.

Businesses with global activities must abide by U.S. laws, even when compliance puts that business at a competitive disadvantage because of local customs. Knowledge of the Foreign Corrupt Practices Act (FCPA) (1977) is the basis for understanding which gifts used to secure sales comply with the law. In some cultures cash payments are the norm, but that is not allowed under the FCPA. Accountants must monitor internal controls in a business to recognize problems (Lee & Slear, 2007). Accounting education must provide that technical expertise to students to prevent FCPA problems.

International business operations involve transactions in foreign currencies. Accountants must be able to provide advice on exchange rate risk and the reporting issues associated with it (Mooney & Karantonis, 1987). Foreign currency translations and transactions require complicated reporting in financial statements, and businesses need to anticipate and manage the effect of fluctuating exchange rates. In addition, the tax laws associated with income earned in foreign countries are mutable depending on the political mood. Students must be ready to take on these challenges in a multinational company through technical knowledge of relevant topics.

Globalization is a force for change in accounting education because international business activities require well-developed soft skills and specialized technical knowledge. Students must acquire the skills to work with culturally diverse colleagues either face to face or electronically. Students must also acquire technical knowledge of laws and reporting standards associated with doing business in foreign companies. Accounting education must develop a curriculum to prepare students for businesses operating in a global economy.

Macro-level changes in society and the world produce new environments for business. To prepare students for work in that environment, accounting education must keep pace. Advances in technology have changed the way accounting education is delivered, sometimes exposing a gulf of capability between instructors and students. The Great Recession has changed the level of funding and the accountability requirements for secondary and higher education, forcing more efficiency and proof of effectiveness. Globalization has pushed new soft skills and complex topics into the curriculum.

SUMMARY

This chapter was introduced with the question, "Who or what causes changes to accounting education?" The answer is many entities and developments. Some, such as professional organizations, have the future professional in mind and influence changes through certifying exams. Professional organizations also connect directly with educational institutions through committees and programs designed to advise faculty on what new accountants need to be successful. Professional organizations call for changes in accounting education to meet the needs of the accounting profession in the future.

Other entities—regulators—have the goal of protecting the public interest and cause change to accounting education. Regulators specify requirements for licensing or practice to ensure competent accountants necessary for commerce. Institutions construct their curricula to meet those requirements to enhance their own reputation for producing successful professionals.

In addition to identifiable entities causing change to education, developments in society and the world also influence how and what is taught. The characteristics of the student population necessitate change in teaching methods and materials to achieve learning more effectively. Technology, economic realities, and globalization are transforming education at all levels by enabling new methods and by requiring new topics.

The process of change is difficult, but necessary. The forces of change on accounting education are varied and represent professionals, protectors of the public, and world developments. Successful change will benefit students and the profession.

REFERENCES

AICPA. (n.d.-a). *About the AICPA.* Retrieved from http://www.aicpa.org/About/Pages/About.aspx

AICPA. (n.d.-b). *Core competency framework & educational competency assessment Web site.* Retrieved from http://www.aicpa.org/interestareas/accountingeducation/resources/pages/corecompetency.aspx

AICPA. (n.d.-c). *The Pre-certification Education Executive Committee (PcEEC).* Retrieved from http://www.aicpa.org/interestareas/accountingeducation/community/pages/pre-certification-education-executive-committee.aspx

Advisory Committee on the Auditing Profession. (2008). *Final report of the advisory committee on the auditing profession to the U.S. Department of the Treasury.* Retrieved from http://www.treasury.gov/about/organizational-structure/offices/ Documents/final-report.pdf

Alsop, R. (2008). *The trophy kids grow up.* San Francisco, CA: Jossey-Bass.

Anderson, N. (2010, May 27). 100,000 teachers nationwide face layoffs. *The Washington Post,* p. A01.

Bisoux, T. (2005, July/August). The Sarbanes-Oxley effect. *BizEd,* pp. 24–29.

Callahan, D. (2004). *The cheating culture: Why more Americans are doing wrong to get ahead.* San Diego, CA: Harcourt.

Foreign Corrupt Practices Act of 1977. S. 305, 95th Cong. Pub. L. 95-213, 91 Stat. 1495 (1977) (enacted).

Harris, D., & Taylor, L. (2008). *The resource costs of standards, assessments, and accountability: A final report to the National Research Council.* Retrieved from http://www7. nationalacademies.org/cfe/HarrisTaylor%20Paper.pdf

Institute of Internal Auditors. (n.d.-a). *Academic Relations Program.* Retrieved from http://www.theiia.org/guidance/academic-relations

Institute of Internal Auditors. (n.d.-b). *Internal Auditing Educational Partnership Program.* Retrieved from http://www.theiia.org/guidance/academic-relations/ internal-auditing-education-partnership-program

IMA [Institute of Management Accountants]. (n.d.-a). *Current CMA candidates.* Retrieved from http://www.imanet.org/cma_certification/current_cma_candidates/ flexible_study_options

IMA. (n.d.-b). *Statement of ethical professional practice.* Retrieved from http://www. imanet.org/pdfs/statement%20of%20Ethics_web.Pdf

Jonsson, P. (2011, July 5). America's biggest teacher and principal cheating scandal unfolds in Atlanta. *The Christian Science Monitor.*

Lee, J. A., & Slear, J. D. (2007, May/June). Unique problems with FCPA compliance in the People's Republic of China. *Business Law Today, 16*(5). Retrieved from http:// apps.americanbar.org/buslaw/blt/2007-05-06/slear.shtml

McBride, T., & Nief, R. (2011). *The mindset list.* Retrieved from http://www.beloit.edu/ mindset/2011

Minnesota Office of Higher Education, (2009). *Minnesota measures: 2009 report on higher education performance.* Retrieved from http://www.ohe.state.mn.us/pdf/ MinnesotaMeasures2009.pdf

Mooney, S., & Karantonis, A. (1987). Australia and the United States: Still attractive for the foreign investor? *International Real Estate Journal, 19,* 13–17.

NASBA [National Association of State Boards of Accountancy]. (2008, May). Model education rules approved. *State board report.* Retrieved from http://www.nasba.org/ blog/2008/05/01/nonworking-linkmay-2008-model-education-rules-approved

NASBA. (n.d.). *Uniform Accountancy Act (UAA), sixth edition.* Retrieved from http:// www.nasba.org/blog/2011/09/06/24114

No Child Left Behind Act of 2001. H.R. 1, 107th Cong. Pub. L. No. 107-110, 115 Stat. 1426 (2002) (enacted).

Ranier, T., & Ranier, J. (2011). *The Millennials: Connecting to America's largest generation*. Nashville TN: B&H Publishing Group.

Santovec, M. (2004, November 15). Strategies to ensure quality. *Distance Education Report, 8,* 1–7.

Sarbanes-Oxley Act. Pub. L. 107-204, 116 Stat. 745 (2002) (enacted). Retrieved from http://www.govtrack.us/congress/bill.xpd?bill=h107-37

Securities and Exchange Commission. (2010). *Commission statement in support of convergence and global accounting standards* (Release Nos. 33-9109; 34-61578). Retrieved from http://www.sec.gov/rules/other/2010/33-9109.pdf

Shinn, S. (2009, July/August). Ready or not, here comes IFRS. *BizEd,* 44–50.

Texas Higher Education Coordinating Board. (2011). *Summary of higher education legislation: 82nd Texas Legislature.* Retrieved from http://www.thecb.state.tx.us

Toppo, G. (2010, January 6). Recession fuels shift from private to public schools. *USA Today,* p. 1a.

Weiss, J. M. (2011, April). Implementing IFRS curriculum into accounting programs. *The CPA Journal, 81*(4), 62–63.

Wilson, M., & Gerber, L. E. (2008). How generational theory can improve teaching: Strategies for working with the "Millennials." *Currents in Teaching and Learning, 1,* 29–44.

Developing Issues In Economic Education and Personal Finance

Lila Waldman

David Bashaw

University of Wisconsin

Whitewater, WI

M. Scott Niederjohn

Lakeland College

Sheboygan, WI

Two important topics in a business education program are economics and personal finance. Even if not offered as standalone courses, topics from these two areas are incorporated in many courses in the business education curriculum. The recent global economic downturn and overwhelming evidence that young adults are not learning the skills needed for financial success have prompted many institutions to advocate for the teaching of economics and personal financial education in public schools (Gavigan, 2010; Jump$tart Coalition, 2006). Evidence of this need emerges in the number of business education publications focused on the topic published in recent years. The 2009 National Business Education Association (NBEA) yearbook's focus was economics and personal finance education (Wilhelm & Truell, 2009). Two *Keying In* issues (Wagner, 2003; Glenn, 2006) discussed the need and priority for financial education. The Policies Commission for Business and Economic Education's (PCBEE's) Policy Statement 10 (1969) was titled "The Role of Business Education in Economic Education," and the more recent Policy Statement 69 (2001) focused on the role of business education in financial education. In addition, in 2000, Delta Pi Epsilon published two instructional strategy papers on the teaching of consumer finance (Adams, 2000a; Adams, 2000b).

As Clow (2009) stated in the opening chapter of the 2009 NBEA yearbook, the topics of economics and personal finance are important in preparing "students with the skills, knowledge, and attitudes necessary for leading lives that are productive and enjoyable" (p. 2). He went on to state that an informed citizenry is important for the health and welfare of our society. The three serious challenges he felt were facing individuals and the nation were the low level of savings, the overuse of credit, and increased global competition.

Economic and financial literacy serves the public interest in several ways. Citizens need to understand basic economics to participate fully in our nation's market economic system and its system of democratic governance. Economic issues related to topics such as gross domestic product, unemployment, inflation, productivity, monetary policy, and fiscal policy often dominate political campaigns at the federal and state level. This was evident in the November 2010 elections; the economy was the number one issue, and politicians traded barbs, often highly misleading, over the unemployment rate, economic stimulus packages, and international trade (Niederjohn, 2011). Apart from politics, workers in many careers benefit when they can address work-related issues with some understanding of supply and demand, costs, profits, and production. And, of course, people in all walks of life benefit from a practical understanding of personal finance. On the flip side, the costs of economic and financial illiteracy can be great. One needs to look no further than the financial crisis of 2007–2008 to find evidence of that.

THE 2007–2008 FINANCIAL CRISIS
The financial crisis of 2007–2008 provided a painful illustration of the real-world ramifications of economic and financial illiteracy. Although the causes of the crisis are complicated and will be debated by economists for years, the blame list of "greedy" investment bankers, foolish investors, imprudent bankers, incompetent rating agencies, and predatory mortgage brokers must also include financially illiterate consumers. Consumers' lack of knowledge about mortgages, interest rates, risk, debt, and consumer credit played an important part in the crisis (Niederjohn, 2011).

John Bryant, the vice-chairman of the now defunct President's Advisory Council on Financial Literacy formed by President George W. Bush in 2008 said, "Take the greed and the financial misrepresentation out of it, and the root of this crisis is massive levels of financial illiteracy" ("Getting it right," 2008). He may have been referring to large numbers of "subprime" borrowers who, often encouraged by mortgage brokers, took on loans they could not possibly afford, or to others who chose adjustable-rate loans that would only be affordable when their rates reset upward. He might also have been referring to levels of household debt. Between 1950 and 1980, household debt as a share of disposable (after-tax) income ranged from 40% to 60% (Niederjohn, 2011). Since the early 1980s, however, the household debt-to-income ratio has been climbing at an alarming rate, reaching 135% in 2007, more than twice the level of the mid-1980s (Federal Reserve Bank of St. Louis, 2011). All of these factors and many others suggest that a financially illiterate public played a part in the financial crisis that afflicted the United States and several other countries in recent years.

RETIREMENT RESPONSIBILITY, FINANCIAL SECURITY, AND CONFIDENCE

Economic and financial literacy is critical to individuals' efforts to attain short- and long-term financial security. According to the U. S. Bureau of Labor Statistics (2010), fewer than 20% of private-sector employees now have access to defined-benefit pension plans and this percentage has been declining for many years. As fewer and fewer employers commit to providing specific retirement benefits, employees increasingly bear responsibility for providing their own retirement by managing their defined-contribution retirement plans and other investments. Coupled with the increased number of financial services now available to consumers via the Internet and with Social Security's uncertain future, the trend in retirement planning creates an unprecedented need for individuals to be well informed about the options open to them, and the corresponding risks (Niederjohn, 2011).

Unfortunately, many Americans are not well prepared to handle their new responsibilities. According to a 2009 survey conducted by the National Foundation for Credit Counseling, 41% of U.S. adults give themselves a grade of C, D, or F on their knowledge of personal finance. In addition, a recent Harris poll published by the Council for Economic Education (CEE) in 2009 found that on average American adults earned a grade of 57% for their knowledge of basic economic concepts.

BEHAVIORAL INDICATORS OF ECONOMIC AND FINANCIAL ILLITERACY

It is possible, of course, that in their day-to-day conduct Americans show more knowledge about economics and personal finance than the various national assessments suggest. Unfortunately, behavioral indicators do not support this suggestion. According to a 2009 Federal Deposit Insurance Corporation (FDIC) study, 55% of African-American households are either "unbanked" or "under-banked"; that is, they have no checking or savings accounts and they make regular use of nonmainstream financial institutions such as payday-loan stores. Other examples pertain to savings and credit. A 2009 Harris survey reported that only 11% of workers under the age of 35 indicate they are participating in their company's 401(k) plans (CEE, 2009).

A study conducted by the Atlanta Federal Reserve Bank found that 30% of people in the lowest quartile of financial literacy, as measured by a test of basic financial calculation skills, thought they had fixed-rate mortgages when they actually had adjustable rate mortgages. This same study of subprime borrowers in the northeastern United States also found that 20% of people who scored in the bottom quartile experienced home foreclosures. The average was 5% for those in the top quartile (Gerardi, Goette, & Meier, 2010).

Many college students also handle credit poorly. According to a report by Sallie Mae (2009), undergraduates today are carrying record-high credit card balances. The average balance in 2009 was $3,173, and half of all students used four or more credit cards. According to the same survey, 2009's cohort of college seniors graduated with an average of $4,100 in credit card debt. This debt, of course, was placed on top of student loan debts.

CURRENT STATUS OF PERSONAL FINANCE AND ECONOMICS IN K–12 SCHOOLS

In recent years, economics and financial education has become a growing national priority. Under President George W. Bush, a national Advisory Council on Financial Literacy was formed. More recently, the Dodd-Frank financial reform bill included a provision to create an Office of Financial Literacy within the federal government. Interestingly, one state, Wisconsin, has even created a Financial Literacy Resource Center within its Department of Financial Institutions (http://www.finlitwi.org/default/index. html). Given all this attention at the national level, it is only natural to ask how our nation's schools have responded.

Personal finance and economics topics are taught at all K–12 levels, but generally offered as full courses at the secondary level. The Jump$tart Coalition and the CEE continue to promote making such courses a high school graduation requirement. The CEE's (2009) *Survey of the States* reported that 21 states required high school students to take an economics course and 13 states required high school students to take a personal finance course as a graduation requirement. In addition, the National Association of State Boards of Education stated that "financial literacy should be a 'basic feature' of K–12 programs" noting that a number of states already had passed legislation making personal finance a graduation requirement (Black, 2009, p. 44). The Jump$tart Coalition (2006) stated in its mission statement, "Personal finance is included in the education of all students."

Wisconsin's Office of Financial Literacy 2011 report stated that one-fourth of Wisconsin school districts required financial literacy as a graduation requirement. A 2010 survey conducted by the Wisconsin Department of Public Instruction found that 48% of 104 high schools responding required personal finance as a graduation requirement.

According to the survey of states conducted by the CEE (2009), 21 states currently require an economics course for graduation, while 13 require a personal finance course. Interestingly, both of these numbers are up significantly from the last survey, conducted in 2007. At that time, economics was required in only 17 states, while personal finance was mandated in only seven. The national trend seems to be toward more economic and financial education.

CURRICULUM AND RECOMMENDED COURSE CONTENT

In developing courses and units in economics and personal finance, business educators will find several sources with curriculum and course content topics available to them.

Personal Finance

Two sources for national standards in personal finance are the NBEA and the Jump$tart Coalition; there is much overlap between these lists of standards. The NBEA (2007) standards in personal finance offer achievement standards and performance expectations for levels 1–4 (grades K–14) in the following eight areas:

1. Personal decisionmaking
2. Earning and reporting income
3. Managing finances and budgeting
4. Saving and investing
5. Buying goods and services
6. Banking and financial institutions
7. Using credit
8. Protecting against risk

The Jump$tart Coalition's (2007) *National Standards in K–12 Personal Finance Education* offers competencies and performance standards for grades K–12 in the following six areas:

1. Financial responsibility and decisionmaking
2. Income and careers
3. Planning and money management
4. Credit and debt
5. Risk management and insurance
6. Saving and investing

Although titles vary between the NBEA and Jump$tart national standards, there is considerable overlap between the two sets of standards for personal finance.

In addition, state and local standards may exist to assist instructors in planning courses or units in personal finance. For example, the Wisconsin Department of Public Instruction provides a handbook that contains among other resources Wisconsin's Model Academic Standards for Personal Financial Literacy, developed in 2006 (Wisconsin Department of Public Instruction, 2009). These include content and performance standards for students at the end of grades 4, 8, and 12. In addition, the handbook offers instructors tips on how to build an effective financial literacy program, plan instruction (units, resources, and activities), and create assessments. Furthermore, Missouri has developed the *Personal Finance Curriculum Guide*, which contains a curriculum outline and resources for teaching the course (Missouri Center for Career Education, 2006).

Following good curriculum design procedures, the first step is to determine the most important competencies that students should know or be able to exhibit. The NBEA's and Jump$tart Coalition's general categories of standards should be the starting point in this process, as these standards reflect the financial knowledge most needed by citizens in our society. This decision will then provide the basis for determining the length of each unit in the course, lesson plans, and assessments.

Economics

Two sources for national standards in economic education are the NBEA and the Council for Economic Education (2003). The NBEA (2007) standards in business education offer achievement standards and performance expectations for levels 1–4 (grades K–14) in the following nine areas:

1. Allocation of resources
2. Economic systems
3. Economic institutions and incentives
4. Markets and prices
5. Market structures
6. Productivity
7. The role of government
8. Global economic concepts
9. Aggregate supply and aggregate demand

Although the NBEA standards outline a general approach to important principles, the CEE national standards for economics are very specific and thus consist of the following 20 areas:

1. Scarcity
2. Decisionmaking
3. Allocation
4. Incentives
5. Trade
6. Specialization
7. Markets and prices
8. Role of prices
9. Competition and market structures
10. Institutions
11. Money and inflation
12. Interest rates
13. Income
14. Entrepreneurship
15. Economic growth
16. Role of government and market failure
17. Government failure
18. Economic fluctuations
19. Unemployment and inflation
20. Fiscal and monetary policy

Many of the standards from these two sources overlap. The basic economic principles are roughly the same. CEE standards highlight important concepts as individual standards. For instance, the NBEA standard for allocation of resources is a concept that is heavily based on the first three CEE standards for scarcity, decisionmaking, and allocation. The NBEA standards provide a general framework for the teacher, whereas the CEE standards represent a more specific laundry list of concepts that should be taught.

The differences between the two lists are minor. The CEE standards tend to be more balanced between microeconomic and macroeconomic principles, whereas the NBEA standards are more microeconomics based. In addition, CEE standards specifically include entrepreneurship, which in the NBEA standards is a standalone topic, separate from economics.

RECOMMENDED RESOURCES FOR TEACHERS

Although many good textbooks are available for economics and personal finance courses, a large number of resources are offered free or for little cost from a wide variety of organizations today, most online. Because of this, many school districts and teachers are deciding not to purchase textbooks for these courses. Recent NBEA yearbook chapters (Luft, 2008; McEwen, 2009; Perreault, 2009; Snyder, 2009; Yohon & Kesten, 2009) list many resources for teaching personal finance. The North-Central Business Education Association (2010) published a CD with links to the NBEA standards, including 32 links related to economics and personal finance. The Wisconsin Department of Public Instruction's *Planning Curriculum in Personal Financial Literacy* includes an appendix listing more than 34 resources for teaching personal finance (Wisconsin Department of Public Instruction, 2009).

This section lists of some of the more widely used resources and a few more recent resources not included in the 2008 and 2009 NBEA yearbooks. When selecting resources, it is important to choose those that will assist in meeting curriculum standards.

Personal Finance Resources

Comparing the resources already mentioned above, the following Web sites appeared in at least three sources, indicating the popularity and continuing relevance of the resources.

- **Jump$tart Coalition Clearinghouse:** http://www.jumpstart.org
  A clearinghouse for resources from a variety of organizations.

- **Junior Achievement:** http://www.ja.org
  A partnership with the business community, providing programs for elementary, middle school, and high school programs. Community volunteers work with educators to facilitate programs.

- **Federal Reserve Banks:** http://federalreserveeducation.org
  Federal Reserve Education provides information about the Federal Reserve System. In addition, the individual Federal Reserve Banks provide a variety of useful teaching resources.

- **National Endowment for Financial Education:** http://nefe.org
  The High School Financial Planning Program is a very comprehensive, free source, including booklets that can be used as textbooks in a personal finance class.

- **Practical Money Skills for Life:** http://practicalmoneyskills.com
  Tools and resources for teaching personal finance, including "It All Adds Up."

- **Public Broadcasting System:** http://www.pbs.org/teachers
  A variety of resources for teachers, including activities and projects related to personal finance.

In addition to the six resources listed above, two other resources may be considered for use in a personal finance program/course. MoneySKILL (http://www.moneyskill.org) provides free modules and quizzes for high school students. Consumer Jungle (http://consumerjungle.org) provides free quizzes, worksheets, and resources related to cars, computers, credit, health, independent living, and wireless phones. Although there is a charge for Dave Ramsey's personal finance program (http://daveramsey.com), it provides a comprehensive program that meets the national standards.

The Brass Student Program (http://www.studentprogram.com) provides free student magazines and a variety of online resources appropriate for teaching personal finance to high schoolers. Family Economics and Financial Education (http://ag.arizona.edu/sfcs/fefe) for a charge offers curriculum packages for a complete eight-week course with supplements. Free lesson plans are also available.

A relatively new program, FoolProof (https://www.ecu.com/educational/consumer/classroom/foolproof) offered by the Educators' Credit Union includes five financial education modules, a testing system, and a teacher's guide with lesson plans.

The Wisconsin Educational Communications Board's Financial Literacy–Teach It Web site (http://www.ecb.org/finance) offers video clips showing ideas for teaching personal finance lessons in seven categories for grade levels K–4, 5–8, and 9–12.

The Center for Student Credit Card Education now offers the free credit card literacy program "The ABCs of Credit Card Finance" through their Web site (http://theabcsofcredit.com). In addition, The Ford Motor Company has a five-chapter unit, "Understanding Credit: Fun and Game, Credit-Style," (http://www.fordcredit.com/companyInfo/crediteducation.jhtml).

Economics Resources
In keeping with the above format, the following are popular resources for teaching economics that can be accessed online for free.

The CEE provides many resources—from texts to lesson plans to technological applications—to aid the teacher. Many resources are designed to help the teacher infuse economics into the teaching of other disciplines such as history or mathematics. This wealth of information can be found at http://www.councilforeconed.org/resources.

Contained in this list of resources is Econedlink (http://www.econedlink.org), one that deserves special mention. Econedlink is a database of economics lesson plans the teacher can search by concept, topic, grade level, or economic standard. Lesson plans are submitted by professors and teachers throughout the world and are available at no cost for all interested.

National Stock Market Simulation is a very popular activity that allows students to manage an imaginary portfolio of stocks, bonds, mutual funds, and commodities with real-time quotes. A national competition is held to reward those whose portfolios have the highest return over time and many states have their own competitions as well. Information on this competition and access to teacher resources and lesson plans can be found at http://www.nationalsms.com.

Federal Reserve Banks also provide a number of classroom and teaching resources for economics educators. Its Web site (http://www.federalreserveeducation.org/resources/topics/teacher_economics.cfm) contains lesson plans and activities for students. Economic indicator data available from the Federal Reserve allows for ample information to fuel case studies and investigations. The resources can also be searched by grade or topic, and information is also provided on tours and programs that the various Federal Reserve Banks offer.

Junior Achievement focuses its economic instruction on entrepreneurship, data analysis, critical thinking, and problem solving. These concepts are conveyed through various projects that allow students to apply their knowledge to real-world situations. Its Web site (http://www.ja.org/programs/programs_high_econ.shtml) offers instruction for elementary, middle, and high school students.

The Foundation for Teaching Economics offers lesson plans (http://www.fte.org/teacher-resources/lesson-plans) focusing on the economics of various events, such as the demise of the Soviet Union and natural disasters. Heavy emphasis is given to the popular topic of economics and the environment.

WHO IS TEACHING PERSONAL FINANCE AND ECONOMICS IN U.S. K–12 SCHOOLS?

A recent national study conducted by two University of Wisconsin-Madison professors surveyed more than 1,200 K–12 teachers in eight states on preparation to teach personal finance. Their results included the following troubling facts (Way & Holden, 2010):

- As many as 63.8% of the teachers feel unqualified to address their state's financial literacy standards.

- Only 29.7% of the teachers are teaching financial education in any way.

- Only 37% of the teachers had taken a college course in personal finance.

- Fewer than 20% of the teachers reported feeling very competent to teach any of the personal finance topics mentioned on the survey.

The elementary teacher respondents were used as a control group for the study. Two interesting statistics were discovered when comparisons of teacher preparation backgrounds were made with this control group: vocational/technical education teachers (including business education) were nearly five times as likely and social studies teachers were more than three-and-a-half times as likely to have taken a course with personal finance content than the elementary teachers. Vocational/technical and social studies teachers were also more likely to be teaching a personal finance course (Way & Holden, 2010).

The subject areas in which teachers are licensed to teach personal finance and economics vary from state to state. In addition to business education teachers, personal finance may be taught by family and consumer science education, social studies, mathematics, and elementary teachers (Way & Holden, 2010). In many states economics falls under the umbrella of social studies. Although other subject areas can be licensed to teach these topics, business educators are highly qualified based on coursework required in teacher preparation programs. For example, pre-service business education students at a Midwestern National Association for Business Teacher Education member university are required to take two economics courses and one personal finance course for licensure in business education (University of Wisconsin-Whitewater, 2011a). Social studies pre-service teachers at the same institution, in contrast, are not required to take economics courses unless they are pursuing the economics concentration, and no personal finance courses are required (University of Wisconsin-Whitewater, 2011b).

We suggest that the teaching of high school economics be decoupled from regulations governing the social studies curriculum in all states. In many cases, teachers certified in business education are equally well qualified, if not better qualified, to teach courses in economics. Which teacher teaches an economics course in a district should be determined by school boards and administrators in that district, based on the qualifications of prospective instructors.

Recognizing that school districts take most seriously the content that is contained on state tests, the authors suggest that testing students for knowledge about economics and personal finance should be an important part of any state's assessment system. Testing for knowledge of economics and personal finance should be placed on equal footing with testing for other social studies strands, including history.

SUMMARY

The importance of economic and personal finance education is well documented. In addition, the root causes of the recent financial crisis in the United States reinforce the need for these types of classes. Many institutions and states are recognizing this need, and states are beginning to include economic and/or financial literacy content, if not courses, as graduation requirements.

In addition to NBEA standards, the Jump$tart Coalition and the Council for Economic Education have developed national standards. Some states have also developed their own standards and curriculum guidelines. Teacher resources in economics and personal finance are plentiful. This chapter provides a list of widely used resources not published in previous NBEA yearbooks dealing with these topics.

There are no national guidelines, however, on who can teach these courses; this decision is left to states' licensure divisions. Based on related courses taken, business education teachers would appear to be the most qualified to teach economics and personal finance content and courses. Social studies teachers who have taken economics courses are also highly qualified to teach that subject. Because of the current national call for accountability, testing of students for knowledge about economics and personal finance should be incorporated as an end-of-course activity.

REFERENCES

Adams, E. (2000a, September). Consumer finance: A teaching framework including strategies, activities, and resources, part 1. *Instructional Strategies: An Applied Research Series, 16*(3).

Adams, E. (2000b, December). Consumer finance: A teaching framework including strategies, activities, and resources, part 2. *Instructional Strategies: An Applied Research Series, 16*(4).

Black, S. (2009, February). An investment in literacy. *American School Board Journal, 196*(2), 44–45.

CEE. (2003). *Council for economic education standards in economics: Survey of students and the public.* Retrieved from http://www.councilforeconed.org/cel/results.php

CEE. (2009). *Survey of the states: Economic, personal finance & entrepreneurship education in our nation's schools in 2009. A report card.* Retrieved from http://www.councilforeconed.org

CEE. (2011). *EconomicsAmerica: National standards.* Retrieved from http://www.councilforeconed.org/ea/standards

Clow, J. E. (2009) Importance of economics and personal finance education. In W. J. Wilhelm, & A. D. Truell (Eds.), *Economics and personal finance education*: NBEA *2009 yearbook* (Vol. 47, pp. 1–14). Reston, VA: NBEA.

Federal Deposit Insurance Corporation. (2009, December). *FDIC national survey of unbanked and underbanked households executive summary.* Retrieved from http://www.fdic.gov/householdsurvey/executive_summary.pdf

Federal Reserve Bank of St. Louis. (2011). *FRED economic data St. Louis FED: Financial indicators.* Retrieved from http://research.stlouisfed.org/fred2/categories/46

Gavigan, K. (2010, March/April). Show me the money resources: Financial literacy for 21st-century learners. *Library Media Connection, 28*(5), 24–27.

Gerardi, C., Goette, L., & Meier, S. (2010, April). *Financial literacy and subprime mortgage delinquency: Evidence from a survey matched to administrative data* (Working Paper 2020-10). Atlanta, GA: Federal Reserve Bank of Atlanta.

"Getting it right on the money: A global crusade is under way to teach personal finance to the masses." (2008, April 3). *The Economist, 387*(8574). Retrieved from http://www.economist.com/node/10958702

Glenn, J. L. (2006, March). Focus on finance. *Keying In, 16*(4). Reston: NBEA.

Jump$tart Coalition. (2006, January). *Mission statement.* Jump$tart Coalition for Personal Financial Literacy. Retrieved from http://www.jumpstart.org/mission.html

Jump$tart Coalition. (2007). *National standards in K–12 personal finance education.* Retrieved from http://www.jumpstart.org/assets/files/standard_book-ALL.pdf

Luft, R. L. (2008). Economics and personal finance. In M. Rader (Ed.), *NBEA 2008 yearbook: Effective methods of teaching business education in the 21st century* (Vol. 41, pp. 208–223). Reston, VA: NBEA.

McEwen, B. C. (2009). Saving and investing. In W. J. Wilhelm, & A. D. Truell (Eds.), *Economics and personal finance education* (Vol. 47, pp. 140–154). Reston, VA: NBEA.

Missouri Center for Career Education. (2006, August). *Personal finance curriculum guide.* Retrieved from http://www.missouricareereducation.org/index.php?view=project&project=persfin

National Foundation for Credit Counseling. (2009). *The 2009 consumer financial literacy survey: Topline report and data sheet.* Retrieved from http://www.nfcc.org/newsroom/FinancialLiteracy/files/2009FinancialLiteracySurvey.pdf

NBEA. (2007). *National standards for business education* (3rd ed.). Reston, VA: Author.

Niederjohn, M. S. (2011). *Failing our children: Wisconsin's deficit in teaching personal finance and economics.* Hartland, WI: Wisconsin Policy Research Institute.

North-Central Business Education Association. (2010). *Linked into learning* [CD-ROM].

Perreault, H. (2009). Personal decision-making. In W. J. Wilhelm, & A. D. Truell (Eds.), *Economics and personal finance education: NBEA 2009 yearbook* (Vol. 47, pp. 98–111). Reston, VA: NBEA.

PCBEE. (1969). *The role of business education in economic education.* Reston, VA: NBEA.

PCBEE. (2001). *This we believe about the role of business education in financial education.* Reston, VA: NBEA.

Sallie Mae. (2009, April). *How undergraduate students use credit cards: Sallie Mae's National Study of Usage Rates and Trends 2009.* Retrieved from http://static.mgnetwork.com/rtd/pdfs/20090830_iris.pdf

Snyder, L. G. (2009). Buying goods and services. In W. J. Wilhelm, & A. D. Truell (Eds.), *Economics and personal finance education: NBEA 2009 yearbook* (Vol. 47, pp. 155–169). Reston, VA: NBEA.

University of Wisconsin-Whitewater. (2011a). *Planning guide: Business education (250).* Retrieved from http://www.uww.edu/coe/docs/planning/Secondary_Business_Ed_BSE.pdf

University of Wisconsin-Whitewater. (2011b). *Teacher licensing.* Retrieved from http://academics.uww.edu/cni/degrees/secnded/ss/licensing.html

U.S. Bureau of Labor Statistics. (2010). *Employee benefits survey.* Retrieved from http://www.bls.gov/ncs/ebs/benefits/2010/benefits_retirement.htm

Wagner, J. (2003, January). Personal finance. *Keying In, 13*(3). Reston: NBEA.

Way, W. L., & Holden, K. (2010). *Final report. Teachers' background and capacity to teach personal finance: Results of a national study.* Denver, CO: National Endowment for Financial Education. Retrieved from http://www.nefe.org/LinkClick.aspx?fileticket=q9Ahp7m5Cbg%3d&tabid=246

Wilhelm, W. J., & Truell, A. D. (Eds.). (2009). *Economics and personal finance education: NBEA 2009 yearbook* (Vol. 47). Reston, VA: NBEA.

Wisconsin Department of Public Instruction. (2009). *Planning curriculum in personal financial literacy.* Madison, WI: Author.

Wisconsin Department of Public Instruction. (2010, May). *Personal finance report.* Retrieved from http://dpi.wi.gov/bit/pdf/personalfinanceresults.pdf

Wisconsin Office of Financial Literacy (2011, January). *Wisconsin financial literacy report: An interim view of Wisconsin's financial literacy legacy and future.* Retrieved from http://dpi.wi.gov/bit/pdf/financialliteracyreport.pdf

Yohon, T., & Kesten, C. (2009). Managing finances and budgeting. In W. J. Wilhelm, and A. D. Truell (Eds.), *Economics and personal finance education: NBEA 2009 yearbook* (Vol. 47, pp. 125–139). Reston, VA: NBEA.

Entrepreneurship and Basic Business Skills

Tena B. Crews
Moody E. Crews
University of South Carolina
Columbia, SC

This chapter provides an overview of entrepreneurship and basic business skills, including management, marketing, business law, and insurance. Because entrepreneurs play an integral role in today's economy, the chapter also explores the entrepreneurial spirit. Discussion of the career development process will help those interested in careers in business evolve to become competent employees or employers. The chapter concludes with information on the States' Career Cluster Initiative (SCCI) with its clusters and pathways, and the National Standards for Business Education (NBEA, 2007), which are pertinent to entrepreneurship, as well as other resources.

ENTREPRENEURSHIP

The following definitions provide an overview of entrepreneurship and a framework for this section. In common terms, entrepreneurship is typically thought of as a system through which a person starts a new business or develops a new product or service. For a more in-depth definition, Shane and Venkataraman (2000) defined entrepreneurship as "the scholarly examination of how, by whom, and with what effects opportunities to create future goods and services are discovered, evaluated, and exploited" (p. 218).

Greene (2009) defined entrepreneurs as "people who own, operate, and take the risk of a business venture" (p. 5). Obviously, the term *entrepreneur* can be defined in a variety of ways; however, typical definitions include a person who develops or discovers goods and/or services and not only organizes a business venture, but assumes the risks involved. Key terms included in these definitions provide for further investigation into entrepreneurship.

Business ventures must involve individuals with appropriate financing to fund the operation as well as visionaries who are creative thinkers to develop the idea. Individuals involved in an entrepreneurial vision may generate a new idea or invention, bring together resources to take an idea to the marketplace, or improve existing products or services (Federal Reserve Bank of Dallas, n.d.). All individuals involved in the business venture must understand the idea, be active in planning for success, and be engaged in the development and implementation of the business plan.

The business plan should describe and provide an analysis of the business and include detailed projections about the future of the business (McKeever, 2010). Typical business plan components include the introduction/executive summary, marketing research plan, risks and financial plan, operational plan, and summary statement with appendices (Greene, 2009; Mentors, Ventures, & Plans, 2010). Throughout the implementation of the business plan, risks are involved. The entrepreneur must not only be aware of such risks but also be "willing to assume the responsibility, risks, and rewards of starting and operating a business" (Community Futures, 2010, p. 1). "Entrepreneurs are simply those who understand that there is little difference between obstacle and opportunity and are able to turn both to their advantage" (Kiam, n.d.).

Small Business Impact on the Economy

Entrepreneurship is often equated with small business ownership. The definition of a small business is determined by the U.S. Small Business Administration (SBA). The definition includes the number of employees, annual income of the business, and type of business (SBA, 2010b). Overall, the SBA defines a small business as an independent business having fewer than 500 employees (SBA, 2010a).

McGibbon and Moutray (2009) compiled *The Small Business Economy: A Report to the President*, which states that "small businesses create most of the nation's new jobs, employ about half of the nation's private sector work force, and provide half of the nation's nonfarm, private real gross domestic product" (p. 1). Entrepreneurs are noted as innovators, as they develop or introduce new methods, products, and/or sources of supply (Schumpeter, 2000). By engaging in these activities, they provide a source for economic change. "The entrepreneur is the *persona causa* of economic growth" (Link & Ruhm, 2011, p. 1). Recognizing an entrepreneur as an innovator, the Massachusetts Institute for Technology (MIT) offers an entrepreneurship and innovation track within its master of business administration (MBA) program (MIT Entrepreneurship Center, 2010).

"The growth of the economy depends upon entrepreneurial activities leading to the formation of new businesses and the production of new goods and services"

(Gohmann, Hobbs, & McCrickard, 2008, p. 855). As noted by Carland and Carland (2004), entrepreneurial efforts and innovation emerged as the leading factors of employment growth and economic development in the 1990s and 2000s. In 2006 more than 5 million small businesses with fewer than 20 employees were operating in the United States (McGibbon & Moutray, 2009).

Innovation and Financial Readiness

Small business owners face uncertainty and must not only be innovative but also resourceful. They must be resourceful in using their business skills appropriately and securing financial support. A small business owner must be creative when developing a business. However, the entrepreneur must distinguish between invention, discovery, and innovation. An estimate has been made that up to 80% of the small businesses created fail annually within the first five years of operation (Nickels, McHugh, & McHugh, 1999; Silvestri, 1999). However, when less innovative and efficient companies fail and close, more innovative and more efficient companies take their place. In 2005–2006, a reported 3,682,455 firms were born and 1,999,214 firms went out of business, compared with 3,609,285 and 1,931,018, respectively in 2004–2005 (Nickels, et al., 1999).

Figure 1 provides an overview of the entrepreneurial journey. As shown, individuals have entrepreneurial thoughts and begin with an idea. Entrepreneurs need skills and financial support to begin the business and additional skills to help the business succeed. Education and business associations are crucial to the success of the business.

Figure 1: The Entrepreneurial Journey

The learning journey:
from being entrepreneurial to be a successful entrepreneur

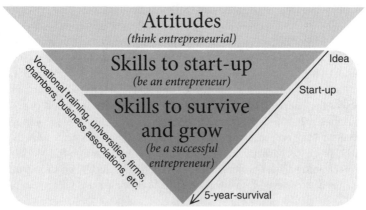

(Potter, Marchese, & Hofer, 2010)

Banking institutions require entrepreneurs to provide information to show they are financially competent, and their business plan should demonstrate financial feasibility. As noted by Careers in Business (2010), poor business skills account for the failure of most entrepreneurs. It also noted managerial incompetence, inexperience, ineffective business controls, lack of planning, and undercapitalization.

The initial steps in becoming an entrepreneur may be developing the idea and completing market research, but arranging for capital is essential to begin and sustain the business venture. Entrepreneurs rely on bank credit and investments, which average about $80,000 a year (Robb, et al., 2010).

Having enough start-up capital is essential. Start-up capital consists of "the funds a business owner will need to finance the production of a good and the sale of that good until the business reaches a break-even point" (Financial Web, n.d., para. 1). Entrepreneurs must also develop a budget and a business plan appropriate for their start-up goal. Therefore, as entrepreneurs begin to plan their business and develop their ideas, they need to be aware of specific basic business skills to help them in their venture.

BASIC BUSINESS SKILLS

Many skills are necessary for success in business. Bryce (2007) indicates the following basic business skills categories: computer/technology, Internet, and communication. Within each category are key components of the skills. For example, computer/technology skills include e-mail, word processing, spreadsheets, desktop publishing, graphics, and multimedia. Internet skills include search skills, determining reliable sources on the Internet, social media, etc. Communication skills include oral, written, and interpersonal skills. Entrepreneurs should have a basic knowledge of technology and how it affects success in business.

Overall, entrepreneurs must have good management and marketing skills. However, additional business skills, such as creative thinking, team building, and strategic planning, are specific to entrepreneurial success. These additional skills related to the entrepreneur are discussed in the management and marketing sections below.

Management

Key basic business management skills include planning, organizing, leading, and coordinating. However, an entrepreneur must also be aware of knowledge management components and how to develop a strategic management plan. A strategic management plan consists of developing the company's mission and vision and completing an internal analysis of what the company offers and external analysis of how the company compares with competitors (Brockmann & Lacho, 2010). Strategic management skills are essential and strongly relate to the financial success of small businesses (Ireland, 2007; Katz & Green, 2007).

Management includes developing structure, organizing procedures, enforcing policies, and establishing profitability. Entrepreneurs must ask pertinent questions to develop and sustain their business. Clarkson and Deck (1997) suggested the following questions for entrepreneurs.

- How does the business preserve its vision?
- How does the business balance growth, risk, and profitability?
- How does the business establish a governance system that holds management accountable without undermining its independence and flexibility?

These questions provide a basis for developing a product or service and maintaining the business. However, other business skills are pertinent to entrepreneurs. These skills include the following:

- Communication
- Decisionmaking
- Financial management
- Goal setting
- Organization
- Accounting/record keeping
- Strategic planning
- Team building

An entrepreneur may not have all of these skills initially but will work to develop them and/or employ those who have already developed the skills.

Marketing

Because an entrepreneur is an innovative individual who takes appropriate risks to bring a product to production or a service to the customer, he or she must market a product or service accordingly. Many entrepreneurs begin marketing to a particular segment of the market; therefore, the business plan must include a marketing component as well. To develop an appropriate marketing plan, entrepreneurs must understand the marketing mix: product, price, place, and promotion. However, the entrepreneur must also understand market research, supply and demand, customer behavior, and trends in the particular market in which the product or service will be created.

Through market research, entrepreneurs will analyze the findings to help them design and evaluate marketing strategies. As this happens, an effective marketing plan can be developed. Given that the marketing plan is a component of the overall business plan, this plan is a critical component to share with possible investors to help them understand the business, develop a representation of prospective customers, analyze the supply and demand for the product or service, investigate competitors, and see that a comprehensive analysis of the marketing mix has been completed.

The entrepreneur must also contemplate possible advertising avenues that include the Internet, social media, print-based media, and other advertising outlets. The entrepreneur must decipher not only how and where to advertise, but the best way to manage the marketing project. In summary, essential marketing skills needed by entrepreneurs include the following:

- Analysis
- Collaboration
- Communication
- Creative thinking
- Project management
- Technology

BASIC BUSINESS COMPONENTS

Business skills such as management and marketing are critical to the development of a project or service and success of a business; however, other components in business must be included for sustainability. These additional components include the entrepreneurial spirit, knowledge of laws that affect business, and insurance needs.

Entrepreneurial Spirit

Pierce (2008) noted five characteristics of successful entrepreneurs. These characteristics are (a) passion, (b) positivity, (c) adaptability, (d) leadership, and (e) ambition. According to Mentors, Ventures, & Plans (2010), individuals with a spirit of adventure and who are self-confident, goal oriented, persistent, and hardworking tend to be successful entrepreneurs. Those individuals investigating the possibility of becoming an entrepreneur must understand that they must have a high level of commitment, have initiative, and be innovative.

However, just because individuals start businesses does not mean they have an entrepreneurial spirit. Dawkins (2010) indicated the following characteristics constitute a comprehensive entrepreneurial spirit: uniqueness, creativity, risk taking, business savviness, developing potential, and adaptability, which may ultimately be destructive. Entrepreneurs may be so preoccupied with constant creativity that employees may find the constant change to be a lack of good management and clear direction. Therefore, a business will not succeed with entrepreneurial spirit alone. Knowledge about business law and insurance is also essential to ensure legislation is followed.

Business Law

The first business law decision an entrepreneur should make before pursuing a business is whether to create a sole proprietorship or partnership. A sole proprietorship is owned by one person, whereas a partnership involves more than one individual in the ownership of the business. An important legal aspect to consider when establishing a business is to determine who is legally responsible for the business debts. In other words, if the business is sued, can the person suing the company get business assets as well as the owner's personal assets?

Sole proprietorships and partnerships typically fall into the following three categories: Limited Liability Company (LLC), S-Corporation, and C-Corporation. An entrepreneur should investigate and determine the advantages and disadvantages to each type of business. The main differences among the three categories are how the taxes are distributed and paid and who is responsible for business debt.

Once established, a business must adhere to business legislation related to taxes, including self-employment, social security, and federal and state income taxes. Businesses must also follow the guidelines of the Americans with Disabilities Act (ADA). Entrepreneurs must follow not only federal regulations but also state and local laws. Other business law concerns may include patents and copyright issues. Legal issues pertaining to human resources, employment issues, benefits, and stock options may also pertain to the business venture. Some of these issues are also components of insurance appropriate for the business.

Insurance
Developing an appropriate insurance package for the business and its employees is a part of the financial management plan. Insurance for the employees is one component of the insurance package. Entrepreneurs may provide employee benefits such as life, disability, workers' compensation, and unemployment insurance. However, other insurance components include business liability, risk management, property insurance, and business interruption insurance.

According to Crews (2010), a risk is "any situation in which some kind of loss or misfortune is possible" (p. 4). As the risks are identified in the business venture analysis, every risk that is insurable should be insured. For example, damage to the property owned by the business is insurable and should be incorporated into the business insurance package. However, as noted by Greene (2009), not all risks are insurable. These are examples of uninsurable risks: economic conditions such as a recession, technological changes that may make the product unnecessary, and competitor's actions such as reducing the price for a similar product or service.

Therefore, entrepreneurs must review all legislation relevant to small business ownership. They must ensure that all laws are being followed and they are providing appropriate benefits for employees according to federal, state, and local laws. Entrepreneurs must be legally responsible.

DEVELOPING ENTREPRENEURS
To assist future entrepreneurs with their career development, career planning is essential. The career development process is a critical component in choosing a career

and reaching career goals. Business educators and counselors should be active in helping students understand the career development process, setting career goals, and understanding how to achieve goals students have set.

Career Development Process

The career development process is an ongoing, lifelong process, without a clearly defined start and finish. Career development is a "holistic process which integrates our changing needs, relationships, and situations with the ever-changing world of work" (University of Wisconsin-Madison, 2010, para. 2). Students must self-assess by reviewing their skills, interests, values and personality traits. After the self-assessment, students should explore careers, set career goals, and act to move forward toward those career goals.

The career development process incorporates a partnership among teachers, school counselors, students, and parents and includes the following steps at the various educational levels:

1. Self-awareness and career awareness in elementary school
2. Career exploration in middle school
3. Career planning in high school
4. Career preparation in postsecondary schooling (Zunker, 2006).

The educational levels noted above are not set in stone but instead provide a guide for helping students successfully proceed through the career development process. However, students must realize they may need to re-assess their career goals at some point in their lives as situations, priorities, and other issues arise.

Counseling and Guidance

School counselors should be instrumental in assisting students in creating their personal career development plan. However, business educators may also be key players in the process. If business educators and counselors work in a collaborative environment to assist students in this endeavor, the students benefit. Career guidance should be a top priority for students, parents, teachers, and counselors.

Counselors should coordinate resources for parents and students, conduct career development and planning sessions, and organize career fairs and other activities pertinent to career development. However, all stakeholders must realize that career development needs are different for each student (Bloch, 1991; Clark, 1988; Wadsworth, 2004).

Super, Osborne, Walsh, Brown, & Niles (1992) noted that "career development is an ongoing process, from birth to death. Maturity is a state, usually thought of as the peak of development" (p. 75). This concept of career maturity implies that individuals move through stages based on the individual's age. The stages listed below are based on Super's (1957) original concept of career maturity:

- Growth (birth to age 14 or 15)
- Exploration (ages 15–24)
- Establishment (ages 25–44)
- Maintenance (ages 45–64)
- Decline (age 65 plus) (Zunker, 2006)

Today, the idea of age stage progression has been enhanced by two concepts: (a) recycling and (b) career adaptability. Recycling was introduced by Super et al. (1992) as the ability of individuals to recycle back and forth between stages throughout the lifespan as life and work situations changed. Career adaptability is a concept related to the lifelong career development of adults and is defined by Savickas (1997) as "the readiness to cope with the predictable tasks of preparing for and participating in the work role and with the unpredictable adjustments prompted by changes in work and working conditions" (p. 254).

Super's stages of growth and exploration are still used as a guide for counselors and teachers to understand optimal career development of children and adolescents. Therefore, it is important for educators and counselors to help students understand the career development process and acknowledge that it is an ongoing process.

Courses for Students Interested in Entrepreneurship

Students interested in entrepreneurship will have varying areas of interest. Entrepreneurs have influenced every part of our economy. Consider these: Henry Ford, automobile industry; Walt Disney, entertainment industry; Ray Kroc, restaurant industry; and Bill Gates, technology industry. These are just a few examples of the multitude of entrepreneurs and areas in which goods have been produced and/or services have been provided.

Therefore, once students self-assess their skills, interests, values, and personality traits to develop their career plan, they will have a clearer idea on which courses would enhance their entrepreneurial adventure. A variety of courses are provided through the States' Career Cluster Initiative with its clusters and pathways, and National Standards for Business Education, discussed below.

CLUSTERS, PATHWAYS, AND STANDARDS

Statistics indicate that most entrepreneurs are white (87%), married (71%), and male (67%) and fall into a variety of age groups: the top two age groups are 45–54 (29%) and 35–44 (24%) (McGibbon & Moutray, 2009). However, more than 15% are under the age of 34. Also, 36% of small business owners have completed high school or less schooling (McGibbon & Moutray, 2009). With these statistics in mind, educators must work to provide students with necessary skills to be successful members of the 21st century workforce and/or skills to be successful at the postsecondary level. The following information about career clusters, pathways, and national standards helps educators ensure they are providing students with the opportunity to develop their business skills.

Career Clusters

Sixteen career clusters were developed by the States' Career Cluster Initiative through the National Career Technical Education Foundation (NTEF) as "a tool for seamless transition from education to career in this era of changing workplace demands" (SCCI, 2010, para. 1). They were developed to prepare students for college and/or the workforce and represent all career possibilities. The clusters connect education with employers, industry groups, and parents.

Although several career clusters may have general entrepreneurial connections, a select few will be discussed in this session. "Crosswalks" have been developed to connect specific clusters to O*Net occupations. One cluster, business management and administration, has been connected specifically through the crosswalk with the entrepreneur O*Net occupations. However, other career clusters that would benefit development of basic business and entrepreneurial skills include finance, information technology, and marketing.

The States' Career Cluster Initiative also provides knowledge and skills deemed essential for success in careers through all clusters. They include academic foundations; communications; problem solving and critical thinking; information technology applications; systems; safety, health, and environment; leadership and teamwork; ethics and legal responsibilities; employability and career development; and technical skills. These skills are also essential to the development of basic business and entrepreneurial skills.

Pathways

The career clusters have a variety of subgroups called "pathways." The pathways, listed below each career cluster, provide students with an opportunity to connect their personal interests with a career of their choice.

- Business management and administration
  - General management
  - Business information management
  - Human resources management
  - Operations management
  - Administrative support

- Finance
  - Securities and investments
  - Business finance
  - Accounting
  - Insurance
  - Banking services

- Information technology
  - Network systems
  - Information support and services
  - Web and digital communications
  - Programming and software development

- Marketing
  - Marketing management
  - Professional sales
  - Merchandising
  - Marketing communications
  - Marketing research (Career Clusters, 2011)

Many of these pathways were discussed as business skills, business components, and elements of the entrepreneurial spirit. They also coordinate with National Business Education Association standards, discussed below.

Standards

The National Standards for Business Education were developed and are updated through the National Business Education Association (NBEA, 2010). They provide details about what K–14 students should know and be able to do in business. Several areas of standards support the need for entrepreneurship and basic business skills. They are listed in alphabetical order below.

- Accounting
- Business law
- Career development
- Communication
- Economics and personal finance
- Entrepreneurship
- Information technology
- Management
- Marketing

RESOURCES

Imagine the world without entrepreneurs such as Donald Trump (real estate tycoon), Warren Buffet (investor and philanthropist), Mary Kay Ash (Mary Kay Cosmetics), and Ben Cohen and Jerry Greenfield (Ben & Jerry Ice Cream). These entrepreneurs, along with those mentioned previously in this chapter, had very different interests, educational backgrounds, motivations, and experiences, but all were prosperous. Their career development plans were diverse and ongoing, yet they accomplished a high level of success. As noted, the definition of entrepreneur has diverse components as well; and it is difficult to have one particular definition appropriate for all entrepreneurs. Therefore, an effective way to understand the basics of becoming an entrepreneur is outlined on the Mentors, Ventures, and Plans Web site (http://www.mvp.cfee.org/en).

E	Examine needs, wants, and problems to see how they can improve the way needs and wants are met and problems overcome
N	Narrow the possible opportunities to one specific "best" opportunity
T	Think of innovative ideas and narrow them to the "best" idea
R	Research the opportunity and idea thoroughly
E	Enlist the best sources of advice and assistance that they can find
P	Plan their ventures and look for possible problems that might arise
R	Rank the risks and the possible rewards
E	Evaluate the risks and possible rewards and make their decision to act or not to act
N	Never hang on to an idea, no matter how much they may love it, if research shows it will not work
E	Employ the resources necessary for the venture to succeed
U	Understand that they will have to work long and hard to make their venture succeed
R	Realize a sense of accomplishment from their successful ventures and learn from their failures to help them achieve success in the future

Classroom Ideas
- Invite a local entrepreneur to speak to your class about his/her experience
- Ask local business people to serve as mentors to work with students when developing their business plan or other projects
- Develop a career panel of experts to come to class so students can ask questions
- Invite local entrepreneurs to review students' business plans
- Invite bankers to role play with students as they present their business plans and apply for financial assistance
- In-School Entrepreneurship (http://www.mvp.cfee.org/en)
  - Design, create, and sell
    - Locker decorations for birthdays (students may be willing to pay to have their friends' lockers decorated on their birthdays)
    - Cakes for birthdays
    - Custom-made birthday cards or festive cards for other holidays
    - Custom-made organizers (day planners) for their school
    - Calendars with pictures of families, teachers, or friends
    - CD-ROM yearbooks

Classroom Resources

- **Assess Your Entrepreneurial Skills:** http://www.mvp.cfee.org/en/selfassessskills.html
- **Business Week:** http://www.businessweek.com
- **The Economist:** http://www.economist.com
- **FDIC's Money Smart:** http://www.fdic.gov/consumers/consumer/moneysmart
- **Hispanic Business Magazine:** http://www.ccgdata.com/6015-12.html
- **How to Write a One-Page Business Plan:** http://www.ehow.com/how_2086014_write-one-page-business-plan.html
- **Jump$tart:** http://www.jumpstart.org
- **Morgan Stanley:** http://www.alpfa.org
- **National Society of Hispanic MBAs:** http://www.nshmba.org
- **Occupational Outlook Handbook:** http://www.bls.gov/oco
- **O*Net OnLine:** http://www.onetonline.org
- **Small Business Administration:** http://www.sba.gov/starting_business/index.html
- **Teen Entrepreneurs:** http://app1.sba.gov/faqs/faqindex.cfm?areaID=30
- **Wall Street Journal–Classroom Edition:** http://www.wsjclassroomedition.com/index.html
- **Young Money:** http://www.youngmoney.com

SUMMARY

This chapter provides an overview of entrepreneurship and basic business skills. Entrepreneurs must have the entrepreneurial spirit but also have the attitude and skills to start up and survive. Successful entrepreneurs must be able to communicate effectively, make decisions on a timely basis, have basic business and technology skills, and be able to set and meet goals. They must also be organized, understand accounting principles, and develop a strategic plan that builds a team environment in their business. The ability to analyze important factors, think creatively, and manage projects in a collaborative environment is essential. With these skills, entrepreneurs have an advantage in the competitive market.

REFERENCES

Bloch, D. P. (1991, November). Reducing the risk: Using career information with at-risk youth. *NASSP Bulletin*, 38–44.

Brockmann, E. N., & Lacho, K. J. (2010). Strategic planning: A practical primer for the entrepreneur. *The Entrepreneurial Executive, 15*, 25–32.

Bryce, T. (2007). *Morphing into the real world: The handbook for entering the work force.* Palm Harbor, FL: MBA Press.

Career Clusters. (2011). *The 16 career clusters.* Retrieved from http://www.careertech.org/career-clusters/glance/clusters.html

Careers in Business (2010). *Careers in entrepreneurship.* Retrieved from http://careers-in-business.com/en.htm

Carland, J. C., & Carland, J. W. (2004). Economic development: Changing the policy to support entrepreneurship. *Academy of Entrepreneurship Journal, 10*(1–2), 105–114.

Clark, B. (1988). *Growing up gifted* (3rd ed.). Columbus, OH: Merrill Publishing.

Clarkson, M., & Deck, M. (1997). Effective governance for microfinance institutions. In C. Churchill (Ed.), *Establishing a microfinance industry*, Washington, DC: Microfinance Network.

Community Futures, Cariboo Chilcotin. (2010). *Glossary of business terms.* Retrieved from http://www.cfdccariboo.com/index.php?option=com_content&view=article& id=54:glossary-of-business-terms&catid=17:finances&Itemid=12

Crews, T. B. (2010). *Fundamentals of insurance.* Mason, OH: South-Western Cengage Learning.

Dawkins, J. (2010). *How to define entrepreneurial spirit.* Retrieved from http://ezine articles.com/?How-To-Define-Entrepreneurial-Spirit&id=738736

Federal Reserve Bank of Dallas. (n.d.). *Everyday economics: Entrepreneurs and the economy.* Retrieved from http://www.dallasfed.org/educate/everyday/ev3.html#economy

Financial Web. (n.d.). *How to determine your start up business capital requirements.* Retrieved from http://www.finweb.com/financial-planning/how-to-determine-your-start-up-business-capital-requirements.html

Gohmann, S. F., Hobbs, B. K., & McCrickard, M. (2008, September). Economic freedom and service industry growth in the United States. *Entrepreneurship: Theory and Practice, 32*(5), 855–874.

Greene, C. (2009). *Entrepreneurship: Ideas in action.* Mason, OH: South-Western Cengage Learning.

Ireland, R. D. (2007). Strategy vs. entrepreneurship. *Strategic Entrepreneurship Journal, 1*(1–2), 7–10.

Katz, J. A., & Green, R. P. (2007). *Entrepreneurial small business.* Boston, MA: McGraw-Hill.

Kiam, V. (n.d.). *Introduction to the course: Teaching entrepreneurship.* Retrieved from http://www.aspira.org/files/documents/entrepreneurship/Intro.pdf

Link, A. N., & Ruhm, C. J. (2011, January). Public knowledge, private knowledge: The intellectual capital of entrepreneurs. *Small Business Economics, 36*(1), 1–14.

McGibbon, S. C., & Moutray, C. (2009). *The small business economy: A report to the President.* Small Business Administration, Office of Advocacy. Washington, DC: U.S. Government Printing Office.

McKeever, M. P. (2010). *How to write a business plan* (10th ed.). Berkeley, CA: NOLO.

Mentors, Ventures, & Plans (2010). *About entrepreneurs.* Retrieved from http://www. mvp.cfee.org/en

MIT Entrepreneurship Center. (2010). *The entrepreneurship and innovation track (E&I).* Retrieved from http://entrepreneurship.mit.edu/ei

NBEA. (2007). *National standards for business education* (3rd ed.). Reston, VA: Author.

Nickels, W. G., McHugh, J. M., & McHugh, S. M. (1999). *Understanding business.* Boston, MA: McGraw-Hill.

Pierce, S. (2008, February). *Spirit of the entrepreneur.* Retrieved from http://www. entrepreneur.com/startingabusiness/selfassessment/article190986.html

Potter, J., Marchese, M., & Hofer, A. (2010). *Skills for entrepreneurship: Call for participation 2009*. Organisation for Economic Cooperation and Development, Centre for Entrepreneurship, SMEs and Local Development. Retrieved from http://www.oecd.org/document/0,3746,en_2649_34417_44281759_1_1_1_1,00.html

Robb, A., Reedy, E. J., Ballou, J., DesRoches, D., Potter, F., & Zhao, Z. (2010, May). *An overview of the Kauffman firm survey: Results from the 2004–2008 data*. Social Science Research Network. Retrieved from http://papers.ssrn.com/sol3/papers.cfm?abstract_id=1606933

Savickas, M. L. (1997). Career adaptability: An integrative construct for life-span, life-space theory. *Career Development Quarterly, 45*(3), 247–259.

SBA. (2010a). *Office of Advocacy: Frequently asked questions*. Retrieved from http://www.sba.gov/advo/stats/sbfaq.pdf

SBA. (2010b). *Size standards*. Retrieved from http://www.sba.gov/contracting opportunities/official/size/index.html

SCCI. (2010). *US states' career cluster initiative for CTE*. Retrieved from http://hrd.apec.org/index.php/US_States'_Career_Cluster_Initiative_for_CTE

Schumpeter, J. A. (2000). Entrepreneurship as innovation. In R. Swedberg (Ed.), *Entrepreneurship: The social science view* (pp. 51–75). Oxford, England: Oxford University Press.

Shane, S., & Venkataraman, S. (2000). The promise of entrepreneurship as a field of research. *Academy of Management Review, 25*(1), 217–226.

Silvestri, G. T., (1999, Summer). Considering self-employment: What to think about before starting a business. *Occupational Outlook Quarterly 43*(2), 15–23. Retrieved from http://www.bls.gov/opub/ooq/1999/Summer/art02.pdf

Super, D. E. (1957). *The psychology of careers*. New York: Harper and Row

Super, D. E., Osborne, W. L., Walsh, D. J., Brown, S. D. & Niles, S. G. (1992). Developmental career assessment and counseling: The C-DAC model. *Journal of Counseling and Development, 71*, 74–80.

University of Wisconsin-Madison (2010). *Career development process*. Retrieved from http://www.dcs.wisc.edu/info/careerdevelopment.htm

Wadsworth, J. (2004). Career development for adolescents and young adults with mental retardation. *Professional School Counseling, (8)*2, 141–147.

Zunker, V. G. (2006). *Career counseling: A holistic approach*. Belmont, CA: Thomson Brooks/Cole.

Technological Trends Affecting the Business Education Curriculum and Instruction

Herbert F. Brown
Appalachian State University
Boone, NC

Technology permeates all aspects of our lives today. Computer ownership and global network connectivity continues to grow at an amazing rate in the nation and the world. Students are exposed to technology at a very early time in their lives, and they now represent an image of how technology permeates all aspects of our lives regardless of our diversity. In fact, teen and young adult groups are the most likely to have gone online at least once at a rate of 93%, compared with adults at around 74% (Lenhart, Purcell, Smith, & Zickuhr, 2010).

All individuals—students and adults alike—must now understand and embrace what it means to be a digital citizen. Digital citizenship reflects what it means to be an active and productive citizen in a digital world. Digital media are now integrated into all facets of our lives. This level of technology integration not only creates new opportunities but also creates perils that must be dealt with in a meaningful way. Many years ago business educators were concerned with developing and delivering a curriculum in general business and specific information technology areas; however, because of the depth and breadth that information technology has reached in all students' lives, we recognize now more than ever that the business education curriculum needs to incorporate technology learning across the board. In addition, the previous technology curriculum now needs to grow and develop into a high level of integrative technology instruction as well as advanced topics in information technology. As always, the technology curriculum will grow and develop each day as the landscape of information technology changes. Thus, the purpose of this chapter is to provide insight into some of the developing technology trends and how they will impact the business education curriculum in the coming years.

TECHNOLOGY CURRICULUM: DETERMINING FACTORS

The technology curriculum is a substantial portion of any business education program. Curriculum development should be directed by national standards, industry trends/needs, and industry certifications. Because the purpose of the business education curriculum is to develop students for the workforce or continuation in higher education, the focus of the technology curriculum should support these efforts.

National Standards

If the technology curriculum changes at such a rapid pace, how are business educators expected to modify their curriculum rapidly enough and how should business educators frame and design this curriculum to be innovative? The National Business Education Standards developed by the National Business Education Association (NBEA) in 2007 provide an excellent framework for developing information technology curricula. These standards are developed and updated about every five years by experts in the field. The standards for information technology include these categories: (a) impact on society, (b) hardware, (c) operating systems and utilities, (d) input technologies, (e) productivity software, (f) interactive multimedia, (g) Web development and design, (h) information retrieval and synthesis, (i) database management systems, (j) systems analysis and design, (k) programming and application development, (l) telecommunications and networking infrastructures, (m) information technology planning and acquisition, (n) security, privacy, and risk management, (o) ethical and legal issues, (p) technical support and training, (q) information technology and business functions, and (r) information technology careers. Not only do the standards provide a content framework, but they also provide suggested academic levels at which information technology content can and should be delivered (NBEA, 2007). Many states and local districts use these standards to develop the more specific courses in their respective business education curricula and the specific content, learning objectives, and assessments for each course. Classroom teachers can also use these standards in conjunction with their state and local standards to help drive appropriate curriculum development for their individual schools.

Industry Needs and Trends

National standards provide a framework for curriculum development; however, state and local needs must also be addressed in the development of effective curricula. Every state has unique industries and specific job markets. If business educators are preparing students to obtain employment or continue in higher education, curriculum development must address state and local workforce needs (ASCD, n.d). Through the use of effective advisory groups at the state and local level, educators can obtain essential information on their specific workforce needs.

Another way to determine workforce needs is through needs analysis research. This can be conducted through formal research methods at the state or local level or by advanced business and marketing classes to expose students to this necessary skill. Students can create the research methods (surveys, focus groups, etc.), validate their research instruments, conduct the research, and analyze the results. These results can be used locally or shared through professional presentations at local or regional chambers of commerce, boards of education, and other interested groups. When industry needs are properly identified, joint programs can be developed with the high school and local postsecondary institutions, using articulation agreements to provide students a clear path into the workforce (Fountain, 2010). This process ensures that students are prepared for their local workforce needs and helps ensure the local workforce needs are met.

National/Industry Certifications

Another area driving information technology curricula is national/industry certifications. Although technology-based coursework completed by students does reflect a level of exposure to technology content, it does not ensure a depth of understanding and/or capability necessary for success in an industry. Many states and local education authorities have embraced national industry-standard certifications in combination with standard coursework, so completion of a specific course in a technology area could include an industry-recognized certification at the end of the course with a passing score on the required examination. Some examples include Microsoft Office Specialist Certification for Office Applications (Microsoft, n.d.), A+, and Net+ ("CompTIA," n.d.) for general hardware and network knowledge and even advanced networking certifications in Microsoft Server applications and Linux. When national/industry certifications are used in the curriculum development process, the objectives for those specific certifications drive the specific content in a course.

TECHNOLOGY TRENDS: SOFTWARE

One key area of curriculum development and a major part of most business education programs is computer application software. Software traditionally consisted of coded applications distributed to the end user through traditional media formats (i.e., CD-ROMs and DVDs). The main variations in software applications were the vendor-specific designs of the software and the licensing models under which they were distributed. Today, however, software development, distribution, and licensing have experienced extensive changes. Furthermore, software applications that are taught in most curricula have traditionally focused on the common office application suites and, to a small degree, development platforms (i.e., programming and Web development). Software curricula are now beginning to evolve to include much higher-level applications, such as high-end database systems and enterprise resource–planning (ERP) systems. Software curricula are also helping to change the way we communicate and share information (e.g., e-mail, social media, Web development, and collaboration software such as Google Docs and Microsoft SharePoint) (Parsons & Oja, 2008). The following sections will explore software applications, their evolution into "cloud" computing and Web 2.0 environments, and new licensing models such as open source.

Open Source

When developing curricula around computer software, developers cannot ignore the introduction of the open-source licensing model. The concept of the open source model focuses on a distributed, shared development of the software code and transparency of the process (Open Source Initiative, n.d.). Many developers work to refine the code for a particular software application. They share components of the code and develop a final working application. Other developers can take that code and assist in developing the code beyond the initial design. Because the development and maintenance of the application is a collaborative initiative, the software applications are typically released under one of the dozens of open source licenses. For example, one common open source license—the "GNU" license—allows for free use and distribution of the application (including the source code) and encourages developers to share improvements to the code with the original development team (Open Source Initiative, n.d.). What this means for the classroom is an extensive array of free software that anyone can use and the necessity to discuss current software licensing standards.

Suites

New software licensing models have helped generate new application suites available at no charge such as OpenOffice (http://www.openoffice.org) that are opening up opportunities for students who cannot afford commercial office application suites to download and install. Many applications are available through the open-source licensing model including graphics applications, office application suites, Web development tools, programming development tools, and more. Many commercial applications have an open source or free counterpart, including Microsoft Office through the free limited applications it offers online through Microsoft Live (http://office.microsoft.com/en-us/web-apps). Many of these open source applications are experiencing mainstream implementation in organizations, making it necessary to address these applications in the software curriculum. No longer is it sufficient to teach one commercial office application suite. It is more important than ever to prepare students to generalize their application software experience to more than one software platform. It remains important for students to learn the specifics of productivity applications suites, such as Microsoft Office, OpenOffice, and Corel's WordPerfect Suite; students must also learn how to use each application in the suite appropriately and how to generalize their knowledge among multiple vendors.

Cloud Computing

Not only have software licensing and development models changed, but so have the delivery mechanisms. Software applications are now being delivered through the "cloud." Cloud computing is an environment that provides for ubiquitous computing. Cloud computing involves software that typically runs in a Web-based environment without the extensive hardware footprint required for traditionally installed software (Anderson & Rainie, 2010). For example, a traditional installation of an office application suite may require more than one gigabyte of storage on a computer hard drive, whereas a cloud-based application suite may require no local installation or only a small piece of software to access the cloud-hosted application. Cloud computing is another concept helping to reduce barriers to computing that have contributed to the digital divide in our country (Anderson & Rainie, 2010).

Although cloud computing has included storage tools and application software, it is now being examined as an alternative delivery mechanism for the entire computer operating system. The Google Chrome operating system (OS) is one such emerging tool based on the open-source Chromium OS project (The Chromium Projects, n.d.). When developing the information technology curriculum, including cloud computing is essential not only as a delivery mechanism but also as an alternative to traditional software with analysis of the advantages and disadvantages of software available in the cloud. Although students will likely be working with cloud computing as an end user by experimenting with cloud applications, networking and software development courses should also be examining cloud computing from a development and support approach.

Collaboration Tools

Cloud computing not only opens opportunities for computing anytime, anywhere, but it also helps to facilitate collaboration. The business education curriculum has always been rich with teamwork and collaboration. With the continued changes in technology, it is becoming easier than ever to develop collaboration among students through the use of technology. For example, cloud-based applications such as Google Docs have collaboration tools that allow individuals not only to globally share documents but also to collaborate in real time on those documents (Google Docs, n.d.). Many other commercial applications are also including tools within their applications to facilitate sharing and collaborating on files better, such as Microsoft Groove (n.d.). Collaboration tools fundamentally change the way that individuals work on projects together. Any business education curriculum needs to include collaborative tools and assignments to address these trends.

Web 2.0

Another software trend is the concept behind Web 2.0 and 3.0. Web 2.0 and 3.0 are not direct applications or even standards; they are more conceptions of what individuals believe the Web should resemble. These concepts address the Web environment as a collaborative, media-rich, open-sharing environment wherein individuals can use tools to build and share information in simple and effective ways. These tools can range from communication and sharing tools such as microblogging, blogs, and wikis to applications such as Twitter, Ning, Edmoto, Prezi, and others that facilitate the sharing of information and communication in different, open, and collaborative ways (O'Reilly, 2005).

Web 3.0 technologies strive to incorporate an increasingly media-rich environment that facilitates the sharing and creation of media-rich content and personalization of the Web. It also includes the concept of the "semantic Web" wherein the computer provides an additional layer of information processing using intelligence models to attempt to think for the user (Van Kesteren, 2011). For example, in searching for a movie, a search engine provides additional information on restaurants in the area, assuming the searcher might be interested in dinner with the movie. These concepts are also reflected in the release of the HTML 5 specification for Web development that incorporates new code that facilitates the easier incorporation of media (audio, video, etc.) (Van Kesteren, 2011). The business education curriculum needs to address the advantages of Web 2.0/3.0 and the global sharing of information, as well as the disadvantages of and concerns about copyright and accuracy of information, sources, and citations.

Enterprise Resource Planning and Database Technologies

Business education programs today are attempting to meet the needs of business through their curriculum development efforts. States are exploring curriculum development in the advanced areas of ERP systems and enterprise-level databases. ERP systems from vendors such as SAP and Oracle are typically large-scale, integrated management information systems that an organization relies on to store and manipulate information in all areas of the enterprise (human capital management, operations, corporate services, and financials) (SAP, n.d.). This is a substantial step forward in the traditional business education software curriculum and requires a much higher level of general business knowledge as well as database management and development skills.

Enterprise-level database systems are another curriculum area that supports the ERP curriculum and also many other platforms on which the databases might interact. These databases include such products as Oracle (http://www.oracle.com/us/products/database/index.html), MySQL (http://mysql.com/products), and SQL Server (http://www.microsoft.com/sqlserver/en/us/default.aspx). Many databases now include Web development with back-end database connectivity for easy access for users.

With additional coursework in mathematics and statistics, another area for potential curriculum development is data mining or the ability to extract useful information from vast amounts of stored data. Data analysis and decisionmaking can be completed through the use of "what-if" analysis in Microsoft Excel at a basic level and through statistical packages, such as SPSS,[1] for more advanced statistical analysis of data. Sample business data sets can be created so that all students can analyze different types of data for decisionmaking. More advanced programs can partner with organizations such as SAS through their Global Academic Programs (SAS, n.d.). Although these areas are considered very advanced, states and localities should continue to develop curricula in these areas as they meet workforce needs.

In summary, computer software is one area of information technology curriculum development that has seen many changes. The software curriculum can and should

---

[1]Originally, Statistical Package for the Social Sciences.

be far reaching. The curriculum should meet the needs of business and industry and prepare today's students for the diverse range of software and the methods of delivery they will experience in their education and careers.

TECHNOLOGY TRENDS: HARDWARE

Computer hardware is another area of information technology curriculum development. Hardware continues to change at a very rapid pace. Curricula that encompass the computer hardware area must be fluid and adaptive to remain current and challenging. Multivendor platforms must also be explored, as the landscape of computing hardware rapidly changes.

Rapid Change

Moore's law on computer microprocessor evolution states that the number of transistors on a chip will double about every two years. This concept has held true for over 40 years. More transistors per chip means more processing power in computer hardware. This rate of change suggests an exponential growth in computing power every two years (Intel, n.d.). This change is seen daily in new releases of microprocessors that grow computer speed exponentially over the last revision and hard drives that appear to double in capacity on a monthly basis. Any curriculum involving computer hardware must be fluid and ready to adapt to these rapid changes. Curriculum content in this area needs to be updated at least yearly if not more regularly. Students should also be exposed to ways to deal with this level of rapid change, learning to adapt to change effectively, as detailed in texts such as *Who Moved My Cheese,* by Spencer Johnson (2002), in which he articulates that change is difficult but necessary and the key to success is dealing effectively with that change. To do so, students must be exposed to change management concepts.

System Platforms

Computer hardware rapidly changes but so do operating systems that run on that hardware. The lines between computer hardware and operating system compatibility have changed since the introduction of the Intel-based Macintosh computers. Now there is a common hardware platform with primary differences maintained in the operating system designs. Three main platforms are now available: (a) Microsoft Windows, (b) Apple Mac OSX, and (c) Linux (numerous distributions). Although the Microsoft Windows platform still maintains a large portion of the business organization market share, the Apple Macintosh, Linux, and mobile platforms are experiencing rapid growth (Keizer, 2010). Apple has strongly marketed toward the younger populations with ads and new technology devices that appeal to this generation. Linux distributions have seen growth due to their open-source development and release model that allows individuals to install and run a fully functional graphical user interface–based operating system with software and utilities for free. Businesses have long embraced both Macintosh and Microsoft Windows computer systems, and now many businesses are including Linux installations on the desktop and in the network server infrastructure (Noyes, 2010). The business education curriculum needs to be designed to expose students to all three of these platforms on more than a cursory level. Students need to engage these operating systems on a deeper level in order to understand and develop a working knowledge of each platform. This does not always require buying three computer hardware platforms. Software solutions, such as virtualization technology, can be used to install a single computer platform with all three operating systems, allowing students to experience personally the features and workings of each platform. School districts, therefore, enjoy the cost savings of not having to buy additional hardware for each platform.

Miniaturization and Mobility

Technology developments have also moved computer functionality, typically considered desktop computing technologies, toward small, portable technologies with similar functionality. Computer hardware continues not only to increase in capacity and computing speed, but also to see a reduction in size, allowing for smaller and smaller computing devices such as netbooks, tablets, and smartphones. Laptop computers, around for many years, have now evolved into smaller netbooks with reduced computing power; however, they are still very functional for the average computer user and can complete almost identical computing tasks as a traditional laptop computer (Horowitz, 2008). Laptop classifications have also changed to include tablet computers that are convertible laptops, changing between a traditional laptop and a tablet with the swivel of the screen. Tablet computing has also changed to become a standalone media device with the introduction of the Apple iPad (http://www.apple.com/ipad). The iPad, running a specialized operating system, is now joined by the android-based operating system tablets.

Cell phones have also evolved to become small computers. Smartphones check e-mail, manage documents, and maintain calendars and can perform most of the functions of a normal mobile computer depending on the applications installed. All of these innovations need to be addressed in the business education curriculum.

Technology curricula must be fluid and must match changes in technology. One major concern with these changes is the cost of implementing and maintaining a curriculum that changes as quickly as the technology. Business educators must establish new ways of thinking to incorporate these changes on a restricted budget. Purchasing "sets" of technology, such as tablet computers, and working students through modules has always been one successful method.

Additional funding sources can also be found to help alleviate the financial burden of maintaining technology programs. Programs can also write grants to obtain funding. Foundations and local supporters are also additional potential funding sources. Business educators must find creative ways to fund their programs to provide the students with the most enriching programs available.

With smartphones this is a greater challenge. One solution may be to use "emulators" from the smartphone vendors and build a virtual smartphone that runs on the desktop. Partnerships should be considered at the national level with vendors such as Google to develop a fully functional android emulator that can be installed in a computer lab, which would allow students to experiment with the features of a smartphone without owning the physical device. Virtualization technologies, such as Virtualbox (https://www.virtualbox.org) and Microsoft VirtualPC, should be explored to install multiple operating systems on individual lab computers. The possibilities are endless; however, to provide the most current and rewarding computer hardware curriculum available, educators must think creatively to address the rapid change.

TECHNOLOGY TRENDS: NETWORKING

Growth in connectivity technologies has had a tremendous impact on communications as well as the proliferation of newer technologies such as cloud computing. Without a substantial network communication infrastructure, cloud computing and Web-based application solutions would not be possible today. The growth in connectivity has been through wired, wireless, and mobile environments.

Wired Infrastructure

The United States has developed and long maintained a robust wired network and telecommunications infrastructure. While wireless technologies continue to grow, the wired infrastructure is experiencing renewed interest and investment. In 2010–2011 the federal government announced the National Broadband Plan, connecting America to assist with additional funding and development for rural broadband that will increase the wired infrastructure to additional rural communities where it is not always profitable for telecommunication companies to expand. This initiative is focusing on delivering high-speed fiber optic cabling to the end point (home or business) and general improvements to broadband access across the nation (Broadband.gov, n.d.).

Although a digital divide in broadband connectivity remains between Caucasian (67%) and African-American (56%) households, the gap was almost cut in half just between 2009 and 2010 (Smith, 2010a). Fiber optic infrastructures directly connected to a home or business provide an unparalleled level of connectivity that can handle video, audio, and very high-speed data connections with bandwidth to spare. Although the cost to install the fiber can be high, the potential rewards are great. Greater bandwidth and higher-speed connections open the pathways for the continued convergence of technologies. Examples of convergence include Google TV (n.d.), interactive television with annotations that link to Web content, and more. The use of high-speed wired technologies increases the possible opportunities in the classroom as well. Students with very high-speed Internet access at home can receive almost any type of digital content quickly and easily, which is very important for online learning (Smith, 2010a). It also means that students completing a networking curriculum need exposure to these new technologies and their management, including fiber optic cabling, splicing, and termination; router and gateway configuration; software management tools; and security.

Wireless and Mobile Networking

While many telecommunication companies are reaping the benefits of federal funding to assist with their wired infrastructure, many wireless and cellular providers are enhancing their wireless infrastructures to support the growth of smartphones and other mobile devices. Mobile providers are building extensive data networks into their infrastructure to support all of the new mobile devices requiring network connectivity. Those data networks are expanding from 3G network designs and speeds to the faster 4G network designs. The users of mobile devices will continue to expect higher speeds and greater bandwidth for their devices. Mobile connectivity growth continues at a rapid pace; about 59% of American adults connect wirelessly to the Internet using Wi-Fi or mobile connections (Smith, 2010a, 2010b).

In addition to mobile technologies, the use of Bluetooth personal network devices and Wi-Fi connection speeds has increased. New technologies such as WiMax and others ensure that higher-speed wireless networking solutions are on the horizon. WiMAX is a wireless standard that provides high-speed access to data networks similar to Wi-Fi, but across cellular infrastructures and is defined by the IEEE 802.16 standard (WiMAX Forum, n.d.).

Security is a critical element of any wireless infrastructure, and strides continue to be made to enhance all wireless communications. The proliferation of these technologies means that curricula can now be mobile more than ever before. Students need exposure to mobile and wireless technologies and must understand the impact these technologies have on their personal, work, and academic lives. They need technical skills to connect and manage their wireless devices and security. The business networking curriculum must address wireless infrastructure and security extensively and integrate both into the overall network infrastructure plan. Wireless technologies and mobile communications should be included in curricula and integrated into the students' educational experience.

INFLUENCES OF TECHNOLOGY ON INSTRUCTION: INSTRUCTIONAL TECHNOLOGY

Technology is a curriculum area that is not specific to business education, but must be seen in a larger, cross-curricular framework. Although business educators often design and deliver the majority of the technology curriculum, business educators must be aware of how technology permeates every aspect of students' lives. Educators must ensure all students have the technology skills needed to succeed in elementary, secondary, and higher education; however, students must also be provided the means to develop advanced technology skills for the workforce. Today, technology has a tremendous impact on the instructional environment.

Online Education and Course Management System

With the growth of communication networks and supportive technologies, online education is experiencing tremendous growth in education and business organizations. In fact, the percentage of high school students taking online courses nearly doubled in 2009: 27% of high school students completed at least one online class, compared with 14% in 2008 (Nagel, 2010). Many states and localities are already providing online course offerings. Online courses allow districts to leverage and manage resources more effectively by offering advanced courses online without the need for a specifically trained teacher at the physical location. Many of these online courses are managed through a course management system such as Blackboard (http://www.blackboard.com) or Moodle (http://moodle.org). These server-based software applications provide a simple-to-use, Web-based system that enables teachers to manage the static content (documents), as well as quizzes, grading, and more. The course management systems make it simple enough that technology novices can quickly develop the structure of an online course without understanding any Web coding.

Virtual Schools

As the technology tools have improved online course delivery, the number of virtual schools has also increased. A virtual school model can be a completely online-delivered educational experience or a virtual educational structure that delivers individual online courses within a traditional setting to supplement student educational opportunities. The North Carolina Virtual Public School is one such structure that provides students access to advanced coursework through an online delivery model that students would not otherwise have access to (http://www.ncvps.org). For example, in the North Carolina business education curriculum, the advanced e-commerce II course is delivered through the virtual public school initiative. Online course delivery designs allow states and individual school districts to improve course offerings and opportunities with minimal cost.

Other virtual school models allow for a complete K–12 educational experience. A number of states are incorporating options for school districts to provide students with a virtual (online) education option (North Carolina Virtual Public School, n.d.). Through this model, districts can either create their own educational learning environments or partner with commercial entities to assist with the delivery and management of an online education experience. Home school groups may also use online courses and programs to help facilitate the education experience. With the proliferation of information on the Internet and with many organizations now offering free resources and even free courses, such as MIT's OpenCourseWare Initiative, virtual schools will continue to grow (MIT, n.d.). What this means for the business education curriculum is that developers need to ensure they are considering virtual schools and virtual (online) content delivery in their development process. Additionally, all educators now need experience with online course development and management tools, as many traditional teachers today will facilitate courses in the virtual world tomorrow. This is an excellent area in which business educators can expand their upper-level curricular areas to include training tools, online training, and course delivery and development.

Videoconferencing

Many of the online course and school delivery models include static content hosted in course management systems. Some developers are now beginning to add more videoconferencing to their online delivery tools. Videoconferencing is not a new concept. Hardware-based videoconferencing has been around for many years, as well as desktop videoconferencing solutions. Although the large-scale hardware videoconferencing solutions are experiencing marginal growth in the business enterprise, the desktop solutions are experiencing renewed growth and respect with information technology managers (Turek, 2010). Early desktop videoconferencing solutions involved point-to-point connections with software such as Microsoft Netmeeting and CuSeeMe, whereas individuals today use applications such as Skype. These and other similar tools began to develop into point-to-multipoint solutions that allowed one individual to broadcast to multiple endpoint connections, such as the group version of Skype and Oovoo (http://www.oovoo.com). Applications today include multipoint desktop videoconferencing built around software solutions that allow all connections to interact with video, audio, shared documents, shared whiteboard spaces, chat, and more. These tools, such as Adobe Connect Professional (http://www.adobe.com/products/adobeconnect.html), Wimba (http://www.wimba.com/products/wimba_classroom), Elluminate (http://www.blackboard.com/Platforms/Collaborate/Overview.aspx), and others are complete synchronous learning solutions. Course development using these tools provides students with a more interactive classroom experience that more closely resembles a traditional classroom.

Another video-based delivery method is streaming video. Streaming video can be real-time video streaming or recorded content. Many educators use streaming media Web sites, such as YouTube and Discovery Education Streaming, to augment their classroom experience. Videoconferencing solutions can be incorporated into any business education curriculum to enhance the delivery of the course content. However, business educators should be examining videoconferencing as a business communication tool and how to set up and use videoconferencing tools. The curriculum should also include creating, editing, and delivering original videos for personal, educational, and business use. Today's students are part of the digital generation that expresses itself through all forms of media; therefore, tools should be in place to facilitate this form of student expression.

Mobile Technologies

Access to digital information has changed greatly in the past decade. Access to information does not require a physical location; access can be from anywhere. Today's mobile platforms include more processing capability than the desktop computers of a decade ago. The proliferation of mobile technology and its capabilities is changing the way people work and live. Students are carrying smartphones with e-mail, Web, and document-processing capabilities. The current generation of students is a "texting" generation, using the phone very little in comparison with their texting habits (Smith, 2010a, 2010b). Whole new languages have been developed to facilitate long text communications with minimal typing.

However, many schools still ban cell phones from their schools because they are seen as distractions. In higher education many institutions are requiring students to buy clicker devices for each course they take so they can participate (connect) with commercial response systems. Public schools use response systems that cost thousands of dollars, while students are carrying one of the most robust response systems available—texting with cell phones. Many vendors are now providing commercial and free versions of software that allow instructors to develop audience response systems; these, in turn, allow students to use their cell phones as "clicker" devices and to text responses to a central system that aggregates the responses and displays the results in real-time. Such systems include Poll Everywhere (http://www.polleverywhere.com).

Mobile technology will only continue to grow in the future and should be embraced as part of the educational system. Mobile technology is a topic that influences curricula from business communications to networking (infrastructure and connectivity) to advanced E-commerce (Web development for the mobile platform). Curriculum development should include mobile technologies as delivery tools; but more important, business educators need to educate students on the etiquette and acceptable use of mobile technology.

Tablets, E-Book Readers, E-Books
As delivery platforms change, so do the media that are delivered across those platforms. Traditional paper-based books have a limited future (Neil & Kestner, 2001). Electronic books (e-books) are rapidly gaining market share and continuing to grow in popularity. When e-book readers were released in 2006–2007, they appeared to be another technological fad that might fade with time. However, the past several years have seen renewed growth in e-books and e-readers such as the Kindle, Nook, or Sony Touch. According to Purcell (2011), the number of adults in the United States who owned an e-book reader doubled from 6% in November 2010 to 12% in May 2011. Students in higher education are now beginning to embrace e-textbooks with greater vigor, most likely due to the substantial difference in cost between the electronic and paper versions of textbooks.

Since the e-book reader was released, the tablet device has hit the market, which is viewed as a hybrid e-reader and laptop computer. The tablets, such as the iPad or android-based tablets, are much more than e-readers; they are multimedia-rich productivity tools. These tablets include everything from media players to e-book readers and even include productivity tools and virtual keyboards for entering textual data. Tablets also have full network connectivity, and many include cellular network connectivity as well (e.g., 3G and 4G). All of these devices have changed the way students receive their textbooks, read books for pleasure, and read for work. Books are instantly available across communication networks and can be annotated with notes and comments. They are fully searchable to find necessary information easily. These devices will change the way that students read, think, and explore creative endeavors. The electronic publishing component of the business education curriculum should embrace the educational benefits, ease, and simplicity of these technologies.

Electronic Communication Systems

All of these instructional tools must be delivered across communication networks. These networks must be high-speed, high-bandwidth infrastructures that fully support the media-rich format of data. Electronic communication today means electronic mail, social networking, desktop videoconferencing, texting, chatting, and so much more. The language of electronic communications has also changed to include emoticons and an array of acronyms used in chatting and texting that need their own dictionary. Digital communication allows anyone, anywhere to share ideas, experiences, and opinions with schoolmates, family members, and friends through public or private microblogs, blogs, wikis, and other information-sharing tools such as Facebook and Twitter. Professional networking tools, such as LinkedIn, are allowing individuals to connect through business relationships and professional interests and stay connected. LinkedIn and similar social networking tools have redesigned the idea of professional "networking."

Collaborative Applications

Collaborative, Web-based tools allow business people the opportunity to share and collaborate on documents across the building or across the world. Many of these tools (e.g., Google Docs and Dropbox) are free! Schools have also begun to use social networking tools such as Ning and Edmoto to connect with this digital generation of students. Educators must find new ways to engage and motivate this digital generation of students and use these tools to reach the students and their diverse learning styles. Business educators should also develop curricula that address the advantages and disadvantages of these technologies, while also focusing on the increased use of these tools in business to communicate and collaborate. Advanced curricula should also include the installation, management, and configuration of these many tools.

Technology is having a tremendous impact on the business education classroom in the areas of curriculum and course content delivery. Tools have changed to include social media, synchronous and asynchronous online learning solutions, videoconferencing, and collaborative applications. Business educators need to be ready to adjust and adapt their curricula to remain current in the ever-changing area of instructional technology.

CRITICAL FACTORS INFLUENCING CURRICULUM DEVELOPMENT AND DELIVERY

With technology changing at such a rapid pace, it is imperative that educators remain abreast of the changes and their potential influence on the development and delivery of curricula. Business educators need to see beyond the specific technology tools and reflect on the impact of those tools on critical thinking, global communication, media literacy, and the larger education curriculum. Technology provides endless opportunities for business educators to work on cross-curricular initiatives that not only help academic areas, but also bring greater positive exposure to business education programs. The following sections will explore instructional delivery, 21st century skills, and critical thinking.

Instructional Delivery

Educators must reach beyond button pressing and step-by-step directions to exploratory environments that require students to use and develop problem-solving and critical thinking skills. Students need to be provided with opportunities to communicate and express themselves in the ways of the digital generation, such as through social networking and interaction, media creation, and Web-based tools. Schools and educators need to examine existing policies and procedures that inhibit connections and communication, and look for new and innovative ways to connect with students through new technologies including smartphones and tablet devices. Change has occurred; now the questions are: will it be embraced and how will it be embraced?

21st Century Skills and Critical Thinking

Technology has fundamentally changed society and will continue to do so. Regardless of how technology changes, some fundamental skills are necessary for everyone. The Partnership for 21st Century Skills (http://www.p21.org) identifies student outcomes needed by all students in the 21st century. Businesses have also long embraced the need for all employees to possess the skills identified by this group. The Framework for 21st Century Learning includes four core areas: (a) core subjects and 21st century themes, (b) learning and innovation skills (creativity, innovation, critical thinking, problem solving, communication, and collaboration), (c) information, media, and technology skills, and (d) life and career skills (Partnership for 21st Century Skills, n.d.). The business education curriculum includes information and technology literacy throughout the curricular frameworks as well as many of the other elements incorporated within the 21st Century Skills framework. However, it is imperative that the development and revision of business education curricula include introducing the fundamental skills included in the 21st century framework. These skills are needed by *all* students today, and this opens many additional opportunities for business educators to work across both their curriculum and those of other academic areas to help ensure all students develop the necessary problem-solving and critical thinking skills to be successful in today's world. Students must be able to think independently, analyze information critically, solve problems, and present the solutions in an effective way using an appropriate delivery mechanism (that mechanism is not always a PowerPoint presentation). By developing project-based curricula that require students to think creatively, develop innovative solutions, and present solutions in new ways, educators are ensuring students have the 21st century skills necessary to be effective digital citizens. Incorporating new media and new technology, including social media tools, helps educators to connect students with other students on projects and can even connect students globally. These technologies allow students to collaborate and share their creative ideas in new and innovative ways.

SUMMARY

Technology will always change and evolve; therefore, the business education curriculum must evolve to meet those changes. Educators must not only stay current with the technology, but also find innovative ways to use these technological changes to reach students with diverse learning styles better. Communication is also changing due to evolving technologies, and educators must be ready to reach and teach students using new communication tools. Educators must develop learning communities and collaborate with students in both traditional and online learning environments. Technology curriculum development in business education is ever-changing but can be very rewarding. Business educators must adapt and find new ways to make cross-curricular connections, focusing on developing a next generation of digital citizens who have the 21st century skills they need to succeed in education, work, and life.

REFERENCES

Anderson, J., & Rainie, L. (2010, June 11). *The future of cloud computing.* Retrieved from http://pewinternet.org/Reports/2010/The-future-of-cloud-computing.aspx

ASCD [Association for Supervision and Curriculum Development]. (n.d.) *Thinking about curriculum.* Retrieved from http://webserver3.ascd.org/handbook/demo/curricrenew/pocr/sectioni.html

Broadband.gov. (n.d.). *National broadband plan: Connecting America: Announcing the National Broadband Plan.* Retrieved from http://www.broadband.gov/plan

CompTIA. (n.d.). *CompTIA Certifications.* Retrieved from http://certification.comptia.org/getCertified/certifications.aspx

Fountain, R. S. (2010, December 27). POV: NC articulation helps students plot their own educational paths. *Community College Week.* Fairfax, VA. Retrieved from http://www.ccweek.com/news/templates/template.aspx?articleid=2251&zoneid=7

Google. (n.d.). *An overview of Google Docs.* Retrieved from http://docs.google.com/support/bin/answer.py?answer=49008

Google TV. (n.d.). *Features.* Retrieved from http://www.google.com/tv/features.html

Groove. (n.d.). *Groove virtual office.* Retrieved from http://grv.microsoft.com

Horowitz, M. (2008, October 12). *What is a netbook computer?* Retrieved from http://news.cnet.com/what-is-a-netbook-computer

Intel. (n.d.). *Moore's law and Intel innovation.* Retrieved from http://www.intel.com/about/companyinfo/museum/exhibits/moore.htm

Johnson, S. (2002). *Who moved my cheese?* New York, NY: Penguin Group.

Keizer, G. (2010, January 3). *Windows market share slide resumes.* Retrieved from http://www.computerworld.com/s/article/9142978/Windows_market_share_slide_resumes

Lenhart, A., Purcell, K., Smith, A., & Zickuhr. (2010, February 3). *Social media and young adults.* PewInternet. Retrieved from http://pewinternet.org/Reports/2010/

Social-Media-and-Young-Adults.aspx

Microsoft. (n.d.). *Microsoft Office specialist certification.* (n.d.). Retrieved from http://www.microsoft.com/learning/en/us/certification/mos.aspx#certifications

MIT [Massachusetts Institute of Technology]. (n.d.). *About OCW.* Retrieved from http://ocw.mit.edu/about

Nagel, D. (2010, June 29). *Report: Online learning nearly doubles among high school students.* Retrieved from http://thejournal.com/articles/2010/06/29/report-online-learning-nearly-doubles-among-high-school-students.aspx

NBEA. (2007). *National standards for business education* (3rd ed.). Reston, VA: Author.

Neil, R., & Kestner, R. (2001). *The future of science textbooks.* American Academy of Arts & Sciences. Retrieved from http://www.amacad.org/publications/trans3.aspx

North Carolina Virtual Public School. (n.d.). *The value of your state virtual school.* Retrieved from http://www.ncvps.org/docs/about/value_svs_10.pdf

Noyes, K. (2010, 12 October). *Linux is on the rise for business.* Retrieved from http://www.pcworld.com/businesscenter/article/207479/linux_is_on_the_rise_for_business.html

Open Source Initiative. (n.d.). *The open source definition: Introduction.* (n.d.). Retrieved from http://opensource.org/docs/osd

O'Reilly, T. (2005, September 30). *What is Web 2.0: Design patterns and business models for the next generation of software.* Retrieved from http://oreilly.com/web2/archive/what-is-web-20.html

Parsons, J. J., & Oja, D. (2008). *Computer concepts,* 10th ed., Boston, MA: Thomson Course Technology.

Partnership for 21st Century Skills. (n.d.). *Framework for 21st century learning.* Retrieved from http://www.p21.org/overview/skills-framework

Purcell, K. (2011, June 27). *E-reader ownership doubles in six months.* Retrieved from http://pewinternet.org/Reports/2011/E-readers-and-tablets/Report.aspx

SAP. (n.d.). *ERP Software from SAP.* Retrieved from http://www.sap.com/solutions/business-suite/erp/index.epx

SAS. (n.d.). *SAS Global Academic Program.* Retrieved from http://support.sas.com/learn/ap/brochure.pdf

Smith, A. (2010a, August 11). *Home broadband 2010.* Retrieved from http://pewinternet.org/Reports/2010/Home-Broadband-2010.aspx

Smith, A. (2010b, July 7). *Mobile access 2010.* Retrieved from http://pewinternet.org/Reports/2010/Mobile-Access-2010.aspx

The Chromium Projects. (n.d.). *Chromium OS.* Retrieved from http://www.chromium.org/chromium-os

Turek, M. (2010, September 2). *Frost & Sullivan research on the worldwide videoconferencing endpoints market* . Retrieved from http://www.frost.com/prod/servlet/market-insight-print.pag?docid=210688103

Van Kesteren, A. (2011, January 13). *HTML 5 differences from HTML 4.* Retrieved from http://www.w3.org/TR/2011/WD-html5-diff-20110113

WiMAX Forum. (n.d.). *Frequently asked questions.* Retrieved from http://www.wimaxforum.org/resources/frequently-asked-questions

Social Media and Networking Tools: Meeting Our Stakeholders in Their World

Charlotte Haley

Gold-Burg Independent School District

Bowie, TX

Social media permeate life in a variety of ways. This chapter provides an overview of social media and networking tools and appropriate examples for incorporating them into the business education curriculum. Social networking will be defined, and its past, present, and future will be explored. The inclusion of social media in the classroom will be examined along with any advantages and disadvantages. Specifically, a review of commonly used social media tools that allow users to share, publish, create, discuss, and explore virtual worlds will consider the value of these applications and how they relate to the educational classroom experience. In teaching, modeling, and managing social networking tools in the classroom, educators can create a competitive advantage for students in the 21st century.

DEFINITION

Social networking can be defined as connecting and interacting with others using Web-based services (Boyd & Ellison, 2007). Social networking connects people and ideas in a myriad of ways. Teens and "tweens" are using social networking for hours every day (Harpaz, 2010). Educators must be prepared to meet these so called "digital natives" also known as "Net Gen" within their world (Wehrli, 2009).

Net Geners learn collaboratively. Net Gen students respond to rich, interactive learning environments. They are not passive learners and are easily bored. They spend much of their free time online and embrace technology (Barnes, Marateo, & Ferris,

2007). Incorporating social networking as part of the curriculum is a natural progression to engage students using tools they are already accustomed to using outside the classroom. Discovering ways to implement social networking sites as part of the curriculum is one way to accomplish this task.

Likewise, when implementing any new technology, enthusiasm and motivation are keys to success, as students are naturally motivated by new technologies (Moore, 2008). Also key are the building blocks of 21st century skills identified by the Partnership for 21st Century Skills (http://www.p21.org) as critical thinking, communication, collaboration, creativity, and innovation. By teaching students how to interact and engage in appropriate ways through social media, teachers can help students develop these skills and accomplish the goal of creating 21st century citizens, thus giving students a competitive advantage in their chosen careers.

HISTORY OF SOCIAL NETWORKING

Early social networking focused on communicating in real time in chat rooms. SixDegrees.com, launched in 1997, was the first to combine the ability to create profiles, list friends, and surf friends' lists. Many social network sites have appeared on the Internet horizon since the days of SixDegrees.com. Among those sites, many are still relevant today and have contributed to a social revolution. In 2003 LinkedIn launched its site, followed by MySpace. YouTube launched in 2005. Facebook has been around in different forms since 2004 but became available to everyone in 2006 and has been growing exponentially. Twitter also started in 2006 and has experienced major growth with more than 200 million tweets per day as recently reported by Twitter. Most sites are free and obtain revenue by selling advertising (Boyd & Ellison, 2007).

SOCIAL NETWORKING IN THE PROFESSIONAL WORLD

Businesses make use of social networking tools to communicate with their customers and to reach potential customers. Facebook and Twitter allow businesses to easily connect, communicate, and collaborate with customers. These connections can be a boon for small businesses, as they are able to reach their customers with a small marketing budget (Swartz, 2010). Through this collaboration, customers are able to provide valuable feedback and thus guide company strategy for new products and services. All businesses, large and small, can use social networking as a low-cost method of reaching customers and interacting with customers to gain potentially valuable feedback (Pattison, 2009).

TOP 10 SITES FOR SOCIAL NETWORKING

Social networking is a global concept. A June 2010 survey by The Nielsen Company found that Brazil and Italy ranked at the top of the list of Internet users of social network sites (Nielsen, 2010). The survey also ranked Australia first in users who spend the most time per person on social networking sites (Nielsen, 2010). According to Discovery News (Strickland, n.d.), the following are the top 10 social networking sites worldwide:

1. Facebook: More than 750 million users (http://www.facebook.com/press)
2. Twitter: Popular microblogging site with 200 million tweets per day (http://twitter.com)
3. LinkedIn: Designed for professionals and has 100 million users (http://www.linkedin.com)
4. YouTube: social video site with 92 billion page views per month (http://www.youtube.com)
5. Hi5: Popular in Mexico and other Latin American countries (http://www.hi5.com)
6. Skyrock: The number one site in France (http://www.skyrock.com)
7. Friendster: One of the pioneers of social networking sites (http://www.friendster.com)
8. 51.com: Popular in China (http://www.51.com)
9. Orkut: Owned by Google and popular in Brazil (http://www.orkut.com)
10. MySpace: Once a top site but declining in popularity (http://www.myspace.com)

Although each site has different options, individual users usually have the ability to set profiles and manage privacy settings. The minimum age to join and set up an account differs but generally starts at 13 years of age (Strickland, n.d.).

A new social tool launched by Google named Google Plus might address concerns about privacy issues. One promising feature called "Circles" allows users to establish multiple social networking groups with privacy settings for each circle. Another plus for this application is the future prospect of integration with other Google applications (Watters, 2011).

USAGE STATISTICS

Who uses social networking tools? Teens and tweens "report spending almost as much time using social networking services and Web sites as they spend watching television" according to a study by the National School Boards Association (2007, p.1) in partnership with Grunwald Associates, Microsoft, and Verizon. The majority of students surveyed in the report say they use social networking weekly and education is a common topic. Yet most schools have blocked access to social networking sites and many have policies that forbid electronic communication between teachers and students. Educators and administrators must find ways to bridge the gap (Wehrli, 2009).

Students reported that they regularly post messages, share music, share videos, upload digital images, build Web sites, maintain their own blogs or contribute to blogs, and create new content by participating in collaborative projects, creating new characters, and creating polls, surveys, and quizzes in the National School Boards Association survey (2007). Educators can take advantage of these skills and the opportunity to help students improve information literacy skills for later use in the business world because businesses are also using social media.

Social media business usage continues to rise. Kenna McHugh reported in *The Social Times* that the number of businesses using social media is near 43% according to a Regus survey. The research results show that half of U.S. companies use Twitter and more than half of the companies in the United States use social networks such as LinkedIn. LinkedIn is a professional social network with more than 100 million users according to its Web site (http://www.linkedin.com). The survey also reported that 70% of small businesses use Facebook as a marketing tool to achieve brand loyalty (McHugh, 2011).

BENEFITS FOR THE CLASSROOM

Among the many benefits for including social networking in courses are active student learning and high engagement in the process. High engagement leads to high motivation, which naturally leads to fewer discipline problems in the classroom. Social networking teaches and enhances collaborative skills and works well for project-based learning. Group projects provide a good platform for using social media, as group work fosters communication and collaboration (Reynard, 2008).

Project-based learning develops real-world skills and productivity skills, as students must solve a problem and arrive at a solution within the guidelines of the project. This learning activity requires active participation and provides opportunities for creative thinking, which in turn, develops critical thinking skills. Connecting with peers in this way allows for peer learning and developing valuable networking skills.

Years ago, students often only memorized and recalled information, with little application or evaluation. Today's students must be able to locate and evaluate information and create new information in the learning process. Skills such as sorting, analyzing, and discussing the infinite amounts of information available are more important (Wesch, 2009). Social networking provides opportunities for this to happen.

Moreover, social networking gives students a sense of belonging to a group and gives each student a voice. Students are able to develop communication, collaboration, and peer learning skills. Even when students repeat or re-phrase what another student may post, they are learning, gaining a deeper understanding, and connecting to the curriculum. Communication, collaboration, and connection with others to achieve business objectives are key skills.

Social networking may change the landscape of course management systems, learning management systems, or platforms for distance learning by adding applications that allow new and better communication, collaboration, and connection with other students and teachers.

Students learn effective communication skills. Effective communication is a valuable skill and important to success. Students can hone this skill through social networking. Using social online media, people are able to converse and exchange ideas.

Students have opportunities to practice influencing, persuading, and corresponding within the context of the assignment using these applications.

Within the constraints of the site, people are able to build groups to accomplish a purpose. That purpose may be to communicate with friends and family. Similarly, it could be used as a way to build team communication for business teams or student groups. As students are already using these applications, they can easily transfer these skills modeled in the classroom to future career skills.

Students learn team collaboration skills. The social Web allows users to work together with others of similar interests or common goals to achieve an objective. Promoting collaboration at all levels of education paves the way for students to create new learning experiences. Beginning this process earlier in secondary education encourages higher-level uses in college. Another benefit is that working with others and discussing ideas in cyber space saves time, as participants work at their own pace and within their own schedule with peer learning as a natural outcome.

Students learn social connections skills. At the heart of social networking is connecting people and ideas. In education, administrators and technology directors have done an excellent job of connecting students, teachers, and computers with online access; but more work remains if schools desire to take advantage of all of the educational opportunities technology offers. Cloud computing is one of those opportunities. Cloud computing is defined as using programs and software located on the Internet instead of on a local computer (Glenn, 2010, p. 3), which offers flexibility and inexpensive options for access to Web-based applications.

Connecting with others is as easy as logging in to the Web site or picking up a mobile phone. Connections can be in real time with all parties online at the same time or staggered, as participants leave comments and messages for others to respond to later. E-mail is a daily ritual for many, but the value of connecting with others in a social networking site compared with e-mail is the ability to keep all related messages in a common thread and to include larger groups. Each person in the group can contribute equally and at a convenient time.

As mentioned previously, many students are already communicating, collaborating, and connecting using social networking technology. Teaching and modeling appropriate uses of these technologies is an opportunity for educators to help students gain skills and thus a competitive advantage in their chosen career fields.

Students learn transferable skills. Social networking tools allow students to learn a variety of skills and gain confidence in using these skills in different ways. For example, they learn that all word-processing software programs and tools have the same basic functions and that, in learning one software application and understanding the basics, they can intuitively use any similar program.

Students learn to use productivity tools. Cloud computing is a way for students to learn to use productivity tools with social characteristics. Often referred to as Web 2.0 tools, productivity tools located on the Internet or in the cloud are free on many Web sites such as Google and Zoho. These tools accomplish the same tasks as traditional office software applications, and the social feature is the ability for students to create documents, share documents with a group, and collaborate in real time to complete a project. Some applications such as Google Docs show the contributions of each student, and as long as the student shares the document with the teacher, it can become a valuable classroom tool for monitoring progress. An added benefit is that students do not need to have access to specific software at home; they only need an Internet connection to reach the cloud for anywhere, anytime computing.

Students learn skills in Bloom's digital taxonomy. Another measure of the value of social networking in education is the ability of social networking and online services to make the most of every level of the learning domains in Bloom's Digital Taxonomy (Churches, 2008). The following are some examples:

- Creating (blogging, podcasting, video projects, publishing, and directing)
- Evaluating (blogging and networking)
- Analyzing (outlining, mashing, and editing)
- Applying (sharing, editing, and uploading)
- Understanding (searching and tweeting)
- Remembering (bookmarking and searching)

SAFETY IN THE CLASSROOM

Keeping students safe and teaching students how to use social media safely is of utmost importance. Most K–12 districts have current Internet use policies in place that prohibit social media. According to a National School Boards Association study (2007), school districts must develop new policies and procedures in order to secure online safety for all students and educators and obtain buy-in from all parties. Another part of the answer lies in training students and educators how to harness the power of social media tools through appropriate use. For educators and students, learning how to manage an online identity is essential.

The first lesson should be online safety. Leaving an undesirable image is one of the pitfalls of social networking. Educators and students should realize that once information is posted online, they might not be able to delete it. The information and/or images could still be archived on a server or on friends' sites. It is no longer in their control. Privacy settings should be the primary consideration for everyone when setting up accounts. Educators and students must be aware of the results that a poor online image might convey to a potential employer or college recruiter.

Security and appropriate use. Security of online documents is a concern as well. Students are working in a user-generated environment, and the teacher becomes a facilitator with less control. In the past, schools have solved these problems by blocking access; but they are now looking at ways to incorporate social networking into the curriculum. Early adopters of this technology in the classroom see positive results and believe the benefits outweigh the risks.

As a way to manage those risks, schools have adopted a number of safety programs to allow students to use social media. One option is a private cloud offered by major companies such as Cisco, Dell, and IBM. A private cloud is more secure because the software servers are located within the control of the school district. Other companies provide secure cloud solutions at a low cost; for example, eBackpack monitors student accounts in Facebook and Twitter. Its Web site (http://www.ebackpack.com) provides a complete list of benefits.

Access to inappropriate content. A downside for allowing student access to social networking tools is the lack of control over inappropriate content. Educators and administrators are concerned about the lack of control over content, and this issue becomes a roadblock to obtaining administration buy-in for implementing social media in the classroom. The Children's Internet Protection Act requires K–12 schools to adopt and implement an Internet safety policy. Bridging the gap between current policies and the social, technological revolution is not easy. Schools must develop a plan to identify potential problems and move forward (Wells, 2010). Many students have Internet access at home and should be taught how to use these tools and applications in appropriate ways (Davis, 2010).

EXAMPLES ON USING SOCIAL NETWORKING TOOLS IN THE BUSINESS CLASSROOM

The many forms of social media and how they relate to the educational classroom experience through commonly used applications can transform a classroom. Among the many tools available for teaching and learning are blogging, chat and instant messaging, mashups, microblogging, podcasts, social bookmarking, social media, social networks, text messaging, virtual worlds, and wikis. Creating and sharing content in various ways gives educators many opportunities to develop dynamic curriculum for their students.

Blogging. The term "blog" combines the words Web and log. *Merriam-Webster's Online Dictionary* defines it simply as an online journal ("Blog," n.d.). Blogs have many applications for the classroom such as information sharing, discussion, collaboration, and problem solving. Blogs can be a review or extension of a classroom discussion. As it is not real-time communication, students can use blogs when they miss a class or when they need to review an important topic. Blogs are useful for collaboration and discussion. They provide opportunities for students to further develop reading and writing skills.

An example of using a blog in the classroom is for students to post classroom notes to provide clarification or classroom news. This approach enables teachers to see who has a firm grasp of the classroom topic and who may need additional help. Students can write in their blog to demonstrate understanding of a specific topic. Blogs are used by many teachers to develop and enhance writing and communication skills, such as book reports created by the class through blog postings. Students can also use a blog as a reflection for a completed project in order to add new meaning and gain further understanding. For this purpose, students who complete a stock market simulation project might reflect by using a blog for a "broader discussion of personal financial goals" (Yacht, Siegel, Crosson, & Renner, 2011, p.150). Used in this way, the blog facilitates critical thinking and peer learning opportunities.

Examples of two blog Web sites are Blogger.com, which is accessible by logging into a Google account and Class Blogmeister (http://www.classblogmeister.com). Blogger.com is a free weblog publishing tool from Google. It is easy to set up with pre-made templates. Class Blogmeister is also a free blog site intended for classroom use. Accounts are established and maintained by the classroom teacher. Security is maintained as much as is possible with online accounts.

Chat and instant messaging. Chat rooms are valuable in the classroom for real-time communication. Teachers can use chat rooms to extend classroom discussion or as a review. Some social networking sites such as Facebook, Meebo, and Google Talk have chat access for online users. An example for classroom use is to prepare a list of questions and objectives before the session; copy and paste the questions in as the chat progresses and allow students to respond; set guidelines in advance for how many responses are required of each student; and evaluate the quality of the response using this number and response quality. A rubric would be a quite useful tool here.

Students can also use chat rooms to learn from various students in globally dispersed locations. Locating students in other countries could be a great adventure for an international business class. Yet another application in a business classroom would involve the instructor inviting a guest expert to participate in a classroom chat, setting up the chat, and then having students interact with the guest expert, for example, a mortgage broker or an insurance specialist. Students could prepare questions in advance to ask the experts during the chat in order to learn from experts who may not have the time to travel to the school for a face-to-face classroom presentation.

Gaggle (https://www.gaggle.net) is a company that provides K–12 educators with safe online learning tools. Gaggle offers chat room services and e-mail as part of a free service or a pay service, and it reports any misuse of the site directly to the classroom teacher or administrator. This safety report satisfies Internet safety guidelines for most schools.

The future of chat rooms seems to involve a shift from text-based services to video chats. All that is needed is a microphone and a webcam. Google has applications for voice and video chat, whereas Skype offers similar options. Voice Thread (http://voice thread.com) is an application that facilitates a collaborative multimedia slide show.

Mashups. Mashups are simply the process of using two or more social media tools together to create something new. One example of a mashup is the practice of embedding photos at points on a map such as Google Earth or Google Maps. Yahoo maps and Flickr are other examples of a mashup. Integrating photos with mapping programs allows the user a richer experience. In a classroom, students searching for information on a specific location can view photos taken at that location and posted by a variety of users. Other examples are Facebook applications that allow users to check into locations and iPhone applications that map global positioning system points with digital photos.

Microblogging. Microblogging is a form of blogging that uses short messages. Twitter is the most common microblogging tool used today. Twitter allows users to post short messages of 140 characters or less. Educators can use this tool to communicate with students about assignments or hold class discussions. Summarizing assignments is a good way to use Twitter.

The real value of Twitter is the ability to follow people and organizations of interest to you. This is accomplished by "following" the person or organization on Twitter and checking periodically to read their tweets. For example, a business class could follow a company as it might apply to business research for a project. An economics or finance class might follow the New York Stock Exchange. Business teachers could follow NBEA to get tweets about new technologies for the classroom or to learn about webinars or other opportunities for professional development.

For a business strategy class, students might choose a business and follow that business on Twitter over time. Students could create a list of strengths and weaknesses from this information and gain valuable insight in the process. Students could later develop a strategy based on customer feedback for products and services.

Microblogging is a way to add backchannel communication in the classroom. Imagine a classroom in which the teacher presents new material while students in the room post comments on Twitter. The teacher would also have access to the Twitter feed and be able to respond to students' questions and concerns and adapt the presentation or lecture for clarity based on students' comments. Students in the class could also address their classmates' questions and comments as a way of encouraging peer-to-peer learning and collaboration (Wehrli, 2009).

Podcasts. A podcast is simply a digital media file. It can be audio or video. A vodcast is a video podcast. The process of creating a podcast is to record it and publish it. One place to access educational podcasts is through the iTunes store and iTunes U. ITunes U is a product of Apple, Inc., and according to the company Web site (http://www.apple.com/education/itunes-u), it is a way for students to have access to educational content.

Teachers can use podcasts to record lectures and discussion questions. These podcasts can be downloaded to iPods, MP3 players, and other media devices. Students can create podcasts and use them in a variety of ways.

One example of a podcast would be a lesson to improve interviewing skills. A group of students could create interview questions and record a mock interview. Listening to the podcasts can allow students to hear how their answers might sound and then brainstorm ways to improve the process as a reflection. Other examples are recording school news, interviews or oral histories, book reviews, and critiques.

Audacity is an example of a software program for creating podcasts. Audacity (http://audacity.sourceforge.net) is user friendly and can be downloaded free. One major benefit of Audacity is the ability to edit content to meet time restrictions and to remove unneeded content. Garageband is another program used to create podcasts for Mac users. Users of the free online application Aviary (http://www.aviary.com) can create podcasts with its application called Myna.

Social bookmarking. Bookmarking Web sites such as Delicious and Diigo allow users to bookmark specific URLs for research or other projects and share those bookmarks with others. Instead of being limited to bookmarks saved to a specific computer, users of programs like Delicious can organize bookmarks on the Web so they can be accessed from a computer at any location. Think of having all of your favorite sites available from any Internet connection, organized, and accessible by using keywords. Furthermore, one has the ability to share those sites with a group and to access sites accumulated by similar groups.

Using social bookmarking sites is as simple as downloading a widget to your Internet toolbar and clicking on the widget while on a Web site that you want to add to your collection. Add keywords or tags for easy retrieval, and users will always have easy access in order to revisit and share the location.

In a classroom group project, social bookmarking sites could organize all of the reference Web sites that each person in the group used for research. This shared resource teaches organizational skills and allows other students easy access to all materials for a project.

Social multimedia. Social multimedia sites focus on sharing digital media such as videos and graphics. Flickr and YouTube are two major sources. As inappropriate content is a major concern for school districts, Gaggle also filters YouTube videos for school use. Generally, the best approach for using YouTube is for teachers to find YouTube videos for the class and direct students to specific ones or to download the videos for classroom use. Links to YouTube videos can easily be included in presentations to engage learners, and current versions of presentation software have the ability to embed YouTube videos directly.

YouTube is a rich environment with videos on practically any topic. Students are already using YouTube; so by including this social media tool in the classroom, teachers are providing timely and relevant learning opportunities. Videos are available to teach accounting concepts to discover a variety of careers, and to seek expert advice on numerous topics. All of these resources are free and available 24/7.

Sal Khan of Khan Academy created vodcasts to help his relatives with math and posted the videos on YouTube. He quickly became a YouTube favorite and now creates free teaching videos for a variety of subjects with the support of Google and Microsoft along with user donations. At his Web site (http://www.khanacademy.org), users will see an introduction video by Bill Gates.

Flickr and Picasa are other media-rich sites focusing on digital graphics to share and manage photos. They can be good for classroom use because they allow the user to choose other users who view content. Users can post comments and notes. Teachers can use Flickr or Picasa for creative writing exercises or for sharing photos for specific projects.

Social networks. Most K–12 schools do not have access to social networks such as Facebook and MySpace due to Internet filters, as noted earlier; however, legitimate sites are available to create educational social networks, such as Ning.

Ning is a site where users can create their own educational social network. A classroom Ning allows teachers to limit users and provide students an environment to work on group projects. The value of Ning in the classroom is the ability to limit users, protect privacy, and thus gain more control over content. Ning is easy to set up due to predesigned templates, which allow users to add photos and videos. Users can create blogs and chat in real time. A low-cost mini-plan is available for education that is ad free. For these reasons, Ning is a good social networking tool for classroom use.

Text messaging. Text messaging is a great way to fill time at the beginning or end of class with surveys using a tool such as Poll Everywhere. Poll Everywhere can be used as a classroom response system. With Poll Everywhere, teachers can create polls at the beginning of class as a pre-assessment tool and have access to the results immediately. It can also be used as a reflection or quick assessment of understanding at the end of class. Using applications such as Poll Everywhere engages students and increases participation.

Virtual worlds. SecondLife is a 3D virtual world. Users socialize, collaborate, and live virtual lives. After setting up an account, users create an avatar. An avatar is a graphical representation or character that represents the member. Basic membership in Second Life is free.

An example of using Second Life in the classroom is to build a community and a virtual economy. Users can purchase goods and services in this economy. Another application could be a group project in which students create training for a specific purpose. It could also be a place for a group to meet, plan, and discuss group projects and thus eliminate the need for all group participants to be in the same location at the same time.

Some businesses, such as IBM and Dell, have a presence in Second Life. Businesses can hold meetings, conduct training, and collaborate with associates. Universities such as Notre Dame use Second Life for online collaboration and distance learning. Many possibilities for educational applications may be developed.

Wikis. A wiki is free server software that allows users to create and edit Web page content. According to Wikipedia, which may be the most well-known wiki, the term Wiki is a Hawaiian word meaning quick or fast. The value of a wiki is the ability for collaboration by multiple creators and the ability to add linked pages along with photos and other files. The idea of a wiki is that it will constantly evolve as users correct information and contribute to the content. Wikipedia evolves in an environment of discussion and shared contributions (Wesch, 2009).

Examples of sites for educators to use in creating classroom wikis are PBwiki, Wetpaint, Google Sites, and Wikispaces. Educators should explore options to set up an educational site without ad content. Otherwise, one cannot control the ads that may pop up on any given day. Students should also be aware of privacy issues and use first names only or find another way to protect their identity.

A classroom wiki might contain information about the course of study, in which students add content, such as "what they know," throughout the course thereby creating a classroom resource or portfolio on the subject. Additional interlinked pages can be added to the wiki so an idea of overall structure is available to users before starting. This structure allows content to be organized and easily accessed by users.

Another example is a group wiki. A group could use the wiki to gather and organize information for a group research project. This process allows everyone an opportunity to edit content and allows the teacher to see progress and to make sure that the project is on track.

SUMMARY

By exploring the different aspects of social media and networking tools, educators discover opportunities to meet students in their world and engage them in the process of active learning. Among the many applications explored, Twitter, Facebook, and LinkedIn may offer the most benefit to educators and students, not only because of their popularity but also their high percentage of usage in the business world. Furthermore, schools must address privacy concerns by developing policies for use and security practices in order to make effective use of social media as a teaching tool. In addition, educators and students need training in how to use applications effectively and how to manage an online identity in order to gain the most benefit. Among those benefits, students gain essential skills for success such as effective communication and collaboration skills. As a result, educators can create a competitive advantage for students in the 21st century by teaching, modeling, and managing social networking tools in the classroom.

REFERENCES

Barnes, K., Marateo, R., & Ferris, S. P. (2007). Teaching and learning with the net generation. *Innovate 3*(4). Retrieved from http://www.innovateonline.info/index. php?view=article&id=382

Blog. (n.d.). *Merriam-Webster dictionary online.* Retrieved from http://www.merriam-webster.com/dictionary/blog?show=0&t=1309735731

Boyd, D. M., & Ellison, N. B. (2007). Social network sites: Definition, history, and scholarship. *Journal of Computer-Mediated Communication, 13*(1), article 11. Retrieved from http://jcmc.indiana.edu/vol13/issue1/boyd.ellison.html

Churches, Andrew. (2008) *Bloom's taxonomy blooms digitally.* Retrieved from http://www.techlearning.com/article/blooms-taxonomy-blooms-digitally/44988

Davis, M. (2010). Social networking goes to school. *Education Digest, 76*(3), 14–19. Retrieved from Academic Search Complete database at http://www.ebscohost.com/academic/academic-search-complete

Glenn, J. L. (2010, January). Web 3.0: A work in progress. *Keying In, 20*(3).

Harpaz, B. (2010, November 7). Are texting and Facebook worse for teens than TV? *The Sunday Enterprise.*

McHugh, K. (2011, June 9). *43 percent of U.S. businesses using social media to win new business.* Retrieved from http://socialtimes.com/43-percent-of-u-s-businesses-using-social-media-to-win-new-business_b65728

Moore, M. (2008). Continuing thoughts on social networking. *American Journal of Distance Education, 22*(3), 127–129. DOI: 10.1080/08923640802241067

National School Boards Association (2007). *Creating & connecting: Research and guidelines on online social—and educational—networking.* Retrieved from http://www.nsba.org/site/docs/41400/41340.pdf

Nielsen Company (June 15, 2010). *Social networks/blogs now account for one in every four and a half minutes online.* Retrieved from http://blog.nielsen.com/nielsenwire/online_mobile/social-media-accounts-for-22-percent-of-time-online

Pattison, K. (2009). *How to market your business with Facebook.* Retrieved from http://www.nytimes.com/2009/11/12/business/smallbusiness/12guide.html

Reynard, R. (2008). Social networking: Learning theory in action. *Campus Technology.* Retrieved from http://campustechnology.com/articles/2008/05/social-networking-learning-theory-in-action.aspx

Strickland, J. (n.d.). Top 10 social networking sites. *Discoverynews.* Retrieved from http://news.discovery.com/tech/top-ten-social-networking-sites.html

Swartz, J. (2010, July 21). More small businesses use Twitter, Facebook to promote. *USA Today.* Retrieved from http://www.usatoday.com/tech/news/2010-07-22-techbiz22_ST_N.htm 1/4/2011

Watters, A. (2011, July 2). Google Plus: Is this the social tool schools have been waiting for? *ReadWriteWeb.* Retrieved from http://www.readwriteweb.com/archives/google_plus_education.php

Wehrli, B. (2009, Summer). Technology as a fence and a bridge. *Horace, 25*(1), 1–4. Retrieved from http://www.eric.ed.gov/PDFS/EJ859274.pdf

Wells, C. (2010). Social networking: The essential balancing act in schools. *THE Journal.* Retrieved from http://thejournal.com/articles/2010/11/17/social-networking-the-essential-balancing-act-in-schools.aspx.

Wesch, M. (2009, January 7). From knowledgeable to knowledge-able: Learning in new media environments. *Academic Commons.* Retrieved from http://www.academiccommons.org/commons/essay/knowledgable-knowledge-able

Yacht, C., Siegel, R., Crosson, S., & Renner, B. (2011). Accounting and finance courses. In L. G. Snyder (Ed.), *Online business education, NBEA 2011 yearbook* (Vol. 49, p. 150). Reston, VA: NBEA.

The Role of Middle and High School Business Programs

Frederick W. Polkinghorne
Bowling Green State University
Bowling Green, OH

Business education programs (education for and about business) are an important part of the middle and high school curriculum. The National Center for Education Statistics (NCES) reported in 2009 that nearly 40% of high school graduates earn credit in one or more business-related courses. This chapter will discuss the roles and linkages of business education programs and contemporary influences on them at the middle and high school levels.

THE ROLES OF MIDDLE AND HIGH SCHOOL BUSINESS EDUCATION PROGRAMS

Business education programs address wide-ranging goals and distinct objectives through the development of an organized curriculum (Anderson, 2008). The curriculum allows business educators to guide students in developing both broad and specific business-related knowledge and skills. Theory, research, and professional practice are combined to meet social and economic program commitments (Stitt-Gohdes, 2002).

Business education programs at the middle school level—those schools with no grade level lower than five or higher than eight—develop students' knowledge and skills in technology, basic business, entrepreneurship, and personal finance (NBEA, 2007; NCES, 2000). Middle school business education programs are important, as these programs provide students with the foundation for rigorous and relevant study at the high school level via solidification of technical skills and knowledge that become the schemata for future learning experiences.

At the high school level, programs are normally offered in grades 9 through 12 and develop student competency to become "effective consumers, citizens, workers, and business learners" (NBEA, 2007, p. xii; NCES [National Center for Education Statistics], 2000). Many students do not participate in postsecondary education and/or training programs; as a result, business education programs at the high school level are essential in the development of student experiences that lead toward gainful employment and/or meeting social goals.

The National Business Education Association (NBEA) (2007) indicated that business education programs provide students with experiences that encourage both independent and group decisionmaking through career exploration, technology, work-based skills, business experience, and participation in career and technical student organizations. Via those experiences, students are provided an opportunity to meet important social and economic obligations.

Economic Role

Business education programs have long served the dynamic economic needs of the United States. In fact, business education programs are often developed in unison with shifts in national economic need (Stitt-Gohdes, 2002). Programs are designed to offer students a broad array of courses that often span several occupational areas. Historically, students who concentrated their coursework in career and technical education (CTE) would take several courses in one specialized area, such as business. However, contemporary students who concentrate their study in CTE often stratify their high school study across CTE areas, such as participating in courses in agriculture, family and consumer science, industrial education, and/or business education (NCES, 2009).

The same report indicated that student course-taking decisions regarding course concentration mirror the needs of a complex, challenging, and dynamic global environment (NCES, 2009). In fact, the shift in economic needs reflected a workforce that required participants to have numerous opportunities to integrate knowledge and skills so they are able to make connections, solve complex problems, and participate in a rapidly changing and transdisciplinary global, virtual, and connected world (PCBEE [Policies Commission for Business and Economic Education], 2008b; Railsback & Groneman-Hite, 2008; NASDCTE [National Association of State Directors of Career Technical Education], 2010a).

To meet the dynamic economic workforce needs of the United States, business education content must emphasize interdisciplinary study (PCBEE, 2007; NBEA, 2007). In fact, NBEA (2007) recently spearheaded the revision of program standards for and about business at all levels of the education system. Not all students pursue careers in specific business disciplines, such as accounting and marketing (NBEA, 2007). However, all people, regardless of their career intent, participate in the economic system. Given this participation, NBEA (2007) reported that all people are "entitled to learn how [the economic] system functions and the impact of their role in that system" (p. vii).

Social Role

Beyond the economic role of contemporary middle and high school business education programs, students are provided equitable access to fundamental business knowledge and skills (Scott & Sarkees-Wircenski, 2008). The increasingly diverse body of students has strongly influenced business education programs to provide opportunities to achieve varied social goals (McEwen, 2008). Social goals are targets for obtaining a perceived positive outcome that is generally supported by society. Social goals are quite diverse; however, they often include improvement of academic skill and knowledge, completion of a high school diploma, enrollment in postsecondary programs, and/or obtaining gainful employment (Jones, 1992).

Jones (1992) further indicated that students who are identified as members of a special population often have different social goals from traditional students. Special student populations comprise nearly 39% of all school-age people (United States Census Bureau, 2011). The Carl D. Perkins Career and Technical Education Improvement Act (2006) specifically targeted special populations to include students who are disabled, economically disadvantaged, employed in specialized nontraditional careers, single parents, displaced homemakers, and individuals with limited English proficiency.

Students who belong to a special population find that reaching their social goals can be quite complex (Compton, Laanan, & Starobin, 2010). According to the National Research Center for Career and Technical Education (NRCCTE), business education programs provide an opportunity for those students to increase the probability they will graduate from high school, enter postsecondary education/training programs, and/ or earn occupational credentials (NRCCTE, n.d.).

PROGRAM LINKAGE

Business educators realize that tomorrow's workplace and academic "challenges can't be addressed using yesterday's skills" and/or knowledge (NBEA, 2007, p. vii). Kesten and Lambrecht (2010) reported that business educators believe that programs must support student participation in postsecondary education/training and/or the workplace. Those goals are supported by programmatic standards that guide business educators in developing instruction (NBEA, 2007).

NBEA Standards

The revised National Standards for Business Education, produced by NBEA (2007), emphasize the equitable "access to fundamental business knowledge and skills [that lead toward] an equal opportunity for success" (p vii). In the spirit of equitability, the standards address wide-ranging goals. The revised programmatic goals emphasize the interrelatedness of the basic business content area, elevate technical performance expectations, and recognize the critical thinking requirements of a 21st century workplace. Via the National Standards for Business Education, business educators design a curriculum that link classroom instruction with authentic postsecondary education and training and the workplace.

Postsecondary Education and Training

Business education programs provide a mechanism to support and prepare students for entry into postsecondary education and training programs. According to the 2006 Carl D. Perkins Act, postsecondary programs lead to a credential that requires two or more years of study for the completion of a postsecondary degree, occupational credential, or apprenticeship.

Many first-year postsecondary students, including both participants and nonparticipants in business education programs at the middle and high school level, need remediation in their academic knowledge and/or skill (Allensworth, Nomi, Montgomery, & Lee, 2010). McEwen (2008) reported that middle and high school business education programs provide a context in which to remediate students' deficiencies in academic knowledge and/or skills. The Policies Commission for Business and Economic Education (PCBEE) (2007) supported the premise that middle and high school business education programs, emphasizing interdisciplinary teaching, are likely to ease student transition from high school to postsecondary education/training and/or workplace entry.

Interdisciplinary teaching is the seamless instruction of academic knowledge and skills through teaching business content (Polkinghorne & Hagler, 2010). Through interdisciplinary teaching, business educators are narrowing the gaps among student academic knowledge, skills, and technology (NCES, 2010). As a result, business educators are quite supportive of interdisciplinary teaching (Polkinghorne & Groneman-Hite, 2007).

Several different methods of interdisciplinary teaching exist. Business educators have indicated they support the selection of specific instructional strategies and cooperative instruction between the business educator and their academic peers (Polkinghorne, Hagler, & Anderson, 2010; Laturnas & Kesten, 2010). Polkinghorne, Hagler, and Anderson (2010) reported that many business educators select and implement strategies without cooperation among peer educators.

An example of a strategy that business teachers can implement on their own was suggested by Polkinghorne and Bland (2011). They provided an application of the Max Learning strategy. This strategic example motivates students to acquire information via text to construct labels via a popular word-processing software application. Students are motivated via an explanation of the benefit to constructing mailing labels by connecting the activity to the delivery of graduation invitations and the subsequent mailing of letters to express gratitude for gifts. Furthermore, the activity connects future learning episodes, such as instruction in the integrated use of word processing, spreadsheet, and/or database applications.

In addition to the standard curriculum for business education programs, business educators link the curriculum with authentic learning experiences. In fact, career and technical student organizations motivate, engage, and improve the aspirations of students to enroll in postsecondary education and/or training (Alfeld, et al., 2007; Stanislawski & Haltinner, 2009). For example, Business Professionals of America and Future Business Leaders of America provide students with opportunities to demonstrate their skill and knowledge competencies via state and national competitions. Those experiences provide many students with the motivation to outperform their peers in competition, engage in the learning process, and serve as a catalyst for enrollment in postsecondary training by building students' personal confidence.

Workplace Participation

For some students, receiving an occupational credential and joining the workforce yields a significantly higher return than enrolling in postsecondary education and/or training (Compton, Laanan, & Starobin, 2010). In spite of the idea of "college for all," many students do not continue their education beyond high school. Some students "take several CTE courses [at the middle and high school level] in [an effort to prepare] for employment" (NRCCTE, 2009, p. 9).

Students who concentrate their studies in business education are more likely than students who do not take CTE courses to enter occupations described as other than low wage and/or low skill. Business education tech-prep programs at the high school level provide students with the opportunity to advance well beyond low-wage and/or low-skill occupations. In fact, many tech-prep students enter the workplace in lieu of enrolling in postsecondary education/training programs (NRCCTE, 2009).

EMERGING ISSUES AND TRENDS IN MIDDLE AND HIGH SCHOOL BUSINESS EDUCATION PROGRAMS

A myriad of economic, social, and political issues in the United States cause relentless shifts in the role of middle and high school business education programs. Economic issues and trends are characterized as those events brought about by shifts in the production, distribution, consumption, and management of goods and services; whereas "social issues" and trends are characterized as those events affecting many or all members of a society and are seen as problems and/or controversies related to moral values (Webster's New College Dictionary, 2007). Economic and social issues lead to political pressure to alter program content via requirements posited by state and federal government (Gibton & Goldring, 2001).

The curriculum for business education programs has been impacted by a number of recent trends. Business education programs have been reduced or eliminated as a result of declining funding. The curriculum has been impacted by the growth in English-language learning students and in some cases a reduction in the number of school days. Because of these trends, business education programs and curriculum are rapidly changing to meet the dynamic needs of the United States' workforce. The Association for Career and Technical Education, Delta Pi Epsilon Research Society, NBEA, and PCBEE help to identify emerging issues and trends and/or provide guidance to business educators as they meet dynamic workforce needs (Hosler, 2003).

Contemporary Issues

Contemporary economic and social issues have impacted nearly all content-area programs, including those in business education. Perhaps the most visible trend is a shift away from the teaching of technical skills toward a curriculum that emphasizes both technical and academic knowledge and skill (Stone, Kaminski, & Gloeckner, 2009). The shift in the curriculum is powered by an increased focus on academic skills, in lieu of general labor market preparation (NCES, 2001). Several recent legislative bills and initiatives—such as the revised Carl D. Perkins Act (2006), No Child Left Behind Act of 2001 (2002), and funding tied to the Race to the Top initiative—advocate for college readiness, perhaps at the expense of technical skill preparation.

Data are clear that the quantity and rigor of academic course completion by public high school graduates has increased along with overall achievement in reading and mathematics measured by achievement on standardized assessments, such as those tied to federal legislation (NCES, 2010). At the same time, the technical skills of non-college-bound students have been compromised by the increased focus on academic requirements. As a result, their ability to secure other than low-skill and low-wage careers has become more complex (Handel, 2005). Many high school graduates do not go on for further education or training and are often underprepared to enter the workforce, as indicated by the current rate of unemployment among those with less than postsecondary education/training credentials (Bureau of Labor, 2011). The National Association of State Directors of Career Technical Education Consortium (2010a) indicated that a high-quality technical preparation, such as in business, could assist in meeting the emerging economic needs of the United States.

In addition to traditional learners, business education programs also serve academically at-risk students and the disabled (NCES, 2005). These programs often provide participants with the motivation to remain in school, graduate, and secure jobs (NRCCTE, n.d.). Thus, business education programs continue to transform themselves into catalysts for improved economic and social conditions for all students (NASDCTE Consortium, 2010b). Political leaders have encouraged business educators to continue program transformation via several reform initiatives.

Contemporary Trends

Political leaders have emphasized that all students should have equitable access to educational opportunities for postsecondary education/training and/or entry into the workforce. Middle and high school business education programs are part of the solution and will be held accountable for a positive outcome. As a result, a number of education reform initiatives directly impact middle and high school business education programs. Two of the more recent initiatives include Career Clusters, Career Pathways, and the Common Core Standards.

Middle and high school programs are increasingly structured around career clusters and/or pathways (Office of Vocational and Adult Education, 2007). According to the Policy Commission for Business and Economic Education (2008a), career clusters are groups of courses that are developed around a common occupational outcome, such as business management or finance. The National Career Pathways Network (2010) indicated that career pathways are a sequence of coursework that lead toward completion of a degree of study (such as an associate or baccalaureate), occupational credential (such as specific software application certification), and/or professional licensure. Both the Career Clusters and Career Pathways initiatives strengthen the connection between business and academic programs and lead to improved workforce preparation (PCBEE, 2008a).

The Career Clusters initiative realigns vocational education programs, such as those in business, by developing a structure that further supports programs developed to improve the transition from school to work (Federal Register, 2000). The 16 career clusters integrate business coursework throughout the school experience, but specifically promote business education coursework via clusters aimed at student skills in (a) business, management, and administration, (b) finance, (c) information technology, and (d) marketing, sales, and service (NASDCTE, n.d.).

The Career Pathways initiative provides a sequence of coursework in academic and career/technical courses that leads to postsecondary education and/or training (National Career Pathways Network, 2010). In fact, the same report indicated that the initiative requires opportunities for students to earn college credit through partnerships between secondary schools and postsecondary institutions. The initiative clearly supports business education programs by leading toward a schoolwide philosophy statement that aims to prepare students for the workplace.

In addition to the Career Clusters and Pathways initiatives, the Common Core State Standards Initiative emphasizes a set of internationally benchmarked standards that align program curriculum and "college and career readiness" (Glenn, 2010, p. 7). The common core comprises standards embedded in "authentic contexts" for English language arts and mathematics (Common Core State Standards Initiative, 2010). Glenn (2010) indicated that the Common Core State Standards Initiative may have the capacity to diminish the gap between business education and other academic programs.

Along with these two initiatives, a clear call exists for improved program account-ability. Business educators are concerned about the development and assessment of rigorous, specific, observable, and measurable course standards that are tied to these initiatives. As a result, many business educators report they need additional education/training in the implementation of recent initiatives (Polkinghorne, Railsback, & Groneman-Hite, 2008).

Additional clarity in programmatic requirements is forthcoming. However, it is clear that business educators will make a significant contribution, toward overall student development for college and career readiness.

SUMMARY

Middle and high school business education programs have both an economic and social role. The programs developed along shifts in labor market needs and serve to prepare participants to engage competitively in the economic system and pursue unique social goals. Politicians have suggested a myriad of reform initiatives to assist educators in developing appropriate curricula.

The linkage between middle and high school business education programs and postsecondary education and/or training and the workforce provides students with the opportunity to pursue their personal and career goals. For students who choose not to enter postsecondary education and/or training, there is some evidence that partici-pants in middle and high school business education programs enter careers that are described as other than low skill and/or low wage.

Middle and high school business education programs provide an opportunity for students to be successful. Many of the current program reform initiatives provide for an important role for business education programs. Business educators clearly provide an authentic and relevant education for and about business to nearly 40% of students who are enrolled in the public middle and high schools throughout the United States.

REFERENCES

Alfeld, C., Stone, J. R. II, Aragon, S. R., Hansen, D. M., Zirkle, C., Connors, J., et al. (2007). *Looking inside the black box: The value added by career and technical student organizations to students' high school experience.* Minneapolis, MN: NRCCTE.

Allensworth, E., Nomi, T., Montgomery, N., & Lee, V. E. (2010). College preparatory curriculum for all: Academic and English I for ninth graders in Chicago. *Educational Evaluation and Policy Analysis, 32*(4), 367–391.

Anderson, M. (2008). The business education curriculum in the educational system. In M. H. Rader, G. A. Bailey, & L. A. Kurth (Eds.), *Effective methods of teaching business education: NBEA 2008 yearbook* (Vol. 46, pp. 20–36). Reston, VA: NBEA.

Bureau of Labor. (2011). Employment status of the civilian population 25 years and over by educational attainment. *Bureau of Labor Statistics.* Retrieved from http://data.bls.gov/cgi-bin/print.pl/news.release/empsit.t04.htm

Carl D. Perkins Career and Technical Education Improvement Act of 2006. S. 250, 109th Cong. 20 U.S.C. 2301 (2006) (enacted).

Common Core State Standards Initiative. (2010). *About the standards.* Retrieved from http://corestandards.org/about-the-standards

Compton, J. I., Laanan, F. S., & Starobin, S. S. (2010). Career and technical education as pathways: Factors influencing postcollege earnings of selected career clusters. *Journal of Education for Students Placed at Risk, 15*(1), 93–113.

Federal Register. (2000). *Career clusters—Cooperative agreements.* Retrieved from http://www2.ed.gov/legislation/FedRegister/announcements/2000-4/120600a.html

Gibton, D., & Goldring, E. (2001). The role of legislation in educational decentralization: The case of Israel and Britain. *Peabody Journal of Education, 76*(3/4), 81–101.

Glenn, J. L. (2010). The common core standards initiative and how it might impact business education. *NBEA Business Education Forum, 65*(1), 7–11.

Handel, M. J. (2005). *Worker skills and job requirements: Is there a mismatch?* Washington, DC: Economic Policy Institute.

Hosler, M. M. (2003). The foundations of business education. In M. H. Rader & L. Kurth (Eds.), *Effective methods of teaching business education in the 21st century: NBEA 2003 yearbook* (Vol. 41, pp. 1–16). Reston, VA: NBEA.

Jones, C. J. (1992). *Social and emotional development of exceptional students: Handicapped and gifted.* Springfield, IL: Charles C. Thomas.

Kesten, C. A., & Lambrecht, J. (2010). Future directions for business education: A Delphi study. *Delta Pi Epsilon Journal, 52*(2), 57–76.

Laturnas, H., & Kesten, C. (2010). Making interdisciplinary learning happen in business education. *NBEA Business Education Forum, 65*(1), 41–43.

McEwen, B. (2008). Providing differentiated instruction for diverse student needs. In M. H. Rader, G. A. Bailey, & L. A. Kurth (Eds.), *Effective methods of teaching business education: NBEA 2008 yearbook* (Vol. 46, pp. 53–66). Reston, VA: NBEA.

NASDCTE [National Association of State Directors of Career Technical Education] Consortium. (2010a). *Career technical education: A critical component of states' global economic strategy.* Retrieved from http://www.careertech.org/uploaded_files/Global_Competition_CTE.pdf

NASDCTE. (2010b). *Reflect, transform, lead: A new vision for career technical education.* Retrieved from http://www.careertech.org/career-technical-education/cte-vision.html

NASDCTE. (n.d.). *The 16 career clusters.* Retrieved from http://www.careertech.org/career-clusters/glance/clusters.html

National Career Pathways Network. (2010). *Career pathways.* Retrieved from http://www.cord.org/career-pathways

NBEA. (2007). *National standards for business education* (3rd ed.). Reston, VA: Author.

NCES [National Center for Education Statistics]. (2000). *In the middle: Characteristics of public school with a focus on middle schools.* Retrieved from http://nces.ed.gov/pubsearch/pubsinfo.asp?pubid=2000312

NCES. (2001). *Changes in high school vocational coursetaking in a larger perspective.* Retrieved from http://nces.ed.gov/pubsearch/pubsinfo.asp?pubid=2001026

NCES. (2005). *Table H85. Percentage of public high school graduates who were occupational concentrators, by disability status, limited English proficiency (LEP) status, and occupational area of concentration: 2005.* Retrieved from http://nces.ed.gov/surveys/ctes/tables/archive_2005_h85.asp

NCES. (2009). *New indicators of high school career/technical education coursetaking: Class of 2005.* Retrieved from http://nces.ed.gov/pubsearch/pubsinfo.asp?pubid=2009038

NCES. (2010). *Science achievement and occupational career/technical education coursetaking in high school: The class of 2005.* Retrieved from http://nces.ed.gov/pubsearch/pubsinfo.asp?pubid=2010021

No Child Left Behind Act of 2001. H.R. 1, 107th Cong. Pub. L. No. 107-110, 115 Stat. 1426 (2002) (enacted).

NRCCTE [National Research Center for Career and Technical Education]. (n.d.). *Major research findings 2000–2007: Engagement, achievement, and transition.* Louisville, KY: Author.

Office of Vocational and Adult Education. (2007). *Perkins IV programs of study: State by state review.* Retrieved from http://www2.ed.gov/about/offices/list/ovae/pi/cte/prgms-stdy2007.doc

PCBEE. (2007). *Policy statement 81: This we believe about interdisciplinary teaching.* Retrieved from http://nbea.org/newsite/curriculum/policy/no_81.pdf

PCBEE. (2008a). *Policy statement 82: This we believe about the value of career clusters in business education.* Retrieved from http://nbea.org/newsite/curriculum/policy/no_82.pdf

PCBEE. (2008b). *Policy statement 83: This we believe about the transformation and future of business education.* Retrieved from http://nbea.org/newsite/curriculum/policy/no_83.pdf

Polkinghorne, F., & Bland, Z. (2011). Interdisciplinary instructional strategies: An applied application for business education. *Journal of Applied Research in Business Instruction, 9*(2).

Polkinghorne, F., & Groneman-Hite, N. (2007). Integrated academics? The business of business educators. *Delta Pi Epsilon edited book of readings.* Delta Pi Epsilon: Little Rock, AR.

Polkinghorne, F., & Hagler, B. E. (2010). Integrated academic intervention in high school business courses: A qualitative perspective. *Delta Pi Epsilon edited book of readings.* Delta Pi Epsilon: Little Rock, AR.

Polkinghorne, F., Hagler, B. E., & Anderson, M. (2010). Reading skill development: A survey of need and responsibility. *Delta Pi Epsilon Journal, 52*(1), 32–42.

Polkinghorne, F., Railsback, B., & Groneman-Hite. (2008). Business teacher preparation: Reading and math skill integration. *Business Education Forum, 62*(4), 45–52.

Railsback, B., & Groneman-Hite, N. (2008). The value of business education: Perceptions of high school guidance counselors, principals, and boards of education. *Delta Pi Epsilon Journal, 50*(3), 150–163.

Scott, J. L., & Sarkees-Wircenski, M. (2008). *Overview of career and technical education.* Orland Park, IL: American Technical Publishers.

Stanislawski, D., & Haltinner, U. (2009). Model for preparing marketing and business teachers to meet the challenge of CTSO leadership and advisement. *Delta Pi Epsilon Journal, 51*(3), 166–176.

Stitt-Gohdes, W. L. (2002). *The business education profession: Principles and practices.* Little Rock, AR: Delta Pi Epsilon.

Stone, K. B., Kaminski, K., & Gloeckner, G. (2009). Closing the gap: Education requirements of the 21st century production workforce. *Journal of Industrial Teacher Education, 45*(3), 5–33.

United States Census Bureau. (2011). *School enrollment: Social and economic characteristics of students: October 2008.* Retrieved from http://www.census.gov/population/www/socdemo/school/cps2008.html

Webster's New World College Dictionary. (2007). (4th ed.) Cleveland, OH: Wiley Publishing

Postsecondary Business Career Programs Provide Workplace Skills Necessary for Success

Karen S. Williams
San Diego Mesa College
San Diego, CA

The term career education means different things to different people. The Department of Education and Training in Queensland, Australia, stated that "Career education encompasses the development of knowledge, skills, and attitudes through a planned program of learning experiences in education and training settings that will assist students to make informed decisions about their study and/or work options and enable them to participate effectively in working life" (Queensland, 2001). Although this definition is fairly comprehensive, it does not clearly identify the knowledge, skills, and attitudes students must develop and possess to become successful in today's workplace. Jan Bray, executive director of the Association for Career and Technical Education, indicated that both students bound for college and careers need core academic skills; but students who are planning to start their careers also need employability and technical skills (Roscorla, 2010).

Most career and technical educators would agree that technical skills are those required to master a job successfully and that students need to see the practical application of academic courses in real-life situations. Dave Bunting, executive director of the Iowa chapter of the Association for Career and Technical Education and former executive director of programs at Kirkwood Community College, stated that communication, interpersonal skills, and creativity are just some of the employability skills that employers are demanding, and it is employability skills that will help employees keep a job (Roscorla, 2010). All the skills mentioned by these practitioners are taught and applied in career and technical education (CTE) courses and programs in postsecondary institutions.

This chapter will focus on (a) the history of CTE and the types of postsecondary institutions that offer courses and programs in CTE, (b) CTE areas of business, computer, and business-related curricula at the postsecondary level, (c) credentials that can be earned by students in these CTE areas, (d) job training programs within the curricula, and (e) transferability of courses from one educational level to the next.

HISTORY OF CTE IN POSTSECONDARY INSTITUTIONS

Career and technical education has a rich history and has played a prominent role in postsecondary education. During the Depression of the 1930s, community colleges offered job-training programs as a way of alleviating widespread unemployment. In the 1940s about 70% of community colleges offered career and technical programs (then referred to as terminal programs); more than one-third of the students in these programs were studying a business curriculum. In the 1950s the term career education was used widely, in part to overcome the negative connotation of the word "terminal," but primarily to train people in skills needed in the workplace. During this time, CTE enrollments were significantly lower than those in the liberal arts area; they represented only one-fourth of the total enrollment in community colleges. In the 1960s CTE enrollments began growing at a much faster rate than liberal arts and continued to do so for the next 20 years. Two CTE programs played a significant role in the growth of CTE at this time: business because of the variety of job opportunities it presented and computer studies because of the expansion of computer applications into all facets of an individual's life.

However, the fastest growing sector of postsecondary education since the 1980s has been the proprietary or for-profit schools. This educational sector includes schools that specialize in training for the computer, business, and business-related fields, among others. Students attending proprietary schools are more likely to attend full time and to attain certificates and degrees in less time than at community colleges (Bailey, Gumport, & Badway, 2003). Also during the 1980s, schools were influenced by the report "A Nation at Risk" (National Commission on Excellence in Education, 1983). This report emphasized the fact that education was suffering a disconnect with the changing workplace and what graduates needed to know to be successful in the workplace. In 1991 the Secretary's Commission on Achieving Necessary Skills (SCANS) report was released, whose purpose was to encourage educational institutions that train students in the skills necessary in a highly competitive economy and workplace (U.S. Department of Labor, 1991). This report created a renewed energy for CTE programs.

Where are we today? Career and technical education still has a crucial role in postsecondary educational institutions, made even more important by the reduction of CTE offerings in secondary schools (Bishop & Mane, 2003; Kazis, 2005). Students continue to enroll in postsecondary schools and to study business, computer, and business-related curricula to gain the skills necessary to compete and be successful in today's competitive global workplace. But in addition to technical skills, curricula today include interpersonal and employability skills.

INSTITUTIONS THAT OFFER CTE PROGRAMS

Career and technical education programs, which are designed to prepare students to move into the workplace and experience success, are offered at postsecondary institutions across all levels and sectors: at two-year and less than two-year institutions and in the public, private not-for-profit, and private for-profit sectors. Two-year educational institutions include community colleges, career colleges, technical schools, and trade schools; the latter three terms are often used interchangeably. The majority of their offerings are two years or less in length, and their credentials include certificates, associate degrees, and baccalaureate degrees. There are distinctions, however subtle, among these three types of postsecondary institutions. Career colleges offer courses to prepare students for a specific career with limited coursework and learning outside the scope of the career for which the training is designed. Technical schools also prepare students for a specific career, but they emphasize more the science behind the occupation for which students are being trained. Trade schools tend to focus on the hands-on application of skills necessary to do a specific job (College Degree Guide, n.d.). Community college certificates typically focus on career skills, whereas associate and baccalaureate degrees provide the general education courses that develop a student into a well-rounded employee, as well as providing career-specific programs (American Association of Community Colleges [AACC], 1998).

In 2005, 5,730 postsecondary institutions (including four-year, two-year, and less than two-year institutions) offered CTE curricula and 1,923,400 credentials were awarded. Of all postsecondary institutions offering CTE coursework, 3,685 (about 64%) were two-year and less than two-year educational institutions. In 2005 the two-year institutions awarded 728,110 credentials and those institutions that were less than two years in length awarded 242,338 credentials. That means that, in 2005, two-year institutions awarded 37.9% and less than two-year institutions awarded 12.6% of all postsecondary credentials. Therefore, in 2005 these two types of institutions (both public and private) accounted for just less than 50% of all CTE credentials awarded (U.S. Department of Education, 2008a).

COMMON CURRICULA

The most common majors in 2007 varied somewhat depending on the credential (certificate, associate degree, or baccalaureate degree) that students sought. Among bachelor-degree seekers, business and marketing was the most common major field (33%), followed by education (15%), healthcare (12%), and engineering and architectural sciences (11%). In contrast, healthcare was the most common major field among students in an associate degree program (30%), followed by business and marketing (25%), education (10%), and computer sciences (9%). Healthcare was also the most common field (40%) among certificate seekers, followed by personal and consumer services (16%), trade and industry (13%), and business and marketing (12%) (U.S. Department of Education, 2008a).

Business Administration and Business Support

As businesses continue to streamline, the demand for professionals with a business administration credential and an understanding of core business concepts remains steady and is expected to increase (U.S. Department of Labor, 2010).

Programs in business administration typically provide students with a comprehensive understanding of the fundamentals of business (accounting, economics, law, marketing, and communication), management principles, critical thinking, project planning and implementation, business-oriented technology, and interpersonal skills. Business administration areas of emphasis may include, but are not limited to, accounting, entrepreneurship, marketing, finance, real estate, hospitality management, healthcare administration, and sales management. Curricula in the business support area will need to be updated and adapted to include the new skills and increased responsibilities that business is now requiring of persons in those positions. For example, today's business support personnel are expected to be able to do a variety of tasks: from routine clerical tasks to customer service to Web site maintenance and meeting planning. Courses in a program of study for business support personnel typically include communication (oral and written), business software applications, supervision, management, accounting, human relations, and Web authoring. The 2010–2011 Department of Labor Occupational Outlook Handbook projects that the business support area will have the largest number of openings in the next few years (Bureau of Labor Statistics, 2010).

Computer and Information Technology

Job growth within this category is projected to grow faster in 2008–2018 than the average for all other jobs (U.S. Department of Labor, 2010). As a result, computer and information technology curricula offered in postsecondary colleges need to prepare students for jobs that require a diverse set of computer skills that may be used at a variety of technical levels. The 2010–2011 Occupational Outlook Handbook projects that more than 400,000 new jobs will be added for individuals who have the technical skills to be computer network administrators, systems administrators, database administrators, or computer support specialists. Among the courses offered in the computer and information technology area that will provide the range of skills employers will be seeking are business software applications, systems design, computer networks, programming languages, database management, systems security, project planning, human relations, Web authoring, and spoken and written communication.

Because the Internet has been integrated into every facet of an individual's personal and professional life and is now a vital component in how businesses function in the global environment, curricula that relate to e-commerce, Web site development, and virtual support services have become some of the more popular recent additions to CTE offerings that emphasize computer technologies.

Service-Related Occupations

Programs or certificates at the community college level that prepare students for service-related occupations typically include some general business and "soft" skills courses that serve as a "core" for the curriculum. That core provides the basic skills set required by individuals who are successful in the service area and may consist of courses in interpersonal communication, basic computer skills, business foundations, and ethics. Among the service-related programs offered in community colleges are retail management, customer service, real estate, and financial services.

The course of study pursued within the service-related category will determine the courses that are specific to a particular program or certificate. Retail management programs typically require additional courses in various aspects of retailing, marketing, merchandising, and sales, as well as accounting, marketing, and human resource management. Customer service programs comprise the core discussed earlier with added emphasis on telephone skills, sales techniques, and customer relations.

Another popular service-related curriculum is real estate, which includes specialized courses required for real estate licensure, some of which are particular to a specific geographic area. Another service-related program offered in postsecondary institutions is financial services. Students who are enrolled in this program of study may choose from among several emphases such as banking, investment analysis, or investment management. Personal finance, economics, accounting, law, and financial management courses would likely be required for all programs in the financial services area. Each of these emphasis areas would also require courses relevant to the subject matter. For example, in the investment program, courses in financial analysis, options, securities, commodities, or foreign exchange markets might be required.

Interdisciplinary Studies

Some programs and certificates offered in the postsecondary institutions are a collaborative effort between two or more disciplines. Four popular interdisciplinary programs are Web development, 3D animation and/or video game development, graphic design, and geographic information systems. In each of these programs, courses are taught by business and/or computer faculty, along with faculty with expertise from other academic disciplines.

For example, a majority of the required or elective courses in a Web development program (e.g., programming language, databases, e-commerce, graphics, law, marketing) are taught by business or computer faculty; however, design courses may be taught by someone in the fine arts area. It is conceivable that math faculty might also be involved in teaching the programming language for a Web development course. Three-D animation and video game development programs include courses in programming, graphic design, creative writing, storyboarding, 2D- and 3D- modeling, and animation courses. Some of these courses may be taught by fine arts faculty (design courses), math faculty (possibly programming classes), or English faculty (writing courses), as well as business and/or computer faculty (computer technology courses). Graphic design programs may also be part of an interdisciplinary curriculum. For this program, the fine arts faculty may teach design courses while computer faculty provide instruction on computer software packages. Geographic information system programs are often a collaborative effort between computer faculty who teach the database and computer literacy components and geography faculty who teach the cartography and geography components of the program. Interdisciplinary programs are not taught in isolation and may even be team taught. Having input and expertise from different curricular areas can add real value to the program of study.

STUDENT GOALS

A key to determining student success in a particular program of study is knowing the student's educational goals when he/she enrolled in the program. The purpose of CTE programs is twofold: to prepare students for employment and to meet the needs of business by supplying them with well-educated workers. Therefore, recognizing that not all students who enroll in programs in business or computer studies have a certificate or degree as their goal is important (U.S. Department of Education, 2008b). So it follows that if a student leaves before completing a CTE program in order to work in a related field, he or she should be considered a success. In some CTE programs, "job outs" account for as much as 75% of the students in the program (Cohen & Brawer, 2008).

The Bureau of Labor Statistics projects that nearly half (about 45%) of all job openings between 2004 and 2014 will be in middle-skill occupations of the labor market—those jobs that require more than high school, but less than a four-year degree. Wage gains per year of schooling for those with associate's degrees are comparable to those with bachelor's degrees. Students with certificates in healthcare, construction, and some computer areas have seen wage gains; other fields have not had the same experience (Holzer & Lerman, 2007). In 2007, almost 40% of the undergraduate credentials conferred in the U.S. postsecondary institutions were below the bachelor's degree. Between 1997 and 2007 the number of sub-baccalaureate credentials that were awarded increased 28% to 1.5 million (Horn & Weko, 2009).

Research has shown that two-year degrees and less-than-two-year certificates from community colleges, especially in well-defined occupational areas, are as valuable in terms of salary relative to the time it takes to earn those awards as four-year degrees (Bailey & Jacobs, 2009).

Certificates

College students often enroll in a career and technical program that offers a certificate because it focuses on training and preparation for immediate job placement or advancement in a specialized field of study. Other college students choose to enroll in a certificate program as a starting point to a degree in a chosen field. In either case, certificates are usually completed in a shorter period than an associate degree. Two sources of certificates are postsecondary institutions and industry:

Institutions. Postsecondary institutions offer certificates of varying lengths in business and computer programs. Certificates are often the start of a pathway to an associate or a baccalaureate degree. The names of the certificates vary from school to school and may include certificate of achievement, skills certificate, occupational certificate in business, advanced technical certificate, marketable skills award, certificate of completion, and Level I and Level II certificates. Certificates can be categorized into three different lengths: less than one year (short), between one and two years in length (moderate), two or more years in length (long). The shorter the time frame for completion of the certificate, the more emphasis on the specialized and specific skills in the area of study. In many instances they cover the same coursework as the associate degree but without the general education requirements. This is because the goal is to teach the required skill sets in a relatively short period so the student is available for immediate job placement. To see the scope of certificate programs, the listing below represents a cross-section of certificate offerings across the United States in the business and computer areas:

Administrative assistant	Information record management
Business and technical communication	International business
Business plans	Java application programming
Computer forensics	Leadership in business
Computer help desk	Management/supervisory development
Computer networking and telecommunications	Medical administrative assistant
Computer repair and maintenance	Meeting/event planner
Computerized accounting technician	Quality assurance technology
Customer service	Real estate appraisal
Desktop publishing	Retail sales and service
E-commerce	Small business management
Facility management	Sports management
Financial management/insurance	Supply chain management
Game development business	Tax preparation entrepreneurship
Geographic information systems	Video/animation production
Graphic communication technology	Virtual assistant
Human resource management	Voice over Internet protocol telephony specialist
Information management specialist	Web site development and design

Industry. Industry certification is a process that evaluates the core skills, competencies, and basic knowledge of the student in a specific subject area, process, or technology. The major benefits are validation for potential employers of an individual's competency in a specific skill and standardization of skill level because all persons with that certification have been evaluated using the same criteria. Many postsecondary schools have programs through which a student can earn industry certification. Some professional associations award certifications for their industry. These certifications may include coursework taken at the postsecondary institution to prepare for the certifying exam. Among the fields with this type of certification are real estate, accounting, administrative professional, finance, human resources, e-commerce, project management, virtual assistant, Web development, supply management, and facilities management. Industry certifications may also be vendor specific (e.g., Cisco, Microsoft, Oracle, Novell, Apple, and Red Hat). And yet another category of certifications that may be earned in postsecondary institutions are those sponsored by third-party or vendor-neutral groups (e.g., CompTIA and Certiport).

Degrees

An associate degree can be earned from most postsecondary educational institutions; they may also be earned at four-year colleges or universities. And, some two-year colleges offer baccalaureate degrees in career and technical programs. Both the associate and baccalaureate degrees provide the occupational training necessary to enter a specific business or computer field and then advance in that field. These levels of educational attainment may offer better job prospects and higher salaries.

Associate degrees. An associate degree is an undergraduate degree that usually takes about two years and includes about 60 semester hours or 90 quarter hours of credit. Most associate degrees are earned through the community college; however, private career colleges and some universities also grant them. The three components of course work in the associate degree are major required courses, general education required courses, and electives. Associate degrees are designed to prepare students for a career, immediate entry into the workforce, or transfer to a four-year college or university. In many instances, the associate degree counts as the first two years of a baccalaureate degree, providing the four-year institution has an articulation agreement with the two-year institution (AACC, 1998).

The **associate of arts (AA) degree** is designed as a fully transferable degree to a four-year college or university that offers a bachelor of arts degree in a related field, and it meets most, if not all, of the general education requirements of that four-year institution, including any prerequisites needed in the curriculum major. The degree has a broadly based foundation of courses in the academics in addition to the courses in the student's field of study. In business administration, the AA degree is designed to give students a foundation in theory and knowledge in all aspects of business administration and prepare them for an entry-level job, or it can be transferred to a four-year bachelor-of-arts program in business administration. Some postsecondary schools of-

fer the AA degree in business, economics, computer science, and geographic information systems and attach the prefix "pre-" and the suffix "transfer" to the degree's name,
that is, "pre-AA transfer."

The **associate of science (AS) degree** is designed as a fully transferable degree to a
four-year college or university that grants the bachelor of science degree in a related
field. The AS degree usually requires fewer general education requirements and more
coursework specific to the field that is being studied than an AA degree. Like the AA
degree, the AS degree prepares students for either an entry-level job in a business area
(e.g., computer science, management, business administration, accounting, marketing,
or real estate) or for transfer to a four-year college or university in an area of business
or computer science.

The **associate of applied science (AAS) degree** is for students who intend to enter
the workforce upon graduation or for advancement in an existing job. This degree program requires general education courses, but not as many as for the AA or AS degrees.
The original intent of this degree was not for transferability to a four-year college or
university. However, articulation agreements may be negotiated between the postsecondary institution and the four-year college or university to allow this degree to transfer. A sampling of AAS degrees offered include local area networking systems–security
administration, international business, legal administrative assistant, administrative
professional, financial services, marketing management, entrepreneurship, interactive
media, computer information systems, health information management, accounting,
mortgage banking, and telecommunication technologies.

Baccalaureate degrees. Today a number of community colleges and proprietary or
for-profit colleges offer a baccalaureate degree as an extension of their associate degree
program. The offering of a baccalaureate degree is market driven; it is a response that
enables the postsecondary institution to meet the changing needs of the communities
it serves. Two principal rationales exist for the community college baccalaureate: One
is to increase access to the baccalaureate degree for students whose opportunities are
limited because of existing factors such as geographic location, finances, and learning
styles. The other rationale is to provide a hands-on learning style leading to the baccalaureate called a workforce baccalaureate or an applied baccalaureate degree (Skolnik &
Floyd, 2005).

Applied baccalaureate degree–granting institutions are offered in 39 states. Twenty-
nine of these offer the baccalaureate degree at traditional baccalaureate degree–granting institutions, and 10 states have associate degree–granting institutions (postsecondary institutions) offering the applied baccalaureate degrees. The 10 states in which
postsecondary institutions award applied baccalaureate degrees are Florida, Hawaii,
Nevada, North Dakota, New York, Ohio, Oklahoma, Texas, Washington, and West
Virginia (Bragg, Townsend, & Ruud, 2009). These states offer the applied baccalaureate
degree in banking, technology management, information management, business and

information technology, business administration, supervision and management, and applied management.

Noncredit Courses

Continuing (sometimes called community) education provides a wide array of classes and programs that are offered at no charge or a very low charge to students. These courses are usually noncredit courses; but depending on the school and the course, continuing education credits may be earned. Students taking noncredit courses tend to have short-term goals and are older than the traditional 18- to 21-year old (Cohen & Brawer, 2008). The backgrounds of continuing education students represent a variety of prior school achievement ranging from never having completed high school to being a "swirler" (having a baccalaureate or graduate degree and coming back for additional schooling).

The offerings in continuing education include business and computer courses, professional licensure or re-licensure, industry certification courses, contract training for specific businesses, basic skills courses, and personal enrichment courses. Not only can students take a course in the business or computer field, but they can also complete an entire program in that curricular area. Students taking these courses may be doing so to learn a new skill or skills, upgrade their existing skill set, secure or renew a license (e.g., real estate), gain certification (e.g., Cisco, Microsoft, Oracle, Adobe, and IC3), or take remedial coursework to meet prerequisites for college-level courses.

JOB TRAINING PROGRAMS WITHIN THE CURRICULA

Teachers in CTE programs often subscribe to the three learning strategies of telling the student how to do it, showing the student how to do it, and then letting the student do it in the classroom to reinforce the learning that has taken place. This section discusses real-world application of instructor-led learning.

Work Experience

Students in CTE have an opportunity "to learn while they work" on the job. Work experience, internship, and co-op are all names for this partnership among employers, students, and the college that integrates classroom instruction with hands-on experience. This work experience adds immeasurably to the student's professional, personal, and academic growth.

The benefits of the program for the student are numerous. Students have an opportunity to test their personal abilities in a work environment; they have a more realistic view of the work environment; they build confidence in their technical skills and people skills; they have a better understanding of the human relations dynamic in a job setting; and they develop the skills, habits, and attitudes that will keep them employed once they obtain a job and start their career. All business students can benefit from participating in a work experience program and most schools offer it as part of all CTE curricula.

Apprenticeships

Apprenticeships allow someone with no experience in a chosen career field to work alongside a master in the occupation, who trains the apprentice "on the job." Students are paid for the time spent on the job working and learning; they also attend school for a minimal number of hours each week for other classes related to the duties on the job. Apprenticeships are currently used primarily in the trades areas: plumbing, electrical, construction, machine tool, engineering, and healthcare in the United States. The United Kingdom, however, has apprenticeship programs for business, administration, and law (United Kingdom, 2011).

TRANSFERABILITY OF COURSES

Articulation agreements cover (a) students going from high school to college and from two-year to four-year colleges and universities, (b) "double-reverse transfer" students who go from a two-year to four-year college or university and then back again, and (c) students seeking credit for work experience toward their college credits. The articulation agreements that allow transferability of courses have been formally negotiated between the institutions involved and specifically identify the courses that can be taken and their equivalency.

Dual Enrollment / Dual Credit

College-level courses that students take in high school can earn credit toward high school graduation and toward their college degree (dual credit). Dual enrollment is when students are concurrently enrolled and taking classes in both high school and college. Students in their junior or senior year of high school are the primary participants in this enrollment plan. Dual credit was originally given for academic courses; now it is very common for students in CTE courses to earn dual credit toward a program of study in business or computers at the community college. The courses vary in their eligibility requirements and target populations. Sometimes these variations are regulated by state policies; other times, program structure is determined through cooperative agreements between the partnering institutions (Karp, Calcagno, Hughes, Jeong, & Bailey, 2008). According to the U.S. Department of Education, about 71% of public high schools offer dual enrollment programs (Chen, 2008).

Dual enrollment classes are popular because they provide an early and smoother entry into college coursework for high school students, strengthen the high school curriculum, act as a recruitment tool for community colleges, and accelerate the student's time for earning a degree. It also allows high schools the opportunity to offer CTE courses in technology without having to invest in the costly hardware and software required of those courses.

Course Transferability to Bachelor Degree–Granting Institutions

One of the primary missions of the community college is to provide transferability of coursework to a four-year institution to earn a baccalaureate degree. An associate degree usually qualifies the student to enroll in a four-year college or university with junior status. In some states, it even guarantees the student will be accepted as a junior.

Many community colleges and four-year colleges and universities have entered into articulation agreements with one another, making it easier for students to transfer. The articulation agreements identify which degrees and/or courses will transfer. Practically all liberal arts classes qualify for transfer, but transfer credit for programs or courses in CTE fields are inconsistent (Cohen & Brawer, 2008). All courses for consideration of transfer credit must be numbered at the 100 or higher level to be considered as a transferable course by the admitting university or college. Most community colleges have an individual who works directly with the senior institution to keep the agreements current and to create course equivalency documents. It is important to note that "one size does not fit all" in the transfer process; articulation agreements are with individual four-year colleges and universities.

SUMMARY

This chapter discussed postsecondary preparation available to students in business, computer, and business-related fields for entry into the workplace. Some of the programs of study are very traditional, such as accounting, administrative assistant, computer programming, and marketing. Just as the global business environment is evolving, so are the ways individuals are performing their jobs. With those changes in job tasks comes the need for new or specialized curricular offerings. In addition to the traditional programs of study, more service-related and interdisciplinary courses are now being taught within the business and computer curricula. Among the current nontraditional offerings are virtual assistant, computer forensics, leadership in business, customer service, business plans and projects, interactive media, quality assurance technology, and cybercrime technology.

Credentials awarded in postsecondary institutions include baccalaureate degrees, associate degrees, industry certifications, and certificates. The programs in business and computer studies provide a foundation in basic business concepts and specific skills for the chosen career, as well as employability skills. More jobs are requiring less than a baccalaureate degree, so certificates and associate degrees are appropriate goals for many students.

In addition to coursework, students in postsecondary institutions may participate in work experience. During their work experience, students are able to apply the knowledge and skills learned in their program of study to situations in the real world.

Formalized articulation agreements allow high school students to earn college credits while attending high school and postsecondary students to be able to transfer credits earned at a two-year institution to a four-year college or university in an orderly and timely manner.

Postsecondary institutions play an important role today by preparing individuals to enter the workforce with the necessary skills to succeed and by providing a bridge for career majors to four-year institutions.

REFERENCES

AACC [American Association of Community Colleges]. (1998, July 31). *AACC position statement on the associate degree.* Retrieved from http://www.aacc.nche.edu/About/Positions/Pages/ps08011998.aspx

Ashford, E. (2011, January 31). ACT calls for layered credentialing system. *Community College Times.* Retrieved from http://www.communitycollegetimes.com/Pages/Academic-Programs/ACT-calls-for-layered-skills-credentialing-system.aspx

Bailey, T., Gumport, P. J., & Badway, N. (2003). *For-profit higher education and community colleges.* (CCRC Research Brief No. 16). New York, NY: Community College Research Center.

Bailey, T., & Jacobs, J. (2009, October 22). Can community colleges rise to the occasion? *The American Prospect.* Retrieved from http://www.prospect.org/cs/articles?article=can_community_colleges_rise_to_the_occasion

Bishop, J., & Mane, F. (2003). *The impacts of career-technical education on high school completion and labor market success* (CAHRS WP03-18). Ithaca, NY: Cornell University, Center for Advanced Human Resource Studies. Retrieved from http://digitalcommons.ilr.cornell.edu/cgi/viewcontent.cgi?article=1036&context=cahrswp

Bragg, D. D., Townsend, B. K., & Ruud, C. M. (2009, January). The adult learner and the applied baccalaureate: Emerging lessons for state and local implementation. *In Brief.* Urbana-Champaign, IL: University of Illinois, Office of Community College Research and Learning.

Cohen, A. M., & Brawer, F. B. (2008). *The American community college.* San Francisco, CA: Jossey Bass.

College Degree Guide. (n.d.). *Types of postsecondary schools.* Retrieved from http://www.collegedegreeguide.com/articles-fr/types.htm

Chen, G. (2008, June 3). Dual enrollment programs for high school students. *Public School Review* [Electronic version]. Retrieved from http://www.publicschoolreview.com/articles/26

Holzer, H. J., & Lerman, R. I. (2007). *America's forgotten middle-skill jobs, education and training requirements in the next decade and beyond.* Washington, DC: The Workforce Alliance.

Horn, L., & Weko, T. (2009). *Changes in postsecondary awards below the bachelor's degree: 1997 to 2007* (Report NCES 2010-167). Washington, DC: U.S. Department of Education.

Karp, M. M., Calcagno, J. C., Hughes, K. L., Jeong, D. W., & Bailey, T. (2008). *Dual enrollment students in Florida and New York City: Postsecondary outcomes* (CCRC Research Brief No. 37). New York, NY: Community College Research Center.

Kazis, R. (2005, April). *Remaking career and technical education for the 21st century: What role for high school programs?* Paper presented at the Aspen Institute Program on Education and Society, Aspen, CO. Retrieved from http://www.cew.wisc.edu/docs/resource_collections/Kazis_RemakingCTE.pdf

National Commission on Excellence in Education. (1983, April). *A nation at risk: the imperative for educational reform.* Retrieved from http://www2.ed.gov/pubs/NatAtRisk/index.html

Queensland, Australia, Department of Education and Training. (2001). *Career education.* Retrieved from http://education.qld.gov.au/students/service/career

Roscorla, T. (2010, April 14). Education experts define career readiness. *Converge Magazine.* Retrieved from http://www.convergemag.com/workforce/Education-Experts-Define-Career-Readiness.html

Skolnik, M. L., & Floyd, D. L. (2005). The community college baccalaureate: Toward an agenda for policy and research. In D. L. Floyd, M. L. Skolnik, & K. P. Walker (Eds.), *The community college baccalaureate: Emerging trends and policy issues* (pp. 191–198). Sterling, VA: Stylus Publishing.

United Kingdom, National Apprenticeship Service. (2011). *Business, administration, and law.* Retrieved from http://www.apprenticeships.org.uk/Types-of-Apprenticeships/Business-Administration-and-Law.aspx

U.S. Department of Education, National Center for Education Statistics. (2008a). *Career and technical education in the United States 1990 to 2005* (Report NCES2008 035). Washington, DC: Author.

U.S. Department of Education, National Center for Education Statistics. (2008b). *Community colleges: Special supplement to the condition of education 2008* (Report NCES 2008 033). Washington, DC: Author.

U.S. Department of Labor, Bureau of Labor Statistics. (2010). *Occupational outlook handbook, 2010–11.* Retrieved from http://www.bls.gov/oco

U.S. Department of Labor, Secretary's Commission on Achieving Necessary Skills. (1991). *What work requires of schools: A SCANS report for America 2000.* Retrieved from http://wdr.doleta.gov/SCANS/whatwork/whatwork.pdf

Business Education at the College Level

Priscilla Y. Romkema

Black Hills State University

Spearfish, SD

Business education at the college/university level is delivered primarily through colleges or schools of business or education. This chapter addresses areas that are key to establishing quality business teacher education programs in higher education by defining business teacher education, providing an overview of college/school of business degree programs and national/international/regional business and education accreditations, and summarizing the benefits of internships and advisory boards to business and business teacher education programs.

FROM MISSION STATEMENT TO BUSINESS DEGREE PROGRAMS

A mission statement, while intended to guide the college/school, is also shaped by the individual activities of the college/school, degree programs offered by the college/school, as well as the organizational placement of business teacher education programs within the university structure. Organizational placement has an impact on the mission of that college/school, its promotional/marketing efforts, its role on the university campus and in the community, and its available resources. Specifically, a business department may be one of several departments or divisions within a given college at the university or organized as a stand-alone college/school. In turn, business teacher education may be located in the business or education department, college, or school.

Regardless of the location of business programs, common threads exist among most U.S. universities on the "typical" undergraduate business program/degree offered. The following (or variations thereof) are common among university undergraduate business programs in the United States:

- **Bachelor of arts** in business, business administration, business communications, and business studies

- **Bachelor of science in business administration or management** with or without specializations or concentrations (i.e., accounting, computer information systems, economics, entrepreneurship, finance, management, management information systems, operations management, marketing, and tourism)

- **Bachelor of business administration** with or without majors (i.e., the same areas listed in the previous bullet)

- **Bachelor of science in business education**

DEFINING BUSINESS TEACHER EDUCATION

Business teacher education may be defined broadly as the collegiate/university preparation of individuals to become business education teachers at the middle and high school levels. Although various pathways are available, the typical route for most individuals is either through an undergraduate program in business teacher education or through a program that provides an accelerated pathway for individuals with four-year degrees in business (or related degrees) to obtain secondary teacher certification. Due to state department of education requirements, specific content within programs will vary from state to state; however, similarities exist in the expectations and require-ments across many business teacher education programs—due to state requirements, as well as the leadership of national organizations that focus on business teacher education and business education including the National Association for Business Teacher Education (http://www.nabte.org) and the National Business Education Association (http://www.nbea.org).

Traditional Programs

The traditional undergraduate business teacher education program is a four-year program that includes general education requirements as well as strong emphases in both business content and education. Although the specific coursework may vary somewhat among institutions and states, there are commonalities among most tradi-tional business education programs as noted in the next section.

At the time of graduation, a business teacher education student may be required to take one or more exit exams from the institution. The ETS *Praxis II* may be required of those seeking to "enter the teaching profession as part of the certification process required by many states and professional licensing organizations" (ETS, n.d.). The *Praxis II* Business Education Assessment includes the following content categories: economic systems, money management, business and its environment, professional business education, processing information, office procedures and management, communications and employability skills, and accounting and marketing. Students are required to earn a score determined by the institution and/or state as "passable" or within a certain range. In addition, business education students may be required to take an additional business exit exam such as the ETS Major Field Test in Business (ETS, n.d.).

Coursework

In addition to general education requirements (which may constitute about one-third of the total credits required in the business teacher education program), typical programs include a substantial number of business and education courses designed to provide a foundation in content and pedagogy. The education program content is structured in a manner similar to other teacher education programs; the business content is shaped largely by other business programs at the institution as well as state teaching certification requirements.

Typical business teacher education programs require a solid foundation in the business-related courses commonly taught at the secondary level: accounting, marketing, computers, economics, and communications. Depending on the size of the middle or high school, business education teachers may also have opportunities to teach courses in such areas as entrepreneurship, finance, and international business.

Education courses typically required in a business teacher education program may include American education (foundations), psychology, instructional strategies, teaching of reading, child and adolescent behavior, education of individuals with disabilities, and human relations. Courses required are in accordance with state standards and institutional expectations. Teacher education programs at a given institution are largely the same (see National Council for Accreditation of Teacher Education [NCATE] at http://www.ncate.org).

Unique Features

In addition to business and education courses, business teacher education programs may include a required or optional internship. The internship may include hands-on experiences in one or more content areas (computers and marketing, for example) while the student earns credit. Internships provide additional *know-how* on which the student is able to draw, and serve to complement the student teaching experience in which students are engaged at the end of their academic programs (BHSU, n.d.-a).

Regarding delivery, business education courses may be taught online, via videoconferencing, and/or in a hybrid format (to allow for face-to-face and online instruction and interaction). Variations in delivery provide students with practical experiences that may be encountered in their student teaching experience or employment as a business education teacher. When students are well prepared in terms of content as well as delivery, the teaching experience will be more positive for both the teacher and the students.

New Models

Due to the demands of individuals with recent four-year degrees and those with years of business experience who want to teach business courses at the secondary level, "fast-track" or "accelerated" programs have emerged as a mechanism to become certified in a shorter period. This opportunity has developed due to demand by interested students as well as demand for teachers in particular subject areas.

One example of an accelerated program is "Project Select," currently offered at Black Hills State University in Spearfish, SD. This program was designed to provide

coursework and field experience for students seeking teacher certification as secondary (7–12) teachers within a 10-month timeframe. Candidates must have either their content coursework completed or have a baccalaureate degree in a major. This is a full-time program. The coursework involved includes 41 credits. Individuals (students) are expected to approach this as a job—meaning that they are committing to eight-hour days over 10 months. As there is a strong tie to the public schools in regard to this program, the schedules follow the public school calendars. (BHSU, n.d.-c)

LOCATING BUSINESS TEACHER EDUCATION PROGRAMS

Business teacher education programs are typically located in either a college or school of business or a college or school of education. The location may impact the program in a variety of ways, including level of support and recognition from administration, positioning, marketing, institutional financial support, and unique opportunities with other programs located within the same college/school. As discussed in the following sections, factors vary on where business teacher education is located and why.

College/School of Business

Due to historical, institutional, philosophical, and/or strategic reasons, business teacher education programs may be located in colleges/schools of business. Doing so closely aligns the program with other business administration/management programs; both faculty and students may identify themselves with the "business school" and view their program as a solid business program with essential education courses. The career pathway for business teacher education students is well defined as, upon graduation, graduates are "job ready" for positions at the middle and high school levels. Because of this, these students may closely identify with other business majors due to their "job readiness" along with their keen interest in business content. Another location factor may be that some institutions may require that all education programs are located within the college/school/department that closely aligns with the content area.

College/School of Education

Likewise, due to historical, institutional, philosophical, and/or strategic reasons, business teacher education programs may be located in colleges/schools of education. Doing so permits the possible alignment of the program with other education programs. This location enables education faculty and business teacher education students to interact easily with other future educators from other content areas on the pedagogical aspects of their programs. Student organizations that address the needs and interests of all those in secondary education programs offer opportunities to unite students in their common interest area of education.

Program Location Implications

The location of business teacher education programs has potential implications regarding funding, positioning, recruitment, institutional expectations, and accreditation. Specifically, decisions made within the context of academic affairs and at the college and departmental levels are shaped by the location of the program. Institutions are well served when the various factors that impact this program are carefully reviewed and discussed. There are advantages to all location options as well as challenges that may directly or indirectly influence recruitment, course enrollments, and ultimately, graduation rates.

UNDERSTANDING ACCREDITATION

Accreditation Purpose

The premise of the accreditation process is that there are accepted practices and/or standards in a given profession and that, according to an external accrediting body, a particular entity has or has not met or exceeded the standards established over time. The accreditation process enables faculty, students, and administrators to place direct focus, efforts, and resources on those aspects of its operations that directly impact programs, faculty, and student learning. This focused attention provides real benefit to schools/colleges of business and becomes the impetus for conscious reflection and action. The process of seeking accreditation that includes self-evaluation and self-reflection is as important, if not more important, than being accredited. *Process* is key (Association to Advance Collegiate Schools of Business [AACSB], 2007; n.d.-b).

Once earned, accreditation assures all stakeholders that a given college/school has undertaken a process of close scrutiny by internal and external parties and has achieved standards necessary to join the ranks of previously accredited institutions (Lubinescu, Ratcliff, & Gaffney, 2001).

Assessment Purpose

Assessment is a major focus in most regional and national accreditations. Many colleges/schools conduct annual or periodic internal assessments on the quality of programs, faculty productivity and teaching effectiveness, and student learning. Preparation for accreditation includes establishing program goals and learning objectives, designing assessment instruments/tools, conducting the assessments, reviewing and analyzing the results, and identifying strengths and areas for improvement. Furthermore, the process includes "circling back" so that changes may be made at the course and/or program level. Many schools engage in the assessment process (to varying degrees) and use this process primarily for internal purposes; however, other colleges/

schools use elements of the assessment process to promote (externally) the achievements and accomplishments of their faculty, students, and programs. Conducting assessments on an annual or regular basis enables faculty and administrators to maintain a current check on areas of strength as well as potential areas of concern (AACSB, 2007).

Assessment also provides a mechanism to respond to the larger question of "how are we doing?" Rather than making curriculum decisions based on anecdotal responses, a formal assessment process provides the qualitative and quantitative information needed to make data-driven decisions. The value of assessment is not in the process alone; rather, its value is in the sharing of the results with those who are involved in assessment at the university (i.e., an assessment committee) and those faculty members who are in positions to analyze the assessment results further and lead efforts to update courses and programs. As stated on the Northwest Health Sciences University's Center for Teaching, Learning, and Assessment Web site:

> Assessment is an ongoing process of setting high expectations for student learning, measuring progress toward established learning outcomes, and providing a basis for reflection, discussion, and feedback to improve University academic programs. It is a systematic and cyclic process that makes expectations and standards explicit and public. (Northwest Health Sciences University, n.d.)

As stated earlier, *process* is key!

National/International Accrediting Organizations

In an interview of Dr. Kevin Kinser published with *HigherEdJobs* (n.d.) "Is accreditation the conscience of higher education? And should it feel guilty?" he discussed the geographical differences that exist between national and regional accreditations and that regional accreditations focus on a specific cluster of states, whereas national accreditations embrace the entire country—with a focus on the strengths of the given institution (HigherEdJobs, n.d.).

The reasons for pursuing business accreditation may include campus history, available resources, expectations among various stakeholders, perceived quality of a given accreditation, and regional or national competition. In addition, specialized accreditations may be undertaken for particular programs within the business college or school. For education programs, the National Council for Accreditation of Teacher Education (NCATE) is the most accepted accreditation (see later section).

Various accrediting bodies for undergraduate and graduate business programs are available for schools/colleges of business to pursue. For business programs, the primary accreditation options include the Association to Advance Collegiate Schools of Business, Accreditation Council for Business Schools and Programs (ACBSP), and the International Assembly for Collegiate Business Education (IACBE) (MBA-Options, n.d.).

Some may question the benefit to students in earning their degrees from accredited institutions. What is the value of an accredited program? The answer lies in the credibility that comes with an external body measuring the quality of the program, the faculty, and the students. Although there is not an overall shortage of business programs (online and face to face), accreditation serves as a recognized and valued "screening tool" for prospective students and their parents. An external evaluation is noted and appreciated by employers as well as the general public. These individuals applaud the notion of a "third party" reviewing qualifications of faculty and verifying the quality and outcomes of courses and programs. Accreditation provides the "stamp of approval" in this day of accountability and assessment. Without it, questions may be posed as to the quality, rigor, and relevance of a given program as well as individual courses.

Association to Advance Collegiate Schools of Business (http://www.aacsb.edu). Founded in 1916, this accrediting body provides accreditation opportunities for bachelor-, master-, doctorate-level business and accounting programs. As stated on the its Web site, AACSB accreditation is known worldwide as the longest-standing, most recognized form of specialized/professional accreditation an institution and its business programs can earn. (AACSB, n.d.-a)

AACSB is a membership organization so that schools/colleges that are accepted as members may receive benefits (including resources and conference/workshop training) while they pursue accreditation. Nonmembers may also attend training and make use of online resources. AACSB membership is also available to corporate, nonprofit, and public sector organizations. A membership application and membership dues are required. The AACSB Web site states:

As of July 2011, 633 member institutions hold AACSB Accreditation. Overall, 41 countries and territories are represented by AACSB-accredited schools.

- 41 institutions have undergraduate programs only (6% of accredited members)
- 26 institutions have master's and doctoral programs only (4% of accredited members)
- 177 institutions have AACSB's additional accounting accreditation (28% of accredited members) (AACSB, n.d.-b)

See http://www.aacsb.edu/membership/join.asp for membership details.

Although AACSB accreditation is considered the premier accrediting body for business colleges and schools, a few well-known Ivy League colleges and schools of business are not accredited by AACSB (AACSB, n.d.-c). Factors may include membership and ongoing costs, resources at the institution, philosophy, and curriculum constraints.

Accreditation Council for Business Schools and Programs (http://www.acbsp. org). Founded in 1988, this organization provides accreditation opportunities for undergraduate and graduate business and accounting programs. ACBSP, a membership organization, permits member schools/colleges to receive benefits (including resources and conference/workshop training) while they pursue accreditation. Even nonmembers may attend training and use online resources. Membership is also available to business corporations, foundations, professional associations, and nonprofit organizations. A membership application and membership dues are required. Regarding current membership, the following is stated on the ACBSP Web site:

- 102 institutions that offer both baccalaureate and associate degree are accredited

- 151 institutions that offer only associate degrees are accredited

- 160 institutions that offer baccalaureate/graduate degrees are accredited (ACBSP, n.d.-a)

See http://www.acbsp.org/p/cm/ld/fid=145 for membership details.

International Assembly for Collegiate Business Education (IACBE) (http://www. iacbe.org). Founded in 1997, this body provides accreditation to undergraduate and graduate business programs. The IACBE bases its accreditation reviews on principles, rather than standards. Any academic business unit whose parent institution grants business degrees at the bachelor, master, or doctorate level may apply for academic business unit membership in the IACBE. Schools/colleges accepted as members may receive benefits (including resources and conference/workshop training) while they pursue accreditation (IACBE, n.d.). See http://www.iacbe.org/membership.asp for membership details.

National Council for Accreditation of Teacher Education (http://www.ncate. org). Founded in 1954, NCATE accreditation is a voluntary peer review process that includes a comprehensive evaluation of the professional education unit. The following is stated on the NCATE Web site:

NCATE accredits schools, colleges, and departments of education in U.S. colleges and universities, as well as non-university entities that prepare educators for P–12 schools.

The accreditation covers all educator preparation programs for the purpose of preparing and developing professional educators for work in P–12 school settings, including off-campus programs, distance learning programs, and alternate route programs. However, the accreditation does not include individual education courses that the institution offers to P–12 educators for professional development, re-licensure, or other purposes. (NCATE, n.d.-a)

Regarding current membership, the following is stated on the NCATE Web site under Quick Facts about NCATE:

> Currently, 656 institutions are accredited and nearly 70 others are candidates and precandidates for accreditation. NCATE is recognized by the U.S. Department of Education and the Council for Higher Education Accreditation as a professional accrediting body for teacher preparation. (NCATE, n.d.-b)

Business teacher education programs that are located in colleges/schools of education are often accredited under NCATE. Those located in colleges and schools of business may also be NCATE accredited due to the linkage between the two colleges.

Regional Accrediting Organizations

Regional accreditations of colleges and universities are more common than national/international business accreditations in the United States (in terms of the number of accredited institutions). A regional accreditation provides a measure of assurance to other institutions in the region and other regions around the country on the initial independent review undertaken and ongoing adherence to specific standards. A regional accreditation is critical to a university's credibility, its ability to seek national accreditation, and its ability to comply with other university factors (financial aid issues, for example) (Council for Higher Education Accreditation, n.d.).

The United States has six regional accreditations for higher education programs. These are voluntary, nongovernmental membership associations designed to further educational excellence among a varied group of colleges. A regional accreditation process does not assess specific programs within institutions; rather, the institution as a whole is assessed. Why would an institution pursue a regional accreditation as well as a national accreditation, knowing the time, effort, and expense involved? The reasons are varied but certainly include the added measure of credibility, the external stamp of approval, the expectation of governing boards, and the value added associated with regional accreditation. Likewise, a national accreditation (AACSB, ACBSP, IACBE, and/or NCATE, for example) demonstrates to the internal and external constituencies that the respective program and institution has undertaken a rigorous process of assessment (courses, programs, and faculty) and has passed the standards as set forth by an external body.

The Council for Higher Education Accreditation (CHEA) publishes a directory of accrediting organizations. Inclusion in this directory stands as an endorsement of the standards and processes of the accrediting organization. It follows that this endorsement recognizes the academic quality, improvement, and accountability expectations that CHEA has established. The six regional accreditations available to institutions in the United States are as follows:

The Middle States Association of Colleges and Schools/The Middle States Commission on Higher Education
http://www.middlestates.org
http://www.msche.org
Open to colleges in Delaware, District of Columbia, Maryland, New Jersey, New York, Pennsylvania, and Puerto Rico

The New England Association of Schools & Colleges
http://www.neasc.org
Open to colleges in Connecticut, Maine, Massachusetts, New Hampshire, Rhode Island, and Vermont

The North Central Association of Colleges and Schools/ Higher Learning Commission
http://www.ncahlc.org
Open to colleges in Arkansas, Arizona, Colorado, Iowa, Illinois, Indiana, Kansas, Michigan, Minnesota, Missouri, North Dakota, Nebraska, Ohio, Oklahoma, New Mexico, South Dakota, Wisconsin, West Virginia, and Wyoming

The Northwest Commission on Colleges and Universities
http://www.nwccu.org
Open to colleges in Alaska, Idaho, Montana, Nevada, Oregon, Utah, and Washington

The Southern Association of Colleges and Schools
http://www.sacs.org
Open to colleges in Alabama, Florida, Georgia, Kentucky, Louisiana, Mississippi, North Carolina, South Carolina, Tennessee, Texas, and Virginia

The Western Association of Schools & Colleges
http://www.wascweb.org
Open to colleges in California and Hawaii, the territories of Guam, American Samoa, Federated States of Micronesia, Republic of Palau, Commonwealth of the Northern Marianas Islands, the Pacific Basin and East Asia, and areas of the Pacific and East Asia where American/international schools or colleges may apply to it for service.

ASSESSING BROAD IMPLICATIONS OF ACCREDITATION

University and College/School

A regional, national, or international accreditation provides the comprehensive and systematic review of an institution or programs that benefits both internal and external stakeholders. For the university or college/school, a clear process of program or course improvement may be charted and monitored. "Continuous improvement" and "closing the loop" in the assessment process are concepts faculty and administrators understand must be followed for initial accreditation purposes and for continuous adherence to standards and expectations.

Program

General discussion surrounding program benefits may tie directly or indirectly to the institution, faculty, students, and public and may include the following:

- Credibility for the institution and program(s)
- Pride on the part of internal and external stakeholders
- Clear process for ongoing review of faculty qualifications
- Clear process for ongoing assessment of student learning
- National/international recognition

Along with benefits, accreditation may bring forth challenges that may include the following:

- Budget/financial factors (faculty salaries, accreditation fees/dues, teaching and research technologies, professional development training and travel, and marketing/promotion)
- Perception of accreditation in other colleges on campus
- Close review of all programs and courses
- Potential reorganization of programs for greater efficiencies
- A need to balance student demand, course load, and qualified faculty
- Focused attention to specific course outcomes and, therefore, specific courses
- College/school past practices may need to be reviewed and changed regarding course assignments, overloads, additional assignments, course releases (ACBSP, n.d.-b)

Faculty

Faculty members are impacted by accreditation in terms of rigorous expectations regarding research, teaching, and service. At the same time, the prestige and credibility associated with accreditation is attractive both in terms of recruitment and retention of faculty. Opportunities to attract and retain quality faculty are significantly impacted via accreditation.

Students

Accreditation may directly or indirectly result in improvements in recruitment and retention of students. Among the factors considered in college/university selection may include accreditation (regional as well as national). Students value the prestige and credibility associated with accreditation. In addition, students attracted to accredited programs also value the rigor of the program itself and the quality of the faculty with whom they may engage in the classroom and in research projects.

Public

Accreditation is important to a cross-section of the public, including employers, parents, city and state legislative bodies, and area residents. Earning accreditation is a demonstration of consistent quality (faculty, students, and programs) and the accountability of a given institution or program, both of which are of key importance to the general public as well as specific stakeholders.

MAXIMIZING THE EXPECTATIONS OF ADVISORY BOARDS

Another unique aspect of higher education is the opportunity to benefit from the expertise and guidance of an advisory board. Unlike a board of directors, an advisory board does not have fiduciary accountability; rather, the advisory board members provide ideas and feedback to benefit the university and college/school and, ultimately, the students (Advisory Board Council, n.d.).

As stated on the Ball State University Web site under Miller College of Business the purpose of their college boards is to

promote interaction with industry leaders and play a crucial role in ensuring our ongoing success and vitality. The boards support our mission in education, applied research, and service. Among other things, members offer counsel on curriculum matters, and maintain beneficial relationships with current students. (Ball State University, n.d.)

Other universities, such as Eastern Illinois University, have a specific mission for advisory boards. As stated on its Web site:

The Eastern Illinois University School of Business Advisory Board serves in an advisory role to the Chair of the School of Business and as advocates of the School. The objectives of the Business Advisory Board are to:

- Provide an interface between the School and business community

- Provide advice and support to the Chair on a variety of issues related to the management and offerings of the School

- Promote positive public relations for the School. (Eastern Illinois University, n.d.)

If the board comprises individuals from business and education, administrators and faculty will benefit from the expertise and experience represented by those in business (content knowledge) as well as those in education (pedagogy). However, if the board within the college/school of business is an inclusive, comprehensive business board, deans and chairs are well served to include individuals with expertise in the educational arena.

Short- and long-term benefits of an advisory board to the college/school could include the following:

- Greater awareness among board members on programs, initiatives, faculty, and students within the college or school

- Creation of allies for the college/school among board members
- Constructive feedback from board members on various aspects of the college/school
- Future business and education networking links for administrators, faculty, and students
- Increased knowledge on the part of the college/school on current business practices and realities
- Increased knowledge on the part of the college/school on current practices and realities in education
- Support or guidance for the college/school on funding possibilities
- Formalized pipeline from the community to the university for mutual benefit
- Valuable, timely information provided to those in higher education

SUMMARY

Universities across the United States are in a unique position to prepare quality business leaders and educators. This is accomplished via factors that include strategic organizational positioning of business and business teacher education programs within the university structure and national/international/regional accreditations that address quality programs and faculty. Accreditation provides the internal and external "stamp of approval" to multiple constituencies; this credibility factor is critical to these constituencies and should not be underestimated in terms of its power in the decision-making process for students, their parents, and the faculty.

Other factors play a significant role in rounding out a quality undergraduate education in business. Advisory boards offer a much-needed connection with the business community. Through this formal structure, board members are in a position to provide practical guidance and feedback so that the institution maintains a strong connection with the community at large. Ultimately, students are the beneficiaries of quality programs that are continually assessed, relevant internships that augment the classroom experience, and an engaged advisory board.

REFERENCES

AACSB [Association to Advance Collegiate Schools of Business]. (2007, November 27). *AACSB assurance of learning standards: An interpretation.* (White Paper No. 3) Retrieved from http://www.aacsb.edu/publications/whitepapers/AACSB_Assurance _of_Learning.pdf

AACSB. (n.d.-a). *Business accreditation.* Retrieved from http://www.aacsb.edu/ accreditation

AACSB (n.d.-b). *Accreditation.* Retrieved from http://www.aacsb.edu/accreditation/ accreditedmembers.asp

AACSB. (n.d.-c). *Membership: Educational institutions.* Retrieved from http://www. aacsb.edu/membership/MemberListings/educational.asp

ACBSP [Accreditation Council for Business Schools & Programs]. (n.d.-a). *ACBSP FAQs.* Retrieved from http://www.acbsp.org/index.php?mo=st&op=ld&sid=s1_ 020acc&stpg=25

ACBSP. (n.d.-b). *Value of accreditation.* Retrieved from http://www.acbsp.org/p/cm/ld/fid=75

Advisory Board Council. *Client FAQs.* (n.d.). Retrieved from http://www.advisory boardcouncil.org/ClientFAQs.html

Ball State University. (n.d.). *Miller College of Business advisory boards.* Retrieved from http://cms.bsu.edu/Academics/CollegesandDepartments/MCOB/AboutUs/MCOBAdvisoryBoards.aspx

BHSU [Black Hills State University]. (n.d.-a). *About us.* Retrieved from http://www.bhsu.edu/Academics/TheColleges/CollegeofBusinessandTechnology/About/tabid/178/Default.aspx

BHSU. (n.d.-b). *Internships.* Retrieved from http://www.bhsu.edu/Academics/The Colleges/CollegeofBusinessandTechnology/StudentResources/Internships/tabid/6093/Default.aspx

BHSU. (n.d.-c). *Secondary education learners engaged in constructivist teaching.* Retrieved from http://www.bhsu.edu/Academics/TheColleges/CollegeofEducation andBehavioralSciences/Schools/Education/Programs/ProjectSELECT/tabid/359/Default.aspx

Council for Higher Education Accreditation. (n.d.). *Council for Higher Education Accreditation.* Retrieved from http://www.chea.org/Directories/regional.asp#north-central

Eastern Illinois University. (n.d.). *Business Advisory Board.* Retrieved from http://www.eiu.edu/~business/community_bab.php

ETS: The Praxis Series. (n.d.). *For test takers.* Retrieved from http://www.ets.org/praxis

HigherEdJobs. (n.d.). *Is accreditation the conscience of higher education? And should it feel guilty?* Retrieved from http://www.higheredjobs.com/HigherEdCareers/interviews.cfm?ID=237

IACBE [International Assembly for Collegiate Business Education]. (n.d.). *About the IACBE.* Retrieved from http://www.iacbe.org/about-iacbe.asp

Lubinescu, E. S., Ratcliff, J. L., & Gaffney, M. A. (2001, Spring). Two continuums collide: Accreditation and assessment. *New Directions for Higher Education* (113), pp. 5–21.

MBA-Options.Com. (n.d.). *Business school accreditation.* Retrieved from http://www.mba-options.com/business-school-accreditation.html

NCATE [National Council for Accreditation of Teacher Education]. (n.d.-a). *NCATE Accredited Institutions.* Retrieved from http://www.ncate.org/tabid/176/Default.aspx

NCATE. (n.d.-b). *Quick Facts.* Retrieved from http://www.ncate.org/Public/About NCATE/QuickFacts/tabid/343/Default.aspx

Northwest Health Sciences University, Center for Teaching, Learning and Assessment. (2011). Retrieved October 12, 2011 from http://www.nwhealth.edu/ctl/asmnt/whatis.html

Model Business Education Programs

Peter Meggison

Massasoit Community College

Brockton, MA

Model business education programs are found in high schools, community colleges, and four-year colleges/universities throughout the United States. These programs, by their very nature, share some commonalities, while at the same time being quite diversified. The subject-matter content of these programs includes preparation in business skills necessary for success in today's business environment. Equally important, however, is that they offer students the opportunity to acquire a broad knowledge base of business practices and functions as well as the workplace readiness skills necessary to obtain and advance in today's business environment.

This chapter, devoted to model business education programs in various geographic areas of the United States, examines six very different, yet very similar, programs. Two programs are presented from each of three educational levels: high school, community college, and four-year college/university.

MODEL PROGRAMS

What, then, constitutes a model program? The answer to this question is, of course, subjective. Nonetheless, a useful characterization can be gleaned from the U.S. Department of Education and the National Center for Research in Vocational Education in their identification of outstanding schools that are making great progress in concurrently preparing students for college and the workforce. In these schools, students have the opportunity to do the following:

- Achieve high levels of academic and technical skills
- Prepare for college and careers
- Learn in the context of a career major or other career interest
- Learn by doing—in classrooms, workplaces, or community service
- Work with teachers in small schools within schools
- Receive extra support from adult mentors
- Access a wide range of information on careers and postsecondary education and training
- Use technology to enhance learning
- Benefit from strong links between high schools and postsecondary institutions

(U.S. Department of Education and National Center for Research in Vocational Education, 1996)

The characteristics of the outstanding schools described above are readily apparent in each of the programs described in this chapter. Each program develops a vast array of business competencies as well as preparedness for change.

HIGH SCHOOL PROGRAMS

Finance Academy, Hoover High School

Successful high school business education programs develop and change over time, continually shifting their emphasis to meet the needs of the community, students, and teachers. At Hoover High School in Hoover, Alabama, this re-engineering has included the development of a Finance Academy. The major goals of the Finance Academy are to integrate a smaller learning community within a large comprehensive high school of 2,500 students; develop a curriculum that combines a career focus while meeting college-entrance requirements; and create partnerships with supporting employers, community leaders, and institutions of higher education. Madge Gregg, director of Hoover's Finance Academy, explains, "We emphasize the three Rs in meeting the goals of the Finance Academy: rigor, relevance, and relationships."

Since the Finance Academy consists of a smaller learning community, students feel they are recognized and valued by both their peers and teachers. In this small-group setting, students are given the time, energy, and attention they need to become successful.

The academy's teachers are able to maintain contact with students who may be experiencing any of a myriad of difficulties that typical high school students face and, in turn, can create and implement individualized learning plans to rectify the situation. The academy's features are characteristic of any small learning community (SLC), with its inherent benefits readily identifiable. Oxley (2004) synthesized research in small learning communities and identified the following practices associated with positive outcomes for students:

- SLCs offer an authentic course of study.
- SLCs have a rigorous, standards-based curriculum.
- Teacher teams actively collaborate on curriculum and instruction, as well as student progress.
- Active, authentic (student-centered) work occurs (including collaboration with community partners).
- Teams make innovative, flexible use of time and space to meet the needs of all students.
- Teachers advise and mentor students and collaborate with parents.
- Teams reflect on practice and engage in continuous improvement with stakeholders and other critical friends.
- Teams set and pursue professional development goals that accord with SLC improvement needs.

All of these characteristics are observable in the Finance Academy at Hoover High School. The academy curriculum includes a series of courses that provide students an opportunity for increasing in-depth learning and boosting student interest in a business or finance career. Students also gain knowledge about postsecondary educational opportunities and develop skills that will enhance their lives as consumers and citizens. The academy courses include the following:

- Grade 9: Business Technology Applications and Financial Literacy
- Grade 10: Introduction to Financial Services
- Grade 11: Principles of Accounting
- Grade 12: Entrepreneurship and/or Managerial Accounting

The rigor, richness, and project-based learning activities infused in these classes foster self-discipline and prepare students to handle the demands of higher education and employment. Students refine their own competitive edge through field trips, job shadowing, student conferences, student organizations, leadership roles, and public-speaking opportunities.

By establishing relationships with the business community and postsecondary institutions, SLCs are able to increase the number of students participating in internships and work-based learning experiences as well as receiving postsecondary academic scholarships. To be a Finance Academy graduate, a paid internship is required during the summer between the student's junior and senior years. Gregg further states, "It is our objective to ensure our students' future success by helping them receive relevant work experience, being admitted to the postsecondary institution of their choice, and obtaining academic scholarships."

In coordination with the development of the Finance Academy, a school store—The Buc Stop (based on the school's namesake, the Buccaneers)—has been opened. This venture provides students with a viable, realistic experience in developing the skills and competencies needed to be successful in business, finance, or marketing. With the support of Bryant Bank, one of the local business partners, visually impressive store signage was installed; the resulting exposure increased sales. The store gives students the opportunity to operate a real business with real money and to meet the day-to-day demands of running a successful business. In turn, The Buc Stop earns a substantial profit each school year, which assists educational activities such as state field trips, community-service projects, and classroom materials and software.

In order for the Finance Academy to prosper, an aggressive recruiting approach with middle school students and parents has been necessary. A variety of media are used to communicate the Finance Academy message. Current students are actively involved in the recruitment process through participation in activities such as open houses, Eighth Grade Parent Night, and Eighth Grade Student Orientation Day. The Finance Academy Web site (http://www2.hoover.k12.al.us/schools/hhsfc/teachers/gmoncus/ hhsfinanceacademy/Pages/Default.aspx) is updated regularly and includes pictures of students actively engaged in academy activities. The Finance Academy has a brochure professionally produced each year to distribute at all functions. During the registration process, the academy mails a postcard to all eighth-grade parents and sends an electronic phone call reminding them of the application process for Finance Academy acceptance.

In 2010 a chapter of the National Business Honor Society was installed at Hoover High School to recognize students for their academic achievement. The students understand the importance of membership in an honorary society because it provides them opportunities for leadership, scholarship, and character education. The National Business Honor Society complements the Finance Academy at Hoover High School because it validates the quality of the Finance Academy program.

Virtual Enterprise / Business Management, Virginia Beach City Public Schools

Virtual Enterprise/Business Management, a program offering of the Virginia Beach City Public Schools, provides participants opportunities for both personal growth and business preparation. Virtual Enterprise is a statewide program (http://www.vevirginia. org), as well as part of a national and worldwide network. The coordinator of Business and Information Technology for the Virginia Beach Public Schools also happens to coordinate the state Virtual Enterprise program. In this capacity, she conducts training and major competitive events for Virtual Enterprise across the state. The program attracts students from diverse areas of study, including many who are enrolled in advanced placement courses.

Virtual Enterprise instruction is a task-based curriculum, so students are constantly engaged in the learning process. From the first day of class, students become employees in a simulated online business environment. With their classmates, they design, start, and operate a Virtual Enterprise company as part of an online "economy" of more than 3,000 Virtual Enterprise companies around the world. The Virtual Enterprise of Virginia home page provides links to the national home page as well as links for the international participants.

When deliberation begins at the outset of the course, it is akin to being on a jury. The participants are in an unknown group and must quickly bond and come to consensus on what type of company is desirable. After research and brainstorming sessions, students make their decision and from there produce a company name, logo, and product and service ideas with which to launch their online "virtual" business. This start-up process offers great insight as to which company department will be most appropriate for each student-employee to hone his or her talents and skills. In Virginia Beach most companies begin with predetermined departments: administration, marketing, human resources, and accounting. The company members later decide if they need to incorporate other departments or divide existing departments into two divisions. This process evolves as the company evolves in its set up and organization.

As the start-up process unfolds, students prepare their resumes to seek specific positions within their newly formed company. These positions range from chief executive officer (CEO) to other employees within a specified department. Outside experts are invited to interview those who apply for the CEO position. Class members observe the interviews and complete formal evaluations to relay their opinions about the candidates. After the three top leadership positions are filled (CEO, chief financial officer, and chief information officer), interviews are conducted to select the vice presidents to lead three established departments: accounting, marketing, and human resources. Graduates have returned to the school system and commented on what an excellent learning experience this process for filling positions had been for them. In particular, they indicated how it enabled them to apply for—and succeed in—jobs in the real world. One student attributed his securing a position with Apple to his selling experience in Virtual Enterprise, because a major segment of his final interview involved selling one of Apple's new products.

Once management positions are filled, employees prepare job descriptions for entry-level positions. The student-employees determine salary ranges for each position within the organization. Each employee receives a realistic salary and creates a personal budget. They pay their "virtual" bills online each month through US Network Bank (http://vebankbeta.nycenet.edu/i-bank). In October of each year, the "company" attends a citywide summit with a major emphasis on business plan preparation. Each student attends professional development sessions at which business professionals provide insight on preparing a business plan.

By early December a formal business plan is presented in regional and state competitive events to secure a loan to operate the business. Employees work diligently to prepare the plan based on the National Business Plan Competition rubric (available at http://www.vevirginia.org/business_plans.htm under "Oral Scoring Package").

The written business scoring package is available at http://www.vevirginia.org/bp_guidelenes_2010-11.pdf. Financial statements are prepared, as are sections on industry analysis, target market, the four Ps of marketing, and a SWOT (Strengths, Weaknesses, Opportunities, and Threats) analysis. After the written plan is submitted, the presentation team provides an 8-to-12 minute presentation to a panel of judges consisting of local business persons and bankers. The top two teams from the state in this competitive event advance to the National Business Plan Competition held in New York City. This competition, sponsored by a major bank and organized by the W!SE (Working in Support of Education) Foundation, showcases the best Virtual Enterprise firms in the nation. Since its inception in 2005, Virginia Beach has annually participated in the national competition with at least two teams.

Following the business plan competition, it is time for the "grand opening." After invitations are sent to this event, which is conducted in December or January, displays are developed and students have an opportunity to perfect their selling skills as they meet and greet clientele. Clipboards are ready with product pages and invoices ready to sell the wares of Virtual Enterprise. This event helps prepare the company for the Annual Virtual Enterprise Virginia Trade Fair, a capstone activity at which the firms create a sales booth and participate in 16 competitive events that showcase salesmanship as well as other acquired skills.

Jane Quesenberry and Caroline Myers, facilitators for Virtual Enterprise at First Colonial and Ocean Lakes High Schools, Virginia Beach, Virginia, send the following letter at the start of the school year to participants in the program:

Throughout the year you may have several different jobs and duties in the company—some of them will come easy to you and some will be more difficult. Try your best to learn each role so that your career skills can be expanded.

There will often be times when no one in class is working on the same assignment, yet everyone's assignment must be completed in order for the company to operate smoothly. Therefore, it will be important to help keep yourself and your fellow employees motivated so the company can be successful by winning competitive events and generating enough income to meet the monthly payroll and expenses. If you have the ability to motivate yourself and your fellow employees, you may want to consider applying for a leadership role within the company (be thinking of what you want to say in your leadership essay).

Along with being an employee, you will receive a virtual paycheck. You will have opportunities to use this money to shop for items to buy from other Virtual Enterprise companies around the city, state, country, and world. However, you will also have to pay virtual bills such as rent, utilities, transportation, insurance, and taxes. To manage your budget, you will balance your checking and savings accounts using an online bank.

As the teacher of this class, my role is to be the facilitator. This means that you are responsible for operating the business efficiently and effectively, and I will facilitate this process by providing you with direction, resources, and advice. By participating in this Virtual Enterprise experience, you will enhance your skills in marketing, business, and entrepreneurship. You will also grow and develop in areas such as creativity, responsibility, team work, leadership, communication, and technology.

Your challenge and goal this year as a Virtual Enterprise employee is to design, start, and operate a profitable business that sells the finest products or services available to satisfy customers and employees while making responsible contributions to the community.

Virtual Enterprise meets the needs of a wide array of students and has been approved as a method of instruction for several business content courses. Participants in this simulated business model receive career preparation in employment literacy and in communication, collaboration, personal, interpersonal, critical thinking, and problem-solving skills.

COMMUNITY COLLEGE PROGRAMS

Virtual Assistant Certificate, Owens Community College

The Office Administration Program at Owens Community College in Toledo, Ohio, transformed its two-year office administration degree program by responding to the need for qualified virtual assistant (VA) professionals: in 2005 it implemented the Administrative Virtual Assistant (AVA) Certificate. The purpose of this certificate is to transform an existing administrative or executive assistant who possesses a strong skill set as well as all of the attributes needed as an entrepreneur into an "administrative virtual assistant." To determine the viability of offering this certificate, career opportunities for VA positions were analyzed and a questionnaire administered to currently employed VAs. Professional organizations as well as a former advisory board member who is currently a VA supplied much-valued input.

The AVA certificate is unique because it represents a collaborative effort among departments of the college's School of Business and Information Systems. The school's courses were reviewed to determine which addressed the necessary skills. Office administration faculty collaborated with business faculty in determining the best array of courses needed for developing the skills a VA needs to perform successfully. The result is a unique blend of business, office, and computer-related courses. Currently employed VAs then reviewed the curriculum and provided input, changes were made to the curriculum, and a 24-credit-hour certificate was developed. Courses in marketing, business management, information systems, and office administration comprise the certificate. The certificate program, which can be started conveniently at any time of the year, consists of the following courses:

Small Business Management	3 credits
The Legal Environment of Business	3 credits
Introduction to E-Business	3 credits
Internet for Business	1 credit
Troubleshooting Applications	3 credits
Integrated Office Communications	3 credits
Special Topics: Virtual Assistant Coaching Seminar	2 credits
Information Systems/Office Administration Electives	6 credits

The faculty believes the Virtual Assistant Coaching Seminar facilitated online by a virtual assistant is a particular strength of the AVA certificate. The seminar uses the textbook *Virtual Assistant, The Series: Become a Highly Successful, Sought after VA* by Diana Ennen and Kelly Poelker (2004). Additionally, the elective courses provide students the ability to select topics that may fit their current skill levels and/or a niche of their particular interest. In addition, this certificate can be viewed as "absolutely global," because the courses are offered in both online and face-to-face formats. Moreover, all of the skills used in an online class are paramount to a virtual assistant's success.

Marketing this certificate is essential to the success of this new and relatively unknown field. There are many existing administrative assistants looking to advance their skills to the next level. By "upgrading" their virtual and entrepreneurship skill sets, they can provide business support services to a broad range of clientele locally or even worldwide. Many of these existing administrative assistants are alumni and members of local professional organizations. Owens Community College has sponsored an alumni/recruitment event focusing on the past, present, and future of the office administration field. Not only were alumni invited but advisory committee members and current students also participated in order to hear about the office administration field. Those attending enjoyed reminiscing about the past and hearing about the future, which included a discussion of the Administrative Virtual Assistant Certificate along with a keynote speaker from this burgeoning field. Little documentation is currently available on the topic of entrepreneurs as virtual professionals, which include virtual assistants. For example, few textbooks address this topic except in a limited way or through case studies addressing the benefits of virtual professionals. Nonetheless, many entrepreneurs may become virtual professionals in fields such as real estate, investments, mortgage banking, accounting, and technical specialties. Thus, broadening the scope of existing entrepreneurship courses to include the developing field of virtual professionals is important. Course content needs to emphasize how to conduct business in cyberspace as well as career opportunities as virtual professionals. Students desiring a career path in this area also need to know how to partner successfully with a virtual assistant who is pivotal to the entrepreneur's success.

The faculty is currently considering whether to include Web 2.0 technologies. Recent discussions with VAs indicate major requests for updating Web sites and the need to know how to navigate blogging, Twitter, YouTube, podcasting, Facebook (for business), Flickr, and Second Life.

As business programs continue to lead the way into the 21st century, adapting their curricula to meet the needs of today's students, employees, and employers is necessary. Specifically in administrative/office support professions, the U.S. Department of Labor's (USDOL's) *Occupational Outlook Handbook, 2010–11* reports that employment of secretaries and administrative assistants is "expected to increase by 11 percent, which is about as fast as the average for all occupations between 2008 and 2018." The handbook describes the nature of VA work as follows:

> Some secretaries and administrative assistants, also known as *virtual assistants*, are freelancers who work at a home office. They use the Internet, e-mail, fax, and the phone to communicate with clients. Other duties include medical or legal transcription, writing and editing reports and business correspondence, answering e-mail, data entry, setting appointments, making travel arrangements, bookkeeping, and desktop publishing. (USDOL, 2010)

Rose Marie Kuceyeski, business and information systems professor at Owens Community College, believes, "It becomes necessary, therefore, to ferret out these new growth opportunities and create curriculum that reflects these new skills. Who would have guessed? The revolution that swept the office in the 1970s—word processing—forever changed the office. The virtual assistant field is just one more example of this revolution."

Entrepreneurship Center, Santa Barbara City College

Santa Barbara City College (SBCC) is a comprehensive community college serving the south coast of Santa Barbara County, California. The college has a wide range of associate degree and certificate programs, as well as transfer programs that provide the first two years of study toward the baccalaureate degree. Students are attracted to SBCC by virtue of its outstanding faculty, small classes, state-of-the-art facilities, and numerous student services.

In 2007 SBCC received a permanent endowment to create an entrepreneurship program, the Scheinfeld Center for Entrepreneurship and Innovation (SCEI). The center has been a collaborative effort among administrators, faculty, and community members. The SCEI is a leader in the advancement of excellence in entrepreneurship education and practice and offers an entrepreneurial center in the Santa Barbara area, serving its diverse students and business community. The center's vision is to provide a nexus for entrepreneurship education and training, cultivation and dissemination of new technologies and business models for the 21st century entrepreneur, and resources to small businesses in the community. Melissa Moreno, director of the program, describes the program accordingly: "Academia coupled with a wealth of collaborative resources and guidance to the entrepreneur from the inception of an idea, through the planning stage, and to the execution of an operational, sustainable, and ultimately profitable enterprise defines the Center's mission and its apropos tagline: Dream. Plan. Profit."

Courses are offered for credit through the on-campus Department of Business Administration; noncredit courses are offered through the off-campus Division of Continuing Education. One-on-one business counseling is available at no cost to entrepreneurial students and small businesses in the area through the Santa Barbara County Small Business Development Center, funded by the Small Business Administration and hosted by the SCEI.

At the fulcrum of the SCEI is its for-credit academic program offered as a Skills Competency Award. A series of 10 condensed courses are offered in the evening to attract small business community members and to allow traditional students to easily supplement their regular lower-division curriculum. What is truly unique about the Skills Competency Award is its practical curriculum, which allows students to build an idea from scratch or to "grow" their own business. The courses are sequenced to enable students to walk through the process, step-by-step, from "Introduction to Entrepreneurship and Innovation" to "Business Plan Development." Students exit the program with a product of their own, a market-ready business plan, because they develop a portion of their business plan or strategic growth plan in each course.

In "Start Up to Expansion: Analysis and Assessment," for example, students conduct a feasibility study to determine the viability of their idea or growth plan and work with the instructor to hone their strategy. Course objectives and learning outcomes include identification of opportunities for small business growth or start-up, determination of business opportunities with the greatest possibility of economic success, analysis to assess risks of a new venture or growth plan, identification of significant consumer trends, researching data to help predict sales revenue, and development of a feasibility study for the new venture or growth plan.

A second example is "Entrepreneurial Finance," which results in the creation of a financial plan for the student's business. In this course, students identify the critical determinants affecting the financial requirements of a new or existing business, compare and contrast working capital policies affecting the financial needs of a business, develop a pro forma analysis, apply break-even analysis, identify key factors influencing valuation, compare and contrast options for capital structure and financing of new/existing ventures, and apply capital budgeting techniques.

Complementary to the curriculum is a lecture series entitled the "Enlightened Entrepreneurship Series." This series was created to provide an inspirational and motivational component to the program and to attract community attention. With Yvon Chouinard (founder of Patagonia) as the inaugural speaker, a high-end CEO/ founder series was quickly established. Conducted in an intimate lecture hall and moderated in a fireside chat format, students and community members gain rare insight into how many local entrepreneurs started and eventually experienced success. Pamela Lopker (QAD founder), Doug Otto (Deckers Outdoor founder), Wayne Rosing (former vice-president of engineering at Google), Paul Orfalea (Kinko's founder) are a few of the speakers who have shared their stories.

With grant funding, a supplementary internship program was developed. Outreach to small businesses and entrepreneurs in the community helped to create a large bank of potential employers for students. Under the guise of a "job stimulus" event, the Scheinfeld Center promoted the concept of creating short-term internship positions until businesses recover from the economic downturn and begin hiring once more. The result has been the placement of many students as interns in companies that would not otherwise be available to students.

SCEI raised funds to support an articulated effort with area high schools, which has become known as the New Venture Challenge. The impetus for donors was the creation of this secondary-school relationship, which allows students enrolled in a high school entrepreneurship class or virtual enterprise program to participate in SBCC's entrepreneurship program. Thus, the New Venture Challenge not only encourages entrepreneurial activity on campus (with $15,000 in awards), but also promotes youth entrepreneurship and a pathway from high school to college.

One challenge for most college entrepreneurship programs is providing a mechanism for students to actually launch their businesses and to meet the small business community's start-up and growth needs. With the recent award to the SCEI as the host for the Santa Barbara County Small Business Development Center, assistance with launch and growth has become realistic. The goals for economic impact are threefold: (a) create jobs, (b) increase sales and productivity, and (c) help small businesses procure investment.

COLLEGE/UNIVERSITY PROGRAMS

Sustainable Business, Aquinas College
Sustainable business is defined as a nontraditional business strategy that concurrently builds profits and economic stability, restores the health of natural systems, and promotes prosperous and healthy communities (http://www.aquinas.edu/sb). Since its inception in Europe in the 1980s, the sustainable business concept has also become a very popular movement in the United States.

Aquinas College in Grand Rapids, Michigan, currently offers both a bachelor's and master's degree in sustainable business. The college was the first in the country to offer a bachelor of science degree in sustainable business, and this area of study has become the signature program of the college.

By its very nature, sustainable business is interdisciplinary because it integrates science, business, and environmental studies. The goal of sustainable business is to improve long-term profitability, the health of natural systems, and the social infrastructure of our world community. Sustainable business is now a competitive advantage for organizations and is becoming an essential component of successful business practices. Viewed in the light of traditional business practices, sustainable business represents re-engineering that emphasizes the simultaneous production of financial, natural world, and social values without negative externalities. The design of the program at Aquinas College was initiated by Matthew Tueth, the program's current director, with consultation from an advisory committee made up of 12 early sustainable business practitioners from the Michigan area, as well as faculty from other institutions. This group provided recommendations for program development and evolution during its early stages.

Graduates of both the bachelor's and master's degree programs share these content commonalities:

- Understand conventional business and its systemic problems
- Able to revise business practices with only positive outcomes
- Identify and explore appropriate transition strategies for organizations
- Cultivate ability to apply potent sustainable business theory to a variety of business settings

The undergraduate program's focus consists of four areas:

- Conventional business practices
- Biology, chemistry, and physics
- Environmental studies
- Authentic sustainable business

Students completing the undergraduate program are employed in a variety of business sectors, including healthcare, banking, politics, consulting, manufacturing, food supply, education, and nonprofit organizations. The sustainable business practices emphasized in the program are applicable to all sizes and types of private and nonprofit enterprises.

Besides the sustainable business faculty, the program is supported with classes taught by faculty of business, economics, biology, chemistry, physics, and communications. All sustainable business undergraduates are required to participate in an internship with an organization in which the student routinely applies sustainable business theory within the specific circumstances of the organization; all sustainable business graduate students are required to complete an applied research project in collaboration with an organization in which the graduate student produces a solution for the organization solving an existing problem that inhibited the implementation of a sustainable business process or procedure.

A strength of both the undergraduate and graduate programs is that the sustainable business coursework delves deeply into energy and material issues, while considering the "nature of nature" and the needs of the human community. A variety of current conventional business paradigm components are subjected to meaningful scrutiny and discussion. The program at Aquinas College continues to provide excellent career opportunities for students because, as Tueth states "Sustainable business is mainstream now. It is not a fringe effort, and some of the most successful businesses on our planet have seriously engaged in sustainable business innovations; it has shown to be a competitive advantage to these organizations."

Business teachers can find a wealth of resources to inform themselves about current practices related to the sustainable business concept at Aquinas College's Center for Sustainability Web site (http://www.centerforsustainability.org).

Business Teacher Education, Bloomsburg University of Pennsylvania

Bloomsburg University (BU) of Pennsylvania's business education program, located in Bloomsburg, PA, is the oldest continuous program of its type in the state. From its inception in 1930, the business education program has been a cornerstone of BU, laying the foundation for the College of Business and staying at the forefront of the ever-changing business climate. BU has more than 4,000 business education alumni (BU of Pennsylvania, Business Education, n.d.).

The business education program's history dates back to the days of Bloomsburg State College. At that time, the program focused on certifying students to teach business subjects in grades 7 to 12 and in three content areas: accounting, typing, and shorthand. Today, students in the program meet the requirements of Pennsylvania's Business, Computer, and Information Technology (BCIT) Certification for teaching business/computer courses in kindergarten through grade 12. Students are now prepared to teach in 11 content areas reflecting NBEA's National Standards for Business Education (2012). Dennis Gehris, associate dean of the College of Business, confirms, "From only one small program, you now have a college; it helped initiate business instruction and education on campus and has played a major role ever since."

Students in the program find faculty who are responsive to their needs, small classes, and the opportunity to student teach within miles of the campus. Special attention is placed on matching the student's subject matter expertise, teaching style, and personality type with those of a cooperating teacher. Business education university supervisors observe student teachers a minimum of eight times during the 16-week semester. This frequent supervision allows students to determine their teaching strengths and areas for improvement while working closely with their cooperating teacher and university supervisor.

Before they begin student teaching, students are required to take the course "Instructional Strategies and Assessment in BCIT," which emphasizes various instructional strategies and assessment techniques for teaching business courses. In conjunction with this course, students also complete "BCIT Field Experience," a course that places students in area schools for a minimum of 30 hours. This field experience gives students an opportunity to teach, record, and assess at least three lessons and undertake the responsibilities of a classroom business teacher.

While student teaching, students enroll in "Clinical Studies in BCIT," a course that features seminars on various topics related to teaching business subjects, including principles of education, instructional strategies and assessment techniques, classroom management approaches, applying for a teaching position, nonverbal communication in the classroom, and questioning methods. The course also encourages students to discuss problems, concerns, and opportunities that arise during student teaching.

In addition to an undergraduate program in business education, BU offers a master of education program that provides an opportunity for individuals who already possess an undergraduate degree to obtain BCIT certification. The program content builds on a student's business administration undergraduate degree with education courses in exceptionalities, reading, English language learners, classroom management, training and development, technology applications, diversity in business and education, school law, and research in education. Undergraduate and graduate students from diverse ages, backgrounds, and experiences take four professional business education courses together, resulting in the creation of an energized learning environment.

Bloomsburg University's faculty is in constant contact with public schools as well as the business community to stay current on educational and business trends affecting the preparation of business teachers. Students also attend business conferences to discover new teaching strategies and technologies. "We feel our future teachers need to be involved in the profession," commented John J. Olivo, chair of the Business Education and Information and Technology Management Department. He further stated, "The faculty stay involved at the state, regional, and national levels and serve on advisory boards and national committees as well."

Bloomsburg University's business education undergraduate program is fully accredited by the Association for the Advancement of Collegiate Schools of Business, the National Council for the Accreditation of Teacher Education, and the Pennsylvania Department of Education.

The retention rate for students in the business teacher education programs is more than 70%, and the placement rate is consistently 100%. Because school districts value BU's highly qualified graduates, these business teachers are in constant demand in Pennsylvania as well as the surrounding states of New Jersey, New York, and Maryland. The National Business Education Association's mission—"education for success in business and life"—is readily apparent in the philosophy of this exemplary program in business teacher preparation.

SUMMARY

In a speech on the American Graduation Initiative in 2009, President Barack Obama stated:

> Now is the time to build a firmer, stronger foundation for growth that will not only withstand future economic storms, but one that helps us to thrive and compete in a global economy. It's time to reform our community colleges so that they provide Americans of all ages a chance to learn the skills and knowledge necessary to compete for the jobs of the future. (Obama, 2009)

The six programs illustrated in this chapter, which not only include community colleges but also high schools and four-year colleges/universities, illustrate how innovative business educators are meeting this challenge. By arming our students with the vast array of business competencies developed through model programs such as these, they will be in a position that ensures success in future jobs created by the global economy. As business educators, we will continue to be challenged as the past and present surge into our future; but through proactive vision that brings about decisive action, we can be assured of the continuance of our tradition of excellence in business education.

REFERENCES

BU of Pennsylvania. (n.d.). *Business education (BE)*. Retrieved from http://www.bloomu.edu/be

Ennen, D., and Poelker, K. (2004). *Virtual assistant: The series: Become a highly successful, sought after VA*. O'Fallon, IL: Another 8 Hours Publishing.

NBEA. (2012). *National standards for business education* (4th ed.). Reston, VA: Author.

Obama, Barack. (2009, July 14). *Excerpt from remarks in Warren, Michigan, on the American Graduation Initiative*. Retrieved from http://www.whitehouse.gov/the_press_office/Excerpts-of-the-Presidents-remarks-in-Warren-Michigan-and-fact-sheet-on-the-American-Graduation-Initiative

Oxley, Diane. (2004) *Small learning communities: A review of the research*. Retrieved from http://www.temple.edu/lss/pdf/ReviewOfTheResearchOxley.pdf

U.S. Department of Education and the National Center for Research in Vocational Education. (1996). *The new American high school project*. Retrieved from http://vocserve.berkeley.edu/NAHS

USDOL [U.S. Department of Labor], Bureau of Labor Statistics. (2010). Secretaries and administrative assistants. *Occupational outlook handbook, 2010–11*. Retrieved from http://www.bls.gov/oco/ocos151.htm#outlook

Professional Association Membership: Extending the Community of Practice

Kellie Shumack
Auburn University–Montgomery
Montgomery, AL

Connie Forde
Mississippi State University
Mississippi State, MS

Professional association membership literally brings continuing professional development to one's doorstep. Professional development provides teachers with new insights into the ways their students learn and teaching methods and strategies that ultimately make teaching more effective. Teachers need professional renewal, opportunities to learn from others' experiences, and venues to share their own experiences. This chapter explains the continuing benefits of professional association membership and provides examples of how the resources that these associations provide members may be incorporated into one's professional development practices as a business education professional.

PURPOSE OF PROFESSIONAL DEVELOPMENT

Professional associations within the field of business education serve a fundamental purpose of providing continual professional development of their members. High-quality professional development is considered one of the factors in improving student learning and teaching that takes place in a constantly changing society (Policies Commission for Business and Economics Education [PCBEE], 2006). Professional development has several objectives: "to make a difference in teaching, to help educators reach high standards, and ultimately to have a positive impact on students" (Guskey, 2005,

p. 12). Teachers participate in professional development knowing that it potentially changes the way they teach and, therefore, improves student learning. This change in teaching may mean learning new technologies, new strategies, and/or new motivational techniques, or simply understanding the content of what is taught better; nevertheless, the ultimate goal is to raise student achievement. The three steps (figure 1) in the process of positively affecting student achievement through professional development are as follows:

- Step 1: Improve the teacher's skills and knowledge

- Step 2: Improve classroom teaching through those improved skills

- Step 3: See a positive impact on student achievement (Yoon, Duncan, Lee, Scarloss, & Shapley, 2007, p. 4).

Figure 1: How Professional Development Affects Student Achievement

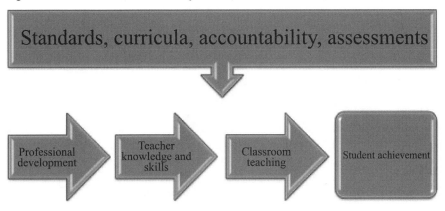

The following discussion expands on how professional development helps educators reach high standards, how teachers make a difference in teaching, and how teachers impact students positively.

Professional Development Helps Educators Reach High Standards

Teachers distinguish themselves as professionals when they participate in professional development because they intentionally take on the matter of lifelong learning, constantly focusing on the need for improving and acquiring knowledge and skills. Business educators have a particular need for ongoing learning due to frequent changes in business and technology. Business education programs must meet multiple standards—that of students, the business world, and the public (Crites, 2006).

Because one of the purposes of professional development is to assist teachers in meeting high standards, it is important for those professional development activities to be high quality. Ostensibly, a professional development activity is considered high quality when there is a positive impact on students, as the students are ultimately the direct or indirect recipients of a teacher's knowledge. Beyond the goal of improving student achievement, quality professional development is referenced in the literature as an activity that "stimulates the mind and leaves much to think about afterward" and one that makes "the learning active" ("Having Your Say," 2002, p. 92) or involves collaborative opportunities with other teachers. The No Child Left Behind Act of 2001 (2002) required quality professional development for teachers setting the following five criteria:

- It is sustained, intensive, and content focused to have a positive and lasting impact on classroom instruction and teacher performance.

- It is aligned with and directly related to state academic content standards, student achievement standards, and assessments.

- It improves and increases teachers' knowledge of the subjects they teach.

- It advances teachers' understanding of effective instructional strategies founded on scientifically based research.

- It is regularly evaluated for effects on teacher effectiveness and student achievement (Yoon et al., 2007, pp. 1–2).

The PCBEE (2010) standards for high-quality virtual professional development include training that is "measureable, collaborative, active and focused on problem solving, and connected directly to local, state, territory, province, and federal education reform initiatives" (p. 2). Professional associations contribute to high-quality professional development by creating opportunities to ensure teachers can provide instruction that makes certain national and professional standards are met.

Professional Development Makes a Difference in Teaching

If teachers participate in professional development activities and what they learn is taken back to the classroom in the form of the application of new ideas or techniques, students will benefit from the time their teachers spent in that professional development (Yoon et al., 2007). In any classroom, real learning is measured by the learner's ability to apply knowledge. Teachers constantly assess students by asking them to apply new concepts through projects, tests, presentations, etc. Professional development for the teacher is the same. To realize the outcome of positive student achievement, teachers must be motivated enough to apply their new skills to classroom teaching. Yoon et al. (2007) wrote that this motivation should be "supported by on-going school collaboration and follow-up consultation with experts," (p. 4) so typical implementation barriers of limited time, materials, and other resources can be overcome.

Professional Development Impacts Students Positively

Research shows a link between teacher skill and student achievement (Holloway, 2003; Mizell, 2003; Sanborn, 2002) and infers an increased difficulty in helping students meet high standards without an improvement in a teacher's own professional development. Professional development is the educator's connection to discovering and improving teaching strategies linked with student achievement. One notable study analyzed the results of nine studies and found that teachers who participated in substantial (more than 49 hours) professional development increased student achievement by 21 percentile points (Yoon et al., 2007).

Schmoker (2002) asserted that students who do poorly on specific standards will improve if teachers work as a team to create strategies to teach those specific standards. He suggested that staff development should be a team effort, and the effort of improving instruction should be focused on linking specific lessons to assessed standards. Holloway (2003) also advocated a professional development model that trains teachers to use state assessment tools that target the specific needs of students.

BENEFITS OF PROFESSIONAL ASSOCIATIONS
"What's in it for me?" That seems to be the general reply when educators are asked to join their professional associations. History shows a movement from a time in the 1970s and 1980s when teachers joined their professional associations because that was the standard for educators and was expected (O'Neil & Willis, 2005). Today educators weigh carefully membership costs vs. benefits while professional associations are challenged to (a) provide abundant membership services that cost more and more to provide, (b) understand how best to use technology in providing membership services, and (c) fulfill the needs of the profession.

What are the benefits of business educators' joining their business education professional associations and becoming actively involved? In a 2006 policy statement, the PCBEE identified several groups benefiting from business educators' active involvement in professional associations. Detailed benefits are explained below, which impact (a) individual members, (b) the business education discipline, (c) students, and (d) employers of educators, business and community partners.

Value to Individual Members
Educators who are members of business education professional associations set themselves apart from business educators who are not professional association members. They not only listen to experts who recommend broadening their horizon when selecting organizations and select industry-specific, interest-specific, and local business groups (Messmer, 2005), but also share what they learn with each other. Business educators who join and become actively involved in professional associations reap the following benefits.

Stay up to date in the field. Membership in a professional association provides access to the most up-to-date publications written by recognized leaders in the field and by educators who wish to share their best practices. Others are written by researchers who are asking important questions of practice and develop or test theoretical perspectives. These publications (journals, magazines, newsletters, white papers, and electronic publications) include valuable information on the trends and issues in the field, curriculum development, and the best practices being advocated at the current time. Annual conferences offer keynote addresses by motivational speakers and a diverse selection of presentations carefully selected to provide the most relevant information to today's business educator. Conference time is also provided for teachers to network and share ideas in small, specialized groups.

Form strong networks. Professional associations are the facilitators of opportunities for building a strong network in the broad context of the profession as well as subgroups for specialized areas of interest. Collaboration with other teachers adds depth to learning experiences. Additionally, these peer relationships strengthen morale, encourage the novice teacher, and play a part in success when ideas are brought back to the classroom.

Opportunities include meeting people at conferences during large sessions, breakout sessions, and social events. Business educators develop lifelong alliances who become a professional family. Often these strong alliances are built over time as members contribute to their profession by working on executive boards as officers and members, committees, and projects.

NBEAConnect is a social network whose goal is to connect business educators across the globe. Subgroups are included for secondary/middle school, secondary, higher education, technical and vocational school, teacher educators, regional association members, and Delta Pi Epsilon (DPE). Groups are added as new groups are identified. Other examples of personal learning networks are discussed in a later section.

Business educators learn from both face-to-face meetings and virtual networks and give of their time and expertise as they serve in leadership roles, participate in social networking discussions, provide advice when members of the network call or e-mail with a need, or stop to chat with the professional in the exhibit hall at a conference. Successful professionals realize that positive reputations are built over time by forming and maintaining a strong professional network.

Develop strong leadership and professional skills. Professional associations are the facilitators of opportunities that can involve members in activities that will build self-confidence and hone essential professional skills, such as communication (both oral and written), human and public relations, marketing, and negotiation and persuasion; the list is infinite. A member must be open and willing to contribute when invited, and professional associations must always be aware of immediately providing opportunities for new members to grow and to be involved. Serving on a state association committee may be the first growth opportunity. With this confidence, the member may be elected an officer of the state association and then encouraged to contribute at regional and later national levels. Through this process, more skills are required to fulfill the job requirements, and the professional accepts these responsibilities and gains the skills necessary to be successful.

Save money. Often professional associations provide free products simply by joining the professional association. For example, by joining the National Business Education Association (NBEA), members receive $250,000 professional liability insurance (U.S. residents only) free of charge that can be upgraded to $1,000,000 and $2,000,000 for a small annual fee. Membership discounts are offered on convention registration fees and publications offered by NBEA.

Value to the Business Education Discipline

Fabian (2008) writes that "associations are much more than just information. Virtually by definition, associations are communities" (p. 78). He further explains that professional associations "help a community of professionals define excellence, the body of knowledge that it practices, and its position on issues" (p. 78). These communities of professionals work relentlessly for business education to define excellence, the knowledge it practices, and its positions on issues. Examples of the contributions of selected business education professional associations are discussed below as examples of the value that active involvement has on the business education discipline.

National Business Education Association. The *National Standards for Business Education* (NBEA, 2007), first released in 1995 and now in its third edition, define the business education profession and establish 11 standard areas. Each area includes standards for the elementary, secondary, and postsecondary levels, and all standard areas are reviewed on a five-year cycle by experts in each specific area.

The *Business Education Forum*, *Keying In*, and *NBEA Yearbook* provide up-to-date literature designed specifically for members of the community. Legislative committees at the state and national levels work together to represent business education throughout the country. Pertinent publications are compiled, and marketing materials are designed and made available to members at http://www.nbea.org/newsite/publications/index.html. Designed by a team of leaders from the various communities, national conferences provide valuable professional development and insight into the profession.

Policies Commission for Business and Economic Education. Comprising leaders from NBEA, the Association for Career and Technical Education (ACTE), and DPE, members of the PCBEE annually collaborate and publish "This We Believe" policy statements to define excellence and position in the profession. Recent statements include "This We Believe about Virtual Professional Development" (PCBEE, 2010) and "This We Believe about the Transformation and Future of Business Education" (PCBEE, 2008). All PCBEE policy statements are available at http://nbea.org/newsite/curriculum/policy.html.

National Association for Business Teacher Education (NABTE). The *Business Teacher Education Curriculum Guide and Program Standards* (NABTE, 2010) guide business teacher education program leaders across the country in the preparation of pre-service business education teachers. This community of business educators revise these standards on a five-year cycle and meet annually with teacher educators to discuss business teacher education issues and plan strategies. In addition, *The Business Teacher Educator* (formerly *NABTE Review*) is the official refereed publication published by NABTE twice annually.

Delta Pi Epsilon. Two publications contributed by this national graduate honorary society for business education professionals are the *Delta Pi Epsilon Journal* and the *Journal of Applied Research for Business Instruction*. Delta Pi Epsilon annually sponsors a national research conference, which provides an avenue for sharing current research in business education.

Value to Students

Not only do the teacher and the professional benefit from teachers joining and becoming actively involved in professional associations, but students are the big winners when they see their teachers involved and when their teachers involve them in the activities of the association. By their membership, teachers model workplace preparation, lifelong learning, volunteerism and contribution to the profession, and the techniques used to balance school, professional, and home duties and responsibilities. Students also benefit from the improved teaching strategies applied in the classroom to impact student achievement. Specific examples of how students benefit are explained below.

Modeled behavior in joining professional associations. Just by joining and participating in professional associations, teachers are sending a message to their students that contributing beyond the classroom walls is important. Students are motivated by the actions of their teachers and are eager to model those behaviors as well.

Engaged students in student organizations. Often teachers who are actively involved in their professional associations will model the importance of professional involvement by sponsoring a student organization and working with students to gain important workplace skills while in school. For students to gain the most from this experience, the teacher must become actively involved and set high expectations for the chapter and its members. Providing opportunities for students to achieve and be recognized will reap great benefits for the students, the teachers, the school, and the community.

Improved student achievement. Teachers gain valuable information and best practices while participating in professional associations and the related professional development opportunities the teacher avails himself/herself. The teacher will choose opportunities wisely that will impact students' achievement. Student achievement can be a natural by-product of teacher professional development.

Enhanced reputation. As the educator grows professionally and becomes an expert in the discipline and the profession, others take notice. Students benefit from the most up-to-date and relevant curricula and instructional strategies. Other teachers in the building seek advice and direction. In higher education, students search for programs with faculty who have national reputations and benefit from their expertise and professional network.

Value to Employers of Educators, Businesses, and Community Partners

School districts, colleges, universities, and other employers of business educators who are actively involved in their professions are benefitting in many areas. These professionals possess the most up-to-date knowledge, skills, and expertise to complete their responsibilities. They bring a well-known and respected reputation beyond the classroom and model professional attitudes that benefit the students and other human resources. The business and community partners also have the opportunity to employ students who have been taught and influenced by this professional.

Benefits to the individual members, the business education discipline, the student, and employers and the business and community partners are many and varied. For many business educators, active involvement has always been considered a standard, and these educators have reaped the many benefits of membership and are respected among their profession as valuable contributors to the business education profession—today and in the future.

PERSONAL LEARNING NETWORKS FOR THE 21ST CENTURY

The business educator as a 21st century learner requires professional development that is accessible virtually. The PCBEE (2010) holds virtual professional development a "must" as a "component of ongoing, sustainable professional development" (p. 1). Personal Learning Networks (PLNs) are a way of individualizing learning to meet individual needs, most often using virtual means. Many educators develop their own PLN via Facebook, Ning, Twitter, LinkedIn, blogs, podcasts, webinars, Second Life, social bookmarking, wikis, and RSS feeds, and professional associations are the stability for these networks that individuals create. Professional associations provide many of the initial contacts for PLNs and provide the resources and networking opportunities for PLNs to expand and thrive. Professional associations are a vital part of harnessing opportunities for the professional development PLN that can be made to fit individual lifestyles, skill levels, and schedules.

Professional associations in general have a valuable Web presence as they provide a variety of opportunities for networking, information gathering, and "just-in-time" training. Just-in-time training is the professional development version of the just-in-time inventory strategy businesses use to reduce costs in inventory storage. Just-in-time training is the training teachers want at the time they choose to get it. Webinars, blogs, and podcasts are examples of how business educators might obtain training digitally and at a time that fits their individual schedules and locations. This section will point out the different professional development opportunities that professional associations offer digitally in the field of business education and offer additional options for business educators who seek virtual professional development. Topics include (a) Web sites, (b) webinars, (c) professional and social networks, (d) blogs, wikis, and social bookmarking, (e) podcasts, and (f) virtual worlds.

Web Sites

Professional association Web sites offer opportunities for professional development by various means and methods. The primary professional association Web sites are explained below:

National Business Education Association. The official Web site of NBEA (http://www.NBEA.org) has links with conference information, publications and other resources, membership, curriculum standards, policy standards, and professional awards. NBEA is represented in different regions and states as well as nationally and internationally.

Delta Pi Epsilon. The national graduate honorary society for professionals in business and business education hosts a Web site (http://www.DPE.org) with information on topics such as membership, research opportunities and awards, publications, and conferences. A listserv helps members stay informed and connected.

The International Society for Business Education (ISBE). ISBE, internationally known as la Société Internationale pour l'Enseignement Commercial or SIEC (http://www.siecisbe.org) offers opportunities for members to network and partner with business educators in other cultures and countries. Each year ISBE holds an international conference to provide attendees the opportunity to learn about the business and education systems of other countries as well as meet business educators from different cultures.

Association for Career and Technical Education. ACTE's core purpose is to "provide leadership in developing an educated, prepared, adaptable, and competitive workforce" (Association for Career and Technical Education, 2011). ACTE promotes the advancement of education that prepares students for careers and encompasses a variety of career technical fields, including agriculture, business, engineering, family and consumer sciences, health, and marketing. ACTE has a resource center for educators and hosts webinars regularly on topics related to public policy, school improvement, and best practices.

The International Society for Technology in Education (ISTE). ISTE has a Web site (http://www.iste.org) bursting with professional development opportunities for educators who wish to support and assess students using technology. Teacher development at this site includes pedagogy as well as skill development in multiple areas.

National Association for Business Teacher Education. The institutional division of NBEA has a Web presence at http://www.nabte.org with links to membership, publications, and the organization's vision.

A list of other associations related to business education can be found at http://www.nbea.org/newsite/about/related_orgs.html.

Webinars

Webinars are synchronous seminars delivered via the Web. Here are some examples of Web sites with available webinars that can help teachers professionally as they try to remain current or learn new skills for the business classroom:

- Business Expert Webinars (http://www.businessexpertwebinars.com)

- Career Builder for Employees (http://www.careerbuilder.com/jobposter/events/webinar)

ACTE, as mentioned previously, provides webinars on various topics related to educational policy and practices related to career and technical education.

Professional and Social Networks

Although this section focuses on professional and social networks that are digital or Web based, it begins with the concept of collaboration in general. This is an important concept when studying professional development and professional associations because it has implications for more than the individual teacher and one classroom; the whole organization or collaborative group has the potential to impact and be positively impacted. Professional associations provide a way for business educators to gain professional development through collaboration. This collaboration taps into the knowledge gained from classroom experience and can transform teachers and schools as people work together to solve problems. Lieberman (1995) wrote that collaboration "involves thinking through how the content and processes of learning can be redefined in ways that engage students and teachers in the active pursuit of learning goals; it involves a joining of experiential learning and content knowledge" (para. 8). The idea of a "culture of support" (Lieberman & Miller, 1999, p. 64) helps educators reach high standards because without it, teachers find it hard to try new ideas, receive comments from peers, and make changes that improve teaching.

Networking in the digital world is a way to "maximize" the return on investment for a professional association membership, as noted by Glenn (2010, p.1). The opportunity is available for intentional networking and those memberships can pay off. Glenn also provided tips for maximizing that return on investment, such as having a goal in mind, joining strategic groups, being active, using technology to help manage information, and being prepared to learn.

NBEAConnect. NBEA has a professional learning network at http://nbeaconnect. ning.com. Currently, this PLN has more than 700 members with 17 groups that represent a variety of interests: Southern Business Education Association, Mountain-Plains Business Education Association, California Business Education Association, business education in Canada, investing, online teaching, DPE, technical/vocational educators, higher education, secondary business education, elementary/middle business education, teacher education, information technology, and administrators of business education programs. Members can add groups, and ongoing discussions relate to the topics in each group. Members can edit personal pages and make "friends" with others. NBEAConnect also has photos, upcoming conference information, educational videos, an events calendar, and a chat feature along with the multiple discussion forums mentioned already.

Facebook. Business educators use this popular social network both professionally and personally. Although the line between personal and professional is more easily blurred with this site's historical use, it does have relevance for professional development. Not only can teachers demonstrate professionalism in yet another venue, they can also remain in contact with fellow educators from across the globe.

A discussion of social and professional networking would be remiss if issues of professionalism were not mentioned. There are effective arguments for and against the use of social networking in professional and academic settings. In business education, there is the added responsibility of training a future workforce, one that does and will continue to face issues related to social networking in the office. Social networks are powerful in their ability to distort the lines between work and play. Lives that were once compartmentalized and segregated are now melded into one for any number of "friends" to witness (more or less depending on privacy settings). Students lose scholarships, employees lose jobs, and candidates lose job opportunities repeatedly as individuals broadcast negative, inappropriate, derogatory, improper, or revealing text, images, etc., on the Internet via social networks, without instituting appropriate privacy settings. As business educators experience the effects of social networking, they have the opportunity to help students navigate this part of the 21st century. Using networks appropriately through professional organizations is an effective way for teachers to bring their professional development learning experiences back to the classroom as well as learn the technology of professional and social networking in order to challenge students to make wise decisions regarding words, attitudes, "friends," and privacy settings.

Twitter. NBEA also has a presence on Twitter at http://twitter.com/NBEA. This site offers the opportunity for brief real-time instant messaging.

Blogs, Wikis, and Social Bookmarking
Blogs, wikis, and social bookmarking are ways to network and collaborate with other educators. This section will briefly describe these tools and provide examples of how they are used as part of an educator's PLN.

Blogs. The term blog is short for weblog and began as a way to journal online. Now it is used as a method for almost anyone to have a voice on the Internet. RSS (rich site summary; also known as really simple syndication) contributes to information-gathering possibilities by allowing someone to monitor the content of various sites without going to each site individually. An RSS reader is employed to gather multiple RSS feeds into one location. For example, Google Reader (http://www.reader.google.com) aggregates blogs so users do not spend time visiting multiple sites, sifting through new posts.

Blogs—such as http://www.mikeroeconomics.blogspot.com—provide opportunities to get new, fresh ideas for teaching. For example, this blog creator records a "pencast" (a podcast using a smartpen) using a LiveScribe pen to provide economics lectures through his blog. Teachers need ideas and resources, and following other teacher blogs is one way to use a PLN to develop new skills and see ideas in action.

Wikis. The term wiki is the Hawaiian word for quick, and in the world of technology it basically means a quick Web site that can be collaborative. Anyone can build a Web site in seconds and start gathering, disseminating, and sharing information using a wiki. An example of a wiki in business education is http://businesseducationtoolbox.wikispaces.com. This wiki contains links to multiple resources, including blogs, lesson plans, and unit plans, and is a great example of teachers collaborating with other teachers to share experiences and information.

Social bookmarking. Business educators may also share their bookmarks by using social bookmarking sites such as http://www.delicious.com and http://www.diigo.com. These tools let users "tag" and categorize sites so that bookmarks follow the user and can be shared with others. Aside from being an effective teaching tool and organizational sensation for the multicomputer user, social bookmarking provides another way for educators to collaborate and share useful information.

Podcasts

Podcasts, including video podcasts, are portable files that can be syndicated. They do not require viewing or listening to an iPod, but the format of a podcast (usually an mp3 or mp4 file) does allow that option. Podcasts represent an excellent mode of acquiring virtual professional development for the business educator: iTunes provides a variety of educational podcasts at no cost, and the iTunesU option has podcasts for students and teachers of all ages who wish to enhance their skills and knowledge on a variety of subjects. Subscribing to a series of podcasts coordinates the automatic delivery of new podcasts to a user's library when iTunes is opened.

ACTE provides podcasts (http://www.acteonline.org/podcasts.aspx?terms=podcasts) of interviews with government policymakers and interesting celebrities.

Virtual Worlds

The 3D virtual world known as Second Life, created by Linden Labs, is a virtual world in which users create an avatar and then navigate by exploring islands, flying, having conversations with other avatars, viewing presentations, playing games, attending workshops, and touring virtual locations within the world—such as museums, factories, zoos, universities, and countries, to name a few. Within Second Life, communities and locations exist that fit particular needs—education, animals, zombies, etc. Professional organizations such as ISTE purchase land and have designers build virtual facilities with meeting rooms, offices, theatres, and more. Virtual worlds can serve as a method of professional development because people meet synchronously at a common virtual location and have conversations, attend classes, teach, and practice skills and have other collaborative opportunities similar to those in real life.

SUMMARY

Professional associations in business education will hopefully continue to embrace the emerging technologies of the era and offer more opportunities such as webinars, blogs, podcasts, a presence in Second Life, and mobile applications specific to associations and members on the go. The underlying purpose of professional associations— that of helping members develop professionally—remains the same regardless of the century and the technology available. The benefits of forming collaborative networks, staying current in the field, promoting national standards and scholarly literature, modeling behaviors, and ultimately improving student achievement will provide members with the tools necessary to succeed in business, education, and the community.

REFERENCES

ACTE [Association for Career and Technical Education]. (2011). *About ACTE.* Retrieved from http://www.acteonline.org/about.aspx

Crites, D. K. (2006). Implementing strategies to journey from good to great. In S. D. Lewis, M. Balachandran, & R. B. Blair (Eds.), *Meeting the challenges of business education through innovative programs, NBEA yearbook* (Vol. 44, pp. 29–41). Reston, VA: NBEA.

Fabian, N. (2008). On the demise of associations… *Journal of Environmental Health, 70*(6), 78, 70–71.

Glenn, J. (2010). Network without leaving your desk. *Keying In, 21*(2), 1–8.

Guskey, T. R. (2005). Taking a second look. *Journal of Staff Development, 26*(1), 10–18. Retrieved from http://www.learningforward.org/news/articleDetails.cfm?article ID=121

Having your say…On professional development, (2002). *Educational leadership 59*(6), 91–92.

Holloway, J. H. (2003). Linking professional development to student learning. *Educational Leadership, 61*(3), 85–87. Retrieved from http://www.ascd.org/publications/ educational-leadership/nov03/vol61/num03/Linking-Professional-Development-to-Student-Learning.aspx

Lieberman, A. (1995). Practices that support teacher development. *Phi Delta Kappan, 76*(8), 591–596.

Lieberman, A., & Miller, L. (1999). *Teachers—Transforming their world and their work.* New York: Teachers College Press.

Messmer, M. (2005, July). Counting the benefits of association involvement. *Strategic Finance, 12,* 14.

Mizell, H. (2003). Facilitator: 10 refreshments: 8 evaluation: 0. *Journal of Staff Development, 24*(4), 10–13. Retrieved from http://www.learningforward.org/news/article Details.cfm?articleID=405

NABTE [National Association for Business Teacher Education]. (2010). *Business teacher education curriculum guide and program standards* (3rd ed.). Reston, VA: National Business Education Association.

NBEA [National Business Education Association]. (2007). *National standards for business education* (3rd ed.). Reston, VA: Author.

No Child Left Behind Act of 2001. H.R. 1, 107th Cong. Pub. L. No. 107-110, 115 Stat. 1426 (2002) (enacted).

O'Neil, S. L., & Willis, C. L. (2005). Challenges for professional organizations: Lessons from the past. *Delta Pi Epsilon Journal, 47*(3), 143–153.

PCBEE [Policies Commission for Business and Economic Education]. (2006). *Policy statement 79: This we believe about the value of professional associations.* Retrieved from http://www.nbea.org/newsite/curriculum/policy/no_79.pdf

PCBEE. (2008). *Policy statement 83: This we believe about the transformation and future of business education.* Retrieved from http://www.nbea.org/newsite/curriculum/ policy/no_83.pdf

PCBEE. (2010). *Policy Statement 87: This we believe about virtual professional development.* Retrieved from http://www.nbea.org/newsite/curriculum/documents/ PCBEEStatement87_000.pdf

Sanborn, J. (2002). Targeted training. *The School Administrator, 59*(11), 16–19. Retrieved from http://www.aasa.org/SchoolAdministratorArticle.aspx?id=9536

Schmoker, M. (2002). Up and away. *Journal of Staff Development, 23*(2), 10–13. Retrieved from http://www.learningforward.org/news/articleDetails.cfm?article ID=443

Yoon, K. S., Duncan, T., Lee, S. W.-Y., Scarloss, B., & Shapley, K. (2007). *Reviewing the evidence on how teacher professional development affects student achievement* (Issues & Answers Report, REL 2007–No.033). Washington, DC: U.S. Department of Education, Institute of Education Sciences, National Center for Education Evaluation and Regional Assistance, Regional Educational Laboratory Southwest.

Research in Business Education: Increasing Capacity and Application in Practice

Marcia Anderson
Southern Illinois University
Carbondale, IL

Business education as a segment of the U.S. education system faces extreme challenges. The movement to a global economy requires an educated workforce possessing skills far beyond those addressed even 30 years ago. Ambitious academic learning for all—what historically was only asked of a few students—has become a unanimous goal. Meanwhile, the changing demography and increased cultural and language diversity of many school systems poses new challenges. Because of these demands and challenges, political and educational leaders and the public are calling for extraordinary efforts to improve the performance of schools.

In other sectors of society, efforts to deal with such situations rely on substantial leadership from their research-and-development communities. Consider the medical profession, for example. Improving patient outcomes in the field of medicine based predominantly on trial and error at the local level or the dictates of fads is unimaginable. Yet, this is a fair description of education reform. Despite calls for "evidence-based practice" and "data-driven decisionmaking" in education, research and development play an inconsiderable role in recent educational improvement efforts (Stipek, 2010).

This chapter presents an overview of research strategies particularly useful in business education. The information is important to both researchers and practitioners in increasing their research capacity and their application of research to practice. In business education, those groups encompass university faculty, business teacher educators, and K–12 teachers.

THE RESEARCH TO PRACTICE IN EDUCATION CONUNDRUM

What is research? McMillan and Schumacher (2010) defined research as "a systematic process of collecting and logically analyzing data for a specific purpose" (p. 490). More than ever before in the history of education, discussions abound and expectations are high about the role of research in improving educational practice. Just as research and development play key roles in medical advances and technological improvement, educational research must enlighten instructional events, how teachers are prepared, and how the role of fields such as business education complement the entire educational system. It is, first, important to understand that discussion about the relationship between research and practice in education has a lengthy history.

Historical Context

The research to practice in education issue has been a central topic of debate almost since the emergence of recognized approaches to educational research in the early 20th century (Coburn & Stein, 2010). But it became a central concern for researchers, practitioners, and policymakers during the 1960s and 1970s in the wake of new federal funding for educational research. For example, concern about the research-practice gap in the 1970s led to the establishment of groups who interpret research findings for people in public schools, and federal funding of a series of regional education laboratories to fulfill the translational role (Clifford, 1973, as cited by Coburn & Stein, 2010).

Continued concern about diffusion of research findings led to the development of the National Diffusion Network, which used up-to-date technology to gather, store, and distribute educational research findings (Hood, 1982). And, more current debate on how to improve the quality of basic and applied research in education as a way to improve schools resulted in the development of the What Works Clearinghouse, a central and trusted source of scientific evidence for what works in education. Established in 2002, as part of the landmark No Child Left Behind Act (2002), the clearinghouse is an initiative of the U.S. Department of Education's Institute of Education Sciences, which does the following:

- Produces user-friendly practice guides for educators that address instructional challenges with research-based recommendations for schools and classrooms

- Assesses the rigor of research evidence on the effectiveness of interventions (programs, products, practices, and policies), giving educators the tools to make informed decisions

- Develops and implements standards for reviewing and synthesizing education research

(U.S. Department of Education, Institute of Education Sciences, What Works Clearinghouse, 2011).

Research does contribute to fundamental changes in educational practice (Mertens & McLaughlin, 1995). However, such changes will not happen unless the research community integrates itself into the groups for which its information has meaning. Through such association, researchers can identify problems and communicate information that can be used to clarify people's understanding of the problems and ultimately help create solutions.

Evolving Frameworks and Themes

Research is often viewed as an obscure process to be left to the work of intellectuals (Takona, 2002). This characterization is far from the truth as educational researchers work to learn about human behavior and to acquire a fuller understanding of the learning/teaching environment (Takona, 2002). Coburn and Stein (2010) focused on the reality and intricacy of how research and practice actually interact with one another through the roles played by a variety of educational researchers. By understanding the potential and the possibility of how things work, new systems, structures, and policies can be identified to help make "what works" the norm rather than the exception. The authors suggested actions that can be taken by key participants to enable "what works" projects to be more widespread and more sustained and thus to touch more teachers, schools, and students.

Those who design curricula, frameworks, and processes should place renewed attention on teacher learning and organizational change. School and district leaders must create opportunities to dialog directly with researchers so they can work together to interpret research findings and engage in more in-depth discussions on implications for district work.

Educational foundations typically have funded the development of a specific project or tool, and when the resources ceased, research partners have gone their separate ways with little integration into the educational mainstream, resulting in a fragmented approach to educational improvement (Coburn & Stein, 2010). Structure of funding for education should acknowledge and encourage a two-way flow of activity: applicants should be able to propose work that is inspired by practice-based observation as well as work that builds on fundamental research. Support must be given to practitioners who can and do conduct research into meaningful educational topics whose findings are often of great value both to themselves and to fellow educators (Mertler & Charles, 2005).

Implications for colleges of education and other institutions training researchers and designers involve new roles for researchers. A primary new role relates to developing trust and shared insights to guide the research. Typically, researchers are trained as if their work is only individual; graduate students in many higher education institutions lack sufficient opportunities to learn how to partner, build trust, and work with people with diverse expertise and status. However, it is exactly these skills that may make the difference between successful research partnerships and unsuccessful ones (Coburn & Stein, 2010).

How might these frameworks come into existence in the education system? Because of its ability to generate information that destroys myths, research can function as a tool for support. For example, before the mid-1900s, a prevailing belief held that persons with mental retardation had conditions that were hereditary and lasting and, therefore, were hostile and dangerous. As such, they should be separated from the rest of society. Research on the condition provided an information base demonstrating that this idea of mental retardation was a myth and essentially unsupported by empirical evidence (Takona, 2002). Educational researchers must also avoid the same trap of faulty observation. To do so, they must use the scientific method, which is based on the collection of solid and observable evidence, accurate description and measurement, precise definitions, controlled observation, and consistent results. Researchers have the responsibility of providing evidence that is defensible (Takona, 2002).

The next sections focus on specific aspects of scientific, evidence-based research and the basics of conducting and evaluating such scientifically based research. To increase their research capacity and application in practice, both researchers and practitioners must understand the process of acquiring and perfecting knowledge in such a way as to minimize the pitfalls of observation and reasoning and produce action toward truth.

RESEARCH DESIGNS

Although too simply stated, according to Takona (2002), research is often categorized as being *quantitative*, that is, using numbers as data to describe events or establish relationships between events, or *qualitative*, that is, using words as data to describe human experience or behavior (phenomenological). Further differences among research designs are discussed below.

Quantitative

Quantitative research involves numbers and statistical manipulation and analysis. It tends to be more scientifically oriented as it involves the systematic and methodical collection and analysis of hard data. Quantitative research tells how many, how much, how often, when, and where, whereas qualitative research seeks to find out why (Takona, 2002; McMillan & Schumacher, 2010). Quantitative analysis often involves computation of statistical measures and tests of significance. This analysis employs deductive logic, moving from the general to the specific, that is, from theory to experience.

Qualitative

Researchers using the qualitative approach seek understanding through inductive analysis, moving from specific observation to the general. The term "qualitative research" implies a process through which rich, thick descriptions of the phenomenon under study are derived, answering the "why" type of questions. In education, the need for answers to the "why" questions has increased for several reasons, including intricate economic, social, and political conditions. The complexity of these conditions has increased the need for greater amounts of qualitative information. Qualitative research is a field of inquiry that cuts across disciplines, fields, and subject content (Takona, 2002; Denzin & Lincoln, 2005).

Data sources for qualitative inquiry include observation and participant observation (fieldwork), interviews and questionnaires, documents and texts, case study, visual methods, and interpretive analysis. These categories of qualitative research have separate and detailed literature as fields of study of their own (Takona, 2002; Denzin & Lincoln, 2005).

Takona (2002) stated that educational research in the past several decades has undergone tremendous change as qualitative studies have come into their own. Previously deemed as unscientific, biased, or just "soft," such research is now established in books and periodicals and is receiving significant interest, respect, and funding.

Mixed Method
A study that combines qualitative and quantitative techniques and/or data analysis within different phases of the research process is referred to as the mixed method approach. A research study using both qualitative and quantitative research approaches in the same study can greatly expand the breadth and depth of understanding of a variety of educational phenomena (McMillan & Schumacher, 2010). Whether research data are quantitative or qualitative, they should be valid so research results reflect what was intended to be measured and are generalizable to similar situations.

Research Method to Use
Differences between qualitative and quantitative research result because each defines problems differently and each looks for different solutions or answers. As stated, qualitative methods lend themselves to discovering meanings and patterns whereas quantitative methods seek to demonstrate causes and relationships statistically without addressing the subjective nature of the groups or individuals of interest.

The choice of research design must be appropriate to the subject under investigation (Patton, 1987). Qualitative data are obviously not suitable to quantification and would not satisfy those who want findings based on numerical data and reports of statistical significance. Nor are findings from qualitative research generalizable from one setting to another. Qualitative inquiry is quite a labor-intensive approach for both data collection and data analysis (Takona, 2002). Given an overview of research design options, the next phase is to go through precise steps in planning, conducting, and reporting the research project.

PLANNING, CONDUCTING, AND REPORTING A RESEARCH PROJECT

Defining Research Design, Research Objective, and Research Questions
A clear statement of the purpose of the research is necessary to define the study clearly. Without clear problem and purpose statements, decisions on the type of data to

collect or what to do with it once it is collected cannot be defined. The study should be designed to answer only the stated problem (objective). A problem often implies that a controversy or difference of opinion exists (Best & Kahn, 2006) or that an issue has not been resolved. Problem statements generally are based on a significant content and an insufficient knowledge base on what to do about the concern. Hillestad (1977) cited several authors who indicated that the research problem should (a) ask a definite question, (b) concern the relationship between two or more variables, (c) concern variables for which the researcher is able to collect data, and (d) contain no value statements.

So how are research questions different from the statement of the research problem? Research questions are distinct areas that are investigated to provide information related to the problem—in essence, breaking apart segments of the problem for investigation. To demonstrate what new light the study will shed on a topic, research questions must be placed in the context of what is already known about the topic. Although the researcher should be aware of value bias, his/her focus must be on trying to acquire factual information, whether qualitative or quantitative. Research is all about collecting sound empirical information about the situation under study.

A review of the extant literature organized around the research questions, as explained in the next section, should identify what is known, how answering the questions will add to existing knowledge, and why it is important to answer these particular questions (Takona, 2002).

Reviewing Relevant Literature

Search process. McMillan and Schumacher (2010) stated that "almost every question about doing new research can be answered by knowing what others have done and reported" (p. 73). Thus, the all-important literature review establishes crucial links between existing knowledge and the research problem under study. The literature review also provides useful information about research methods that can be considered appropriate for the new study.

Literature sources. Literature sources are categorized as primary or secondary. Primary sources of literature are those in which original data and firsthand information are retrieved, whereas secondary sources summarize, review, analyze, or discuss primary source information. Primary sources for quantitative research would be studies published in an article, report, or book, with an analysis of the initial data gathered. The term "empirical research" means that the source is primary. In qualitative studies, primary sources are artifacts and individuals with whom the researcher has direct interaction and the researcher reads firsthand documents, such as memos, reports, minutes, photos, and correspondence (McMillan & Schumacher, 2010).

A secondary source is something written about the primary source of information. Examples of secondary sources are (a) quarterly/annual education reviews and yearbooks, (b) professional books, (c) encyclopedias, and (d) handbooks (McMillan & Schumacher, 2010).

Of course, the Internet is a valuable source of relevant literature related to the research problem. Novice researchers tend to confuse literature obtained through library databases (e.g., Academic Search Premier, Ovid, and FirstSearch) and other information available through general Internet sources. Researchers must understand the source of Internet Web sites. When searching the Internet for current topics, one often finds Web sites of individuals and nonprofit organizations that have a clear agenda to promote. Given this possibility, one must be a critical and judicious user of Internet sources to best gain a more balanced, scholarly perspective. Documenting the Internet sources is critical so other researchers can visit the site used.

Evaluating any type of research requires reading and analyzing the content carefully. It is also helpful to locate a variety of sources that the researchers can compare and contrast in order to get a well-versed view of any topic.

Steps in literature review. McMillan and Schumacher (2010) offered useful steps in conducting the literature review. They stated that the goal in reviewing the literature is not simply to find sources, but to find the best sources that can assist the researcher in establishing significance and in designing the study. The authors suggested that researchers follow this procedure: "Step 1—Identify topic and key terms; Step 2—Identify databases and access locations and software; Step 3—Conduct searches; Step 4—Identify sources as primary or secondary; Step 5—Evaluate and analyze" (McMillan & Schumacher, 2010, p. 77).

When writing the literature review, Best and Kahn (2006) suggested beginning with an outline, which helps determine how and where the references will be used. References for a single topic are placed together and cited together in the review. The review should include studies that disagree with other studies or with the research premise, and an explanation for their contradictory research results.

Identifying Research Strategies

Now that the researcher has identified the research purpose, has succinctly defined the research problem, has developed the research questions to provide information for the problem, and has conducted a thorough literature review, the next task is to identify how data will be collected.

Data sources. The data collection process is accomplished by identifying the types of information needed to answer the research questions. "Population" was defined by Best and Kahn (2006), as "a group of individuals with at least one common characteristic which distinguishes that group from other individuals" (p. 13). Often studying the entire population to arrive at generalizations would be impractical, if not impossible.

To solve the problem of size, a sample of the population to be studied is identified. This sample is a small proportion of the population that is selected for observation and analysis. By studying the characteristics of the sample, researchers can identify certain inferences about the characteristics of the population from which it was drawn. As Takona (2002) stated, "the logic behind sampling is the hopes of collecting a segment of the population that has similar features to the underlying population, and thus provides a balanced reflection of it" (p. 35).

Researchers often overlook data sources already available, such as free data sets and tools available through the U.S. Department of Education, Institute of Education Sciences, National Center for Education Statistics (2011). These data sets represent all aspects of education, gathered by the U.S. Department of Education for legislative reporting purposes.

Data gathering schemes. Takona (2002) provided three useful categorizations of research data collection methods:

- **Survey methods** are those techniques for gathering information from a larger number of people who can provide the needed information to answer the research questions. These techniques include questionnaires and interview scales.

- **Observation methods** require the systematic observation of events, behavior, and artifacts within the setting identified for the research in order to provide a description. The observation could be made either by an individual or individual using a recording device, for example.

- **Experimental methods** include those techniques in which one or more variables are either introduced into a controlled environment or altered systematically for the purpose of recording their impact. This process is called manipulation of the variables, which is effective in measuring cause and effect relationships.

- **Action research** has a variety of definitions but generally refers to those studies conducted by practitioners in educational institutions that address an actual issue in the institution or classroom. Action research typically has both action outcomes and research outcomes.

- **Case study method** describes an in-depth investigation of a single entity. Creswell (2008) referred to a case study as "an in-depth exploration of a bounded system (e.g., an activity, event, process, or individuals) based on extensive data collection" (p. 476). Being *bounded* describes uniqueness according to place, time, and participant characteristics. A variety of case study methods are available.

- **Correlational research studies** allow the researcher to investigate associations among naturally occurring variables, whereas in experimental studies the researchers introduce a change and then monitor its impact.

Developing Data Gathering Instruments

Once the researcher has decided what information is needed to answer the research questions, the next step is to decide instruments to use. An instrument should be identified or developed that includes the questions that will elicit the information needed for each research question. Research instruments are essential to measure such variables as opinion, attitude, size, aptitude, and composition. In education, the instrument might be a questionnaire, a rating scale, taxonomy, a paper and pencil test, or interview schedule. If observations are to be made on subjects, an instrument for making such observations must be furnished.

Existing instruments. The researcher should choose a data-gathering instrument that has established reliability and validity. Although reliability and validity are the most important considerations in selecting an instrument, other factors, such as costs to purchase, copyright, availability, simplicity of administration, and scoring must be considered. Although it is often difficult to locate an instrument that meets all criteria needed, thousands of instruments have defined validity and reliability data, and most likely one can be used intact or modified to meet the specific research purpose. To identify and evaluate existing instruments and those used by other researchers, (a) review the literature and (b) use sources summarizing information on possible measures such as the *Mental Measurements Yearbook*.

Questionnaires. If an existing standardized instrument is not available to provide data needed to answer the research questions, the researcher will need to develop an instrument. Hillestad (1977) offered these steps in developing a valid, reliable questionnaire that encourages responses:

1. Visualize the respondents and how they might interpret how questions are written.

2. Group together questions dealing with each aspect of the study.

3. Arrange questions in either a psychological or logical order. First establish rapport by asking easily answered neutral, interesting questions. Questions should be arranged from the general to the specific.

4. Make apparent that the questions are related to the purpose of the study. Do not ask for some information "because it would be good to have it."

5. Use an easy-to-answer format: (a) decide which questions should be open ended and which will allow appropriate check-off responses, (b) use the simplest language possible, (c) use precise wording that asks exactly what information is needed, (d) use no "loaded" or "leading" questions, (e) use unambiguous questions, (f) use questions that are answerable, (g) use check-off items whenever possible; (h) have responses that relate directly to the question, (i) deal with only one topic in one question, (j) remove emotional overtones from the questions, and (k) keep the response choices in mutually exclusive categories.

6. Prepare dummy tables of anticipated responses to check whether questions will provide usable data and to plan exactly how the data will be classified, tallied, and summarized into tables.

7. Design an attractive questionnaire using the design features for print as well as electronic submission.

8. Supply clear, complete directions.

9. Try out the questions. Ask a number of people to answer the questions in the most "far out" way they can, reading into the questions any misinterpretation they can.

10. Write a good cover letter and follow-up reminders. (Hillestad, 1977, pp. 42–60)

In addition to questionnaires as data sources, scales are another form of data gathering method for researchers to consider.

Scales. A number of options are available for types of scales that can be used:

- **Ranking scales.** Respondents are asked to rank a number of alternative items in order of importance or relevance or against a dimension such as "effectiveness" or "ease of use."

- **Nominal or grade scales.** These yield a single score that indicates both the direction and intensity of a person's attitude. For example, a rating scale designed to measure attitude toward a professor's teaching may have a set of items that relate to attitude toward the lecturer's enthusiasm, another set that relates to organization, or another that relates to presentation characteristics. They are marked with words indicating different grades of the subjective area being measured.

- **Discrete numerical rating scales.** Often, researchers will want to ask questions that may have the same set of answer categories. Takona (2002) suggested such a scale, known as the Likert scale, which is probably the most frequently used method in the social sciences. Respondents are asked to indicate their agreement with each statement on a five-point scale of strongly agree, agree, undecided, disagree, or strongly disagree.

- **Statement rating scales.** This scale is a variation on the numeric rating scale described above in which a number of statements referring to the item under investigation are produced, and participants are asked to decide whether or not they agree with them.

- **Continuous rating scale.** Often referred to as the semantic differential approach, as originally developed, the scale consists of two opposing adjectives such as never/always, good/bad, like/dislike, etc. (McMillan & Schumacher, 2010).

Interviews. The structure of an interview may vary from quite rigid and standard-ized to very flexible and unstructured. The goal is to collect the most complete and accurate information using a thoroughly prepared interview schedule or guide. This guide is a written set of questions outlining specific areas to cover in the interview; the questions must be relevant to the study, directed to appropriate persons, and easily answered.

When composing interview questions, the level of language understood by the inter-viewee must be addressed. Speaking over the interviewee's head by using complex, rare, or foreign words and expressions; words of many syllables; abbreviations; acronyms; and jargon must be avoided. Also speaking down to the interviewee should be avoided (Takona, 2002).

Statements of the researcher's purpose and focus are usually made at the beginning of an interview. Demographic questions may be spread throughout the interview. Interview probes elicit elaboration of detail, further explanations, and clarification of responses. The order of questions varies, although most researchers make choices that enable them to obtain adequate information for each question from the interviewee efficiently. Complex or controversial questions are usually reserved for the middle or later periods in an interview (McMillan & Schumacher, 2010).

Conducting the Research and Analyzing Research Results

Before actually proceeding with data collection, making sure the instruments used are valid and reliable so they will provide accurate and consistent data is critical. A number of techniques are available for ensuring validity and reliability of research instruments. Data collection must be methodical using consistent procedures. If more than one researcher is involved, all must be trained in the consistent procedures to be used.

Once the data have been collected, the data must be systematically examined and analyzed. A variety of techniques is available for analyzing research data. The research-er must select those techniques appropriate for the particular data and use them ef-fectively to generate findings. All quantitative information collected should be assigned codes and entered into whatever computer program is being used to store the data. The data are often classified by division into subgroups and then analyzed and synthesized in such a way that answers the research questions.

A variety of sophisticated statistical analysis procedures are available. A number of factors determine which statistical technique should be used, but two of these are especially important: (a) the type of data being measured, and (b) the objective of the research study. At a minimum, basic descriptive statistics are used in virtually all research reports. These are simply a reporting of the number of responses, the percen-tile, and possibly the mean, which is the most widely used measure of central tendency (McMillan & Schumacher, 2010; Sapre, 1990; Takona, 2002).

Reporting Research Results and the Research Report

Research results are generally presented according to each research question. Frequently, information on research participants and resulting demographic data are presented before research question results. Results according to each research question are usually supported with tables and figures. In answering the questions, the researcher should do the following:

- Take each sub-question separately and select data and the subsequent results related to it.

- Examine the data logically (there are no formulas for this process) and arrive at the answer deemed appropriate (Mertler & Charles, 2005, p. 204).

Conclusions, then, give the researcher the opportunity to interpret, speculate on, and otherwise discuss the meaning of the research results. The researcher subsequently has the opportunity to tell what the findings mean, how they have been interpreted, what they imply for education, and how they relate to existing literature previously cited in the work. Recommendations for further research and practice are addressed next; this is when the researcher can speculate a bit, that is, move a little beyond hard evidence and stringent logic by suggesting some possible avenues to investigate next (Mertler & Charles, 2005).

The *Publication Manual of the American Psychological Association* (6th ed.) must be used as the writing guide. This manual is recognized as the standard for presenting research by "scholars in social and behavioral sciences who wish to enhance the dissemination of knowledge in their respective fields" (American Psychological Association, 2010, p. xiii).

Sapre (1990) suggested an outline for a complete and well-organized research report:

I. Introduction
   A. Need for the study or background of the study
   B. Purpose of the study
   C. Statement of the problem
   D. Research questions
   E. Significance of the problem
   F. Definition of terms
   G. Delimitations of the problem
   H. Limitations of the study
II. Review of the literature
III. Research methodology
   A. Description of population and/or samples and their selection
   B. Description of data-gathering instruments, including validity and reliability data
   C. Procedures used for data collection
   D. Procedures used for data analysis

IV. Research findings and discussion
    A. Description of the results
    B. Discussion of any apparent discrepancies of inconsistencies in the results
    C. Comparison of current findings with those in other studies
V. Summary, conclusions, and recommendations (implications)
VI. Supplementary materials
    A. References
    B. Appendices
        1. Instruments used in gathering data
        2. Raw data (possibly)
        3. Correspondence
            a. Letters of permission to conduct the study
            b. Cover letter for instrument
            c. Follow-up letters
            d. Other pertinent correspondence
        4. Abstract (this may be the first page following title page) (Sapre, 1990)

ISSUES IN EDUCATIONAL RESEARCH

During planning, conducting, and reporting from a research project, the researcher must consider ongoing issues with educational research:

Ethical Considerations

All research must strive to protect the people who are being studied by informing them of its risks, shielding their identities, and upholding any agreements about the nature and conduct of the study. This requirement also pertains to qualitative research where the stakes are higher and the process more intensive. In quantitative studies, researchers typically have little contact with their subjects. Most often, the nature of the research might simply call for the administration of a questionnaire or the limited contact needed to direct participation in an experiment. But carrying out qualitative research often means getting to know people and gaining their trust.

No research should be carried out without an indicated consent from the partici-pants. A researcher is responsible to ensure that participants understand the exact nature of the study and their role as participants. Institutional Review Boards and Human Subjects Committees in colleges and universities have the responsibility of assuring participant confidentiality. It remains the researcher's responsibility to ensure that participants continue to understand their right to withdraw from a study or to refuse to answer questions that make them uncomfortable (Takona, 2002).

Data Analysis Misconceptions

A basic misconception that statistical information is mysterious and difficult to un-derstand remains a problem (Holmes, 1990). Many also believe that statistical analysis cannot be trusted and that statistical information is too filled with technical jargon to be of any practical use (Takona, 2002). In many instances, statistics are not only used but also abused, often a result of ignorance. Takona (2002) discussed several areas of statistical pitfalls: (a) conditions that affect the external validity of statistical results, (b) errors in data gathering, leading to inaccurate or invalid results, (c) interpretation of results, or how statistical results are applied to real-world issues. The bottom line for researchers is to assure professional knowledge of statistical techniques and application before rendering any conclusions on the findings.

CONSIDERATIONS FOR RESEARCH IN BUSINESS EDUCATION

Most of the knowledge base for business education as a field of study comes from two main sources: (a) behavioral and social sciences, particularly psychology and sociology and (b) the content areas of business study such as accounting, economics, finance, management information systems, marketing, and computer information systems. Business education research is intended to seek valid answers to questions of content as well as to the process of instruction (Sapre, 1990).

The leading organization supporting research in business education is Delta Pi Epsilon, the honorary graduate society in business education, founded in 1936. Its two refereed journals reflecting research in the knowledge base described by Sapre are *The Delta Pi Epsilon Journal* and *The Journal of Applied Research for Business Instruction*. In January 2012, Delta Pi Epsilon (to be known as Association for Research in Business Education) became an affiliated division of the National Business Education Association representing the research arm of the business education profession. Other refereed journals publishing business education research are *Business Education Digest, Journal of Education for Business*, NABTE's *Business Teacher Education Journal* (formerly *NABTE Review*), and NBEA's *Business Education Forum*.

Delta Pi Epsilon has periodically published a monograph entitled *Needed Research in Business Education*. Topics included in this monograph are derived from a sizeable number of business educators who have participated in a research project using the Delphi technique (Rader & Wilhelm, 2002). Meggison (1999) asserted that business education research meets the challenge of positive change for the profession.

Gaytan (2007) conducted research to determine the type of research methodologies used for business education manuscripts published in two leading business education research journals between 2001 and 2005. He discovered that most manuscripts used quantitative research methodologies and asserted that much was to be gained from also using qualitative research strategies because qualitative research methods allow researchers to answer questions related to issues that cannot be addressed quantitatively.

O'Connor (2007) further stated that "business education may (emphasize *may*) be suffering from not going beyond our own borders to understand how the economy, demographics, technology, and globalization is affecting our relevance" (p. 50). She went on to suggest some methodological inventiveness and the use of qualitative research methods to expand the inner circles to better understand phenomena. She challenged business education researchers to collaborate more with people outside the traditional business education circles and to disseminate their research beyond business education borders.

SUMMARY

The search for common ground in research practice is destined to be an ongoing challenge. With each new generation of scholars and practitioners, professional norms, traditions, and orientations are passed on from their respective institutional origins with powerful influence. There is hardly a chance that practical research will suddenly assume the lofty status historically reserved for basic research. The institutional mechanisms that produce and continue the dueling domains of research and practice in education are deeply embedded within the profession (as they are in most human service areas) and are not going to disappear anytime soon. Research conducted in service of practical problems can be and should be as rigorous in design, implementation, and analysis as research conducted to advance theory. It behooves practitioners to further develop their research capacity; for researchers the issue becomes one of professional relevance in concert with a moral obligation to align more closely with practitioners (Davis, 2008; Jarvis, 1998).

RESEARCH LITERACY RESOURCES

Online Resources for Understanding Research
- A Guide to Reading Research Articles (http://www.usc.edu/hsc/ebnet/res/Guide%20to%20Reading%20Research.pdf)

- A Guide to Reading Research Articles (for nonresearchers) (http://azrapeprevention.org/updates_2007)

- Mental Measurements Yearbook (http://buros.unl.edu/buros/jsp/searchjsp)

- Reading Research: A Quick Guide to Common Article Layout (http://www.umich.edu/~rsa/dsareads/articlelayout.doc)

- Web Center for Social Research Methods (http://www.socialresearchmethods.net)

- Reading Research in Action (http://www.brookespublishing.com/store/books/mccardle-69643/index.htm)

U.S. Government Resources
- What Works Clearinghouse (http://ies.ed.gov/ncee/wwc)

- Identifying and Implementing Educational Practices Supported by Rigorous Evidence: A User-Friendly Guide (http://www.ed.gov/rschstat/research/pubs/rigorousevid/index.html)

- Institute of Education Sciences (http://www2.ed.gov/about/offices/list/ies/index.html)

- The Condition of Education (http://nces.ed.gov/programs/coe)

- Education Resources Information Center (http://www.eric.ed.gov)

- U.S. Department of Education Publications (free) (http://edpubs.ed.gov)

- Regional Educational Laboratories (http://ies.ed.gov/ncee/edlabs/regions)

REFERENCES

American Psychological Association. (2010). Foreword. *Publication manual of the American Psychological Association* (6th ed.). Washington, DC: Author.

Best J. W., & Kahn, J. V. (2006). *Research in education* (10th ed.). Boston, MA: Pearson.

Coburn, C. E., & Stein, M. K. (Eds.). (2010). *Research and practice in education: Building alliances, bridging the divide.* Lanham, MD: Rowman & Littlefield.

Creswell, J. W. (2008). *Educational research: Planning, conducting, and evaluating quantitative and qualitative research* (2nd ed.). Upper Saddle River, NJ: Merrill/ Prentice Hall.

Davis, S. H. (2008). *Research and practice in education: The search for common ground.* Lanham, MD: Rowman & Littlefield.

Denzin, N. K., & Lincoln, Y. S. (Eds.). (2005). *Handbook of qualitative research* (3rd ed.). Thousand Oaks, CA: Sage.

Gaytan, J. (2007). Qualitative research: Emerging opportunity in business education. *The Delta Pi Epsilon Journal, XLIX*(2) 109–127.

Hillestad, M. (1977). *Research: Process and product.* Little Rock, AR: Delta Pi Epsilon.

Holmes, C. B. (1990). *The honest truth about lying with* statistics. Springfield, MA: Charles C. Thomas.

Hood, P. (1982). *The role of linking agents in education: A review, analysis, and synthesis of recent major studies.* San Francisco, CA: Far West Laboratory.

Jarvis, P. (1998). *The practitioner-researcher: Developing theory from practice.* San Francisco, CA: Jossey-Bass.

McMillan, J., & Schumacher, S. (2010). *Research in education: Evidence-based inquiry* (7th ed.). Boston: Allyn and Bacon.

Mertens, D. M., & McLaughlin, J. A. (1995). *Research methods in special education.* Thousand Oaks, CA: Sage.

Mertler, C. A., & Charles, C. M. (2005). *Introduction to educational research* (5th ed.). Boston, MA: Pearson.

Meggison, P. F. (1999). Research meets the challenge of positive change. *The Delta Pi Epsilon Journal, 40*(1), 1–2.

No Child Left Behind Act of 2001. H.R. 1, 107th Cong. Pub. L. No. 107-110, 115 Stat. 1426 (2002) (enacted).

O'Connor, B. N. (2007). Innovative research strategies for business education. *The Delta Pi Epsilon Journal, XLIX*(1), 50–55.

Patton, M. (1987). *How to use qualitative methods in evaluation.* London: Sage.

Rader, M. H., & Wilhelm, W. J. (2002). Business education research: Identification and prioritization of topics. *The Delta Pi Epsilon Journal, 44*(3), 157–174.

Sapre, P. M. (1990). *Research methods in business education.* Little Rock, AR: Delta Pi Epsilon.

Stipek, D. (2010). Foreword. In C. E. Coburn, & M. K. Stein (Eds.), *Research and practice in education: Building alliances, bridging the divide.* Lanham, MD: Rowman & Littlefield.

Takona, J. P. (2002). *Educational research: Principles and practice.* San Jose, CA: Writer's Club Press.

U.S. Department of Education, Institute of Education Sciences, National Center for Education Statistics. (2011). *Data tools.* Retrieved from http://nces.ed.gov/datatools

U.S. Department of Education, Institute of Education Sciences, What Works Clearinghouse. (2011). *About us.* Retrieved from http://ies.ed.gov/ncee/wwc/aboutus

Business Teacher Education: Preparation and Certification

Diane J. Fisher
The University of Southern Mississippi
Hattiesburg, MS

Barbara Hagler
Southern Illinois University
Carbondale, IL

Researchers have studied the effects of instruction on student learning for many years. After analyzing the achievement scores of more than 100,000 students, Wright, Horn, and Sanders (1997) concluded that the most important factor affecting student achievement is the teacher. In a 2004 study, Nye, Konstantopoulos, and Hedges determined that effective teachers make a significant difference in student achievement.

The preparation of all future educators is of critical importance to student achievement; the pedagogical skills learned in teacher preparation programs lay the foundation for the effectiveness of potential teachers. The purpose of this chapter is to report on business teacher education preparation practices, explore traditional versus alternative certification pathways, understand the challenge of recruiting future business teachers, and identify important factors in business teacher retention.

BUSINESS TEACHER EDUCATION PREPARATION PRACTICES

People enter business teacher education via a myriad of pathways. The following section will discuss the major routes to business teacher certification.

Baccalaureate-Level Program Preparation

Business teacher education programs are designed to prepare business teacher candidates for elementary, middle, secondary, and postsecondary schools. Individuals seeking admission into teacher preparation programs must meet admissions requirements established by the institution's professional education program. Some of these requirements may include passing the Praxis I test or equivalent, maintaining a cumulative grade point average set by the program, clearing a background check via a system established by the program, and completing student teaching. According to Feistritzer (1999), credit hours required to complete most teacher preparation programs in the United States range from 120 to 133 hours, comprising general studies, major studies, professional education studies, and clinical experiences.

Field-based experiences provide actual classroom practice to teacher candidates. The typical length of the practicum / student teaching experience is 14½–16 weeks of placement in varied classroom settings. About 86% of the field-based experiences available to students in initial teacher preparation programs have various clinical experiences throughout the program, and 72.3% have field-based experiences in a variety of demographically different schools (Feistritzer, 1999). To determine the skills most needed by student teachers, Crews and Bodenhamer (2009) obtained feedback from business educators currently in the field. The advice most frequently recommended was "Teach and complete grading and administrative duties" (p. 48). In addition, the researchers found the most important topic to teach in a business education methods course was classroom management and discipline followed by the development of lesson plans, projects, rubrics, assessments, etc.

In a study of nearly 3,000 beginning teachers, Darling-Hammond, Chung, and Frelow (2002) examined the differences among the preparation perceptions of teachers from different teacher education programs versus those who entered teaching without prior preparation. The study concluded that teachers prepared through a professional education program felt better equipped than those who entered the teaching field through alternative programs that minimized preservice training. Trends influencing teacher preparation indicate a need for additional "subject matter preparation, more intensive coursework on content pedagogy and strategies for meeting the needs of diverse learners, and more systematic and connected clinical experiences" (Darling-Hammond, et al., 2002, p. 290).

Statement No. 78 of the Policies Commission for Business and Economic Education (2006) supported the idea that business teacher education programs are developmental, cohesive, and collaborative. Business teacher program outcomes guide prospective teachers to become effective teachers through participation in multifaceted experiences.

Business teacher education programs are guided by the Business Teacher Education Program Standards developed by the National Association for Business Teacher Education (NABTE). NABTE is the official teacher education institutional division of the National Business Education Association (NBEA). The 16 preparatory program standards provide guidance for business education programs that lead to initial teacher preparation. The advanced business education program contains 17 standards to direct programs beyond the initial teacher certification (NBEA, 2010).

Graduate-Level Program Preparation

The purpose of graduate-level program preparation is to continue the development of knowledge, skills, and attitudes as an effective teacher. Business teachers study issues, trends, and problems in business education. In graduate programs, students learn ways to improve instruction, plan curriculum, use effectual assessment, and engage in meaningful research that informs educational planning. Graduate-level licensing is attractive to individuals who possess a bachelor's degree in business and then decide they want to teach (StateUniversity.Com, n.d.). Individuals with a nonteaching degree can earn initial certification from graduate-level teacher preparation programs.

A 1999 survey of institutions of higher education by the National Center for Education Information (NCEI) found that "55 percent of the individuals who were admitted into Teacher Preparation Programs at the post-baccalaureate level within the last year were transitioning into teaching from an occupation outside the field of education" (NCEI, n.d., para. 15). In 2011 the NCEI surveyed 2,500 randomly selected K–12 public school teachers and found that, whereas 65% (two-thirds) of teachers surveyed entered the teaching profession through a traditional teacher preparation program, 18% entered through a traditional graduate teacher education program and 16% entered the profession through alternate routes (Feistritzer, 2011).

Although most teachers are prepared as undergraduates, a growing number of teachers enter teacher preparation programs as graduate students. Twenty-eight percent of students studying to become teachers have at least one degree, and 79% of the degrees are in non-education fields (Roth & Swail, 2000).

Some graduate-level programs do not include a field-based experience component. Programs requiring a clinical experience reported that about 49% of the field-based experiences available to students in post-baccalaureate teacher preparation programs have various clinical experiences throughout the program and 44.7% have field-based experiences in a variety of demographically different schools (Feistritzer, 1999). Darling-Hammond (2000) reported that "teachers prepared in extended teacher education programs enter and remain in teaching at higher rates than teachers in traditional four-year programs, and remain at much higher rates than those prepared in short-term, alternative certification programs." (p. 21).

Alternative Certification Program Preparation

Alternate route preparation programs require teachers to be college graduates, and about 80% of the programs require teachers to demonstrate knowledge of subject matter by completing course work or passing a test. Alternate route degrees/programs include the master of arts in teaching (MAT), Teach for America, and urban teacher residencies (Wilson, 2009). The MAT degree program usually requires a minimum of

30 semester hours beyond the bachelor's degree. This graduate teacher preparation program can be beneficial to middle and secondary school teachers who earn degrees in a subject area and then acquire pedagogical skills during the MAT program (Wikipedia, 2010). Teach for America recruits individuals to be "corps members" for a two-year period in schools located in rural and urban low-income communities. Corps members receive intensive summer training before they begin teaching on an emergency credential. An urban residency model used by several programs selects candidates to work with an expert mentor teacher in a year-long residency. At the conclusion of the residency year, the candidate becomes credentialed, earns a master's degree from the partner university, and commits to teach in that district for three to five years (Wilson, 2009).

The Interstate New Teacher Assessment and Support Consortium, the National Board for Professional Teaching Standards, and the National Council for Accreditation of Teacher Education all support effective teaching and good classroom practice. "Where there is great concern is in the area of alternate and emergency certification and the ability of those teachers meeting the levels defined by these national groups" (Roth & Swail, 2000, p. 7). Although pre-service preparation of teachers typically occurs through state-accredited programs in institutions of higher learning, a variety of alternate programs now prepare teachers for the classroom. "More than a third of new teachers in California, New Jersey, and Texas enter teaching not from university programs but through alternate route programs offered by universities or districts" (Wilson, 2009, p. 2).

Alternative certification programs are designed to "increase the number of teachers available in specific subject areas, increase the number of teachers from underrepresented backgrounds, bring more teachers to rural or inner-city areas, and decrease the need for emergency certification" (Kwiatkowski, 1999, p. 216). Although limited research reports that alternate route programs indicate positive results for teacher success and retention, studies have not been completed that indicate the ability of alternative route programs to produce teachers who increase student achievement.

Business teacher education preparation practices typically follow the traditional pathway, through which students graduate from successful business teacher education programs guided by National Council for Accreditation of Teacher Education, Interstate New Teacher Assessment and Support Consortium, and NBEA standards. Statistics from NABTE show a decline in business teacher preparation programs from 305 NABTE programs in 1980 (Hagler, 2009) to 78 in 2011—a 74% decrease. As the number of business teacher education programs declines, individuals interested in becoming a business teacher will look to alternate certification program preparation. The next section of this chapter will address traditional versus alternative certification pathways.

TRADITIONAL VERSUS ALTERNATIVE CERTIFICATION PATHWAYS

Students desiring to become business teachers can choose between traditional certification programs and alternative certification programs. A student's educational background may make them eligible for an alternative certification program.

Traditional Certification

Cronin (as cited in Roth & Swail, 2000) stated "Certification is the process of deciding that an individual meets the minimum standards of competence in a profession. Licensing is the legal process of permitting a person to practice a trade or profession once he or she has met certification standards" (p. 9). The legal process of issuing licenses is handled by each state. When a student completes professional education programs at institutions authorized by the state, the student becomes a certified teacher and is licensed to teach in that state. Even though teachers are certified and licensed to teach in one state, they may not be licensed to teach in another state. Many states have created reciprocity agreements allowing teachers to teach across states. In addition, states accept teachers who have completed their education from member institutions of the National Council for Accreditation of Teacher Education (Roth & Swail, 2000).

Although licensure and certification requirements differ from state to state, most experts agree that teacher candidates should hold a bachelor's degree, complete an accredited education program with a major or minor in education (for elementary education) or a major in the subject area in which they plan to teach (for middle- or high-school teaching), and pass the appropriate exam. This traditional route to certification has received scrutiny as evidenced by the abundance of programs designed to provide alternative methods of certification.

Alternative and Emergency Certification

For the past century, institutions of higher learning have been educating prospective teachers and certifying to the state that these teachers are qualified to teach. A significant increase in states allowing alternative methods of certification is occurring. In 1983 only eight states allowed alternative certification (Roth & Swail, 2000), while currently 48 states and the District of Columbia offer alternative teacher certification (National Center for Alternative Certification, n.d.-a). According to the National Center for Alternative Certification, 27 states offer alternative certification in technology education and 21 states offer alternative certification in vocational/technical education (National Center for Alternative Certification, n.d.-b).

The purpose of alternative certification is to offer a pathway for individuals to enter teaching without graduating from a four-year traditional undergraduate teacher preparation program. Alternate route certification allows individuals who hold bachelor's degrees in areas other than education to earn professional teaching certificates or licensure. These certificates/licenses are normally issued to potential teachers who plan to teach in their major field of study. Alternate route certification allows professionals to begin teaching while they are concurrently enrolled in an alternative certification preparation program (The Teacher Center, n.d.). Alternatively certified teachers are typically more diverse and older, and have significant professional experience other than education. These teachers "are able to teach in areas with context-specific needs, while traditional certification places more emphasis on expanding a prospective teacher's grasp of effective pedagogy" (Stoddart & Floden, cited in Roth & Swail, 2000, p. 12).

NCEI estimated that more than 125,000 teachers have been certified through alternative methods in the past 20 years. Interest in alternative certification programs stems from a need to address teacher shortage issues, a concern with teacher quality, and a desire to allow individuals who are perceived to have skills needed by schools to enter teaching. The movement from the traditional certification pathway to alternative methods of teacher certification may indicate that the quality of teaching is far more important than the method by which a teacher became credentialed. Alternative pathways to teacher certification are attracting teachers into the classroom (Roth & Swail, 2000).

In addition, emergency certification is used in specific and crisis situations such as teacher shortages, subject-need areas, or geographic-need areas and is issued on a temporary basis. Teachers are typically granted emergency certification for a certain period and are expected to become fully licensed within that time frame. If the teacher working under emergency certification does not become certified, he or she is replaced by a fully certified teacher.

Future Delivery of Business Education

Good teachers produce successful students. A 1996 report by the National Commission on Teaching and America's Future indicated that "fully prepared teachers are more highly rated and more effective with students than those whose background lacks one or more of the elements of formal teacher education—subject matter preparation, knowledge about teaching and learning, and guided clinical experience" (Roth & Swail, 2000, p. 20).

To make the best use of teacher resources, decisionmakers must determine how business education is going to be offered in each state. Although existing business teacher education programs offer a successful pathway to teacher certification, a broader, more flexible pathway may include offering more online courses and developing more online programs.

A study conducted by Fisher (2004) revealed that most business education courses for pre-service teachers are not offered online. Only 14% of the faculty surveyed who teach a methods course teach the course online. Changes to teacher preparation programs may include the development of online programs to attract future business teachers. The flexibility of online learning may be beneficial for students who must work while completing a degree and for professionals who are considering entering the teaching field. Additionally, research shows that traditionally trained teachers are more likely to remain in the classroom, which leads to the challenges of recruiting future teachers.

CHALLENGES OF RECRUITING FUTURE BUSINESS TEACHERS

Several challenges exist when recruiting future business teachers. Hagler (2009) reported that 57% of the respondents to the NABTE survey believed demand exceeded supply for secondary business teachers. Based on many predictions by business education associations, there will be a great need for business teachers in the near future. One of the main reasons for this increased need for business teachers is the retirement of many baby boomer teachers. Another reason identified by Hagler (2009) was the fact that low teacher pay made it difficult to recruit business education teachers. Students are often attracted to highly publicized occupations with high salaries. Carnevale, Strohl, and Melton (2011) of the Georgetown University Center on Education and the Workforce recently released a report summarizing the economic value of 171 specific majors. The highest-earning major, petroleum engineering, reported a median income of $120,000. An education major was among the lowest paying with a median income of $42,000. Gaytan (2008) cited low salary as a reason students choose to not enter business education. The next section introduces some current recruiting practices that appear to be successful.

Recruitment Practices

Teacher recruitment practices vary from area to area. Some recruiting practices are based on the special needs of the area. For example, urban areas have some unique challenges, as do rural areas. Urban areas face critical shortages. According to Morgan and Kristonis (2008):

> A shortage of quality teachers in high-risk urban schools has compelled school leaders to examine innovative methods of recruiting and retaining new teachers to hard-to-staff campuses. Principals must work aggressively to attract new teachers to their campuses by forming university partnerships for early recruitment, and initiating on the job training for new recruits as early as the previous school year. (p. 1)

Rural schools, according to Beesley, Atwill, Blair, and Barley (2010) have problems with recruiting because they often offer lower salaries and have smaller schools in remote locations. Teachers in these schools often teach several different courses, possibly in more than one subject area. A business education teacher in a rural school may find he/she is the only business education teacher in that school. Thus, a shortage of subject-matter mentors may exist.

California is one state experiencing a shortage of teachers. Among several suggestions made by the California Department of Education on recruitment of highly qualified teachers in a 2006 white paper by the California Department of Education are the following:

- Statewide teacher recruitment centers that provide online information on teaching opportunities and submission of applications.

- Teacher recruitment incentives, including signing bonuses, salary enhancements, improved working conditions, and housing subsidies, as well as bonuses and differential pay in the teacher shortage areas of science and mathematics, English learners, and special education.

- Recruitment of individuals from high-tech industry, state and federal government, and the military to become teachers (e.g., Troops to Teachers Program). Credential reciprocation with other states to facilitate recruitment of teachers from out of state. (para. 5)

Impact of Certification Requirements

Teacher certification requirements vary from state to state. Even within each state, certification requirements may differ for initial versus alternative certification. Most teacher education programs require a series of classroom observations before student teaching.

Effectiveness of Pre-Service Teacher Preparation

Pre-service teacher preparation programs vary in their effectiveness according to the literature (Gaytan, 2008). Some of the harshest criticism regarding teacher preparation programs is related to the alternative certification programs. Darling-Hammond (2000) reported that about 60% of individuals who enter through alternative certification programs leave teaching by their third year, compared with about 30% of traditionally trained teachers. Some alternative certification programs do not require the in-depth observations and methods courses of initial certification programs.

In addition, with the decline in the number of institutions offering traditional business education teacher certification programs, some institutions do not have specialized methods courses for their students. Some of these students criticized the lack of preparation, especially in areas of classroom management (Darling-Hammond & Berry, n.d.; Yohon, 2005). This lack of quality pre-service teacher preparation may result in teachers leaving the profession. The next section of this chapter addresses the issues of retention of new business teachers.

RETENTION OF NEW BUSINESS TEACHERS

Business education teachers, like other professionals, often do not stay at their first job for very long. According to the National Education Association (NEA) (2010), more than 40% of new teachers leave the profession in the first five years. Sometimes they use the first job as an opportunity to get some experience and then move to the location of their choice. At other times and what is more alarming in many ways, the business education teacher does not feel he or she made a wise career choice and leaves the school as well as the profession. What can be done to retain business education teachers?

Primary Factors Affecting Teacher Retention

Many factors affect teacher retention, including personal reasons. When a teacher leaves for personal reasons, there may not be anything that could or should be changed. However, in some situations, there are concerns about preparation or job-related factors that affect a teacher's decision to resign.

"Inadequate ongoing job-embedded professional development" was identified by the American Federation of Teachers (2007, p. 21) as a factor contributing to teachers leaving a school or the profession. Hiring schools should be willing to invest in professional development for their new teachers. Allowing teachers to attend professional conferences may be a way for them to learn strategies for their success. These conferences also allow them to network with other teachers who may be experiencing the same issues or who have experienced the same issues and were able to resolve them.

Ruhland (2001) identified retention factors of business education teachers. Some of these factors were salaries, stress, classroom management issues, and lack of administrative support. A factor that increased retention was a positive work climate. Administrators should consider all of these factors and do whatever they can to retain their teachers.

Another factor affecting teaching retention identified by McLaurin, Smith, and Smillie (2009) was accountability under the No Child Left Behind Act of 2001 (2002). To meet this act's highly qualified teacher criteria, some technically qualified teachers were required to return to school. However, some teachers were certified quickly and placed in the classroom before they were fully prepared for the classroom experience. Darling-Hammond (2003) also identified the lack of teacher preparation as a major factor affecting retention and recommended a five-year preparation as opposed to the regular four-year preparation. She reported that graduates of five-year programs reported "higher levels of satisfaction with their preparation and received higher ratings from principals and colleagues" (p. 5).

Teacher Accountability

Standards established by the NBEA are closely aligned with what teachers actually need to know and be able to do. When teachers are confident about what is expected of them, they become more effective. Effective teachers are usually more likely to remain in the profession. Stress will not be as great a factor, and teachers will feel more positive about teaching. Because of less stress and more positive feelings about teaching, these effective teachers will be more likely to continue teaching.

Gillies, Hite, and Evans (2003) reported that teachers without intense preparation left teaching in greater numbers than teachers with strong initial preparation. Their findings supported many other studies indicating that weak preparation is a major factor in the effectiveness of teachers as well as determining the length of time teachers remain in the profession.

Teacher retention is related to multiple factors. School leaders have many important roles and responsibilities to retain the teachers in whom their districts have invested. The American Federation of Teachers offered the following statement:

> It is clear from this list that teachers are attracted to, and most likely to remain in, schools in which the environment is conducive to teaching and learning, where safety and order are priorities, where they have influence over decisions that affect their school and its programs, where they feel supported by those in charge and where they have opportunities to develop professionally. (2007, p. 4)

School administrators need to consider seriously all of these factors and implement as many things as they can to create a positive environment for the teachers.

New Teacher Mentoring

Mentoring has been supported by many studies and is considered to be critical to teacher retention (Ingersoll & Kralik, 2004; Yohon, 2005). If the teacher has a mentor, even if not in the same building or school, they tend to remain on the job. If they do not have a mentor, they are more likely to leave the job and even the profession. Morgan and Kristonis (2008) suggested that "Hard-to-staff campuses must invest in a full-time teacher mentor as well as retired teachers to provide intense mentorship and relevant professional training" (p. 1).

Yohon (2005) found that "experienced teachers are willing to mentor new teachers via e-mail" (p. 63.) Even if the mentor is in another school, the relationship between mentor and mentee can be meaningful. A new teacher has many things to learn, and having a mentor to support them in this learning process can make the process much less stressful.

SUMMARY

This chapter has examined business teacher education practices and pathways, as well as recruitment and retention of teachers. Individuals may enter the teaching profession via baccalaureate-level program preparation, graduate-level program preparation, or alternative certification program preparation. Although many new business teachers receive their degrees through traditional baccalaureate teacher preparation programs, alternative certification programs are steadily attracting increasing numbers of students. Furthermore, research indicates that individuals obtaining licensure through graduate-level program preparation enter and remain in teaching at higher rates than four-year or alternative certification programs.

The No Child Left Behind Act of 2001 (2002) requires schools to hire highly qualified teachers. Because effective teachers make a significant difference in student achievement, business teacher preparation programs must follow the NABTE Business Teacher Education Program Standards and work hard to recruit and retain students in their programs to ensure that qualified teachers are available to fill business education positions at all educational levels. The better prepared new teachers are for the classroom, the more likely they will stay in the field and continue to be an asset to business education.

With the expected shortage of business teachers on the horizon, school leaders must engage in innovative teacher recruitment practices and/or incentives. By investing in professional development and providing mentors to new teachers, school leaders support teachers, making it more likely they will remain at their current schools and in the business education profession.

REFERENCES

American Federation of Teachers. (2007). *Meeting the challenge: Retaining teachers in hard-to-staff schools.* Washington, DC: Author.

Beesley, A. D., Atwill, K., Blair, P., & Barley, Z. A. (2010). Strategies for recruitment and retention of secondary teachers in central U.S. rural schools. *Rural Educator 31*(2), 1–9.

StateUniversity.com. (n.d.). Business education—Preparation of teachers. *Education Encyclopedia.* Retrieved from http://education.stateuniversity.com/pages/1806/Business-Education-PREPARATION-TEACHERS.html

California Department of Education. (2006). *Developing highly qualified teachers and administrators: A white paper on developing highly qualified teachers and administrators for California Schools.* Sacramento, CA: California Department of Education.

Carnevale, A. P., Strohl, J., & Melton, M. (2011). *What's it worth? The economic value of college majors.* Retrieved from http://www9.georgetown.edu/grad/gppi/hpi/cew/pdfs/whatsitworth-complete.pdf

Crews, T. B., & Bodenhamer, J. (2009). Preparing student teaching interns: Advice from current business educators. *Delta Pi Epsilon Journal, LI*(1), 43–55.

Darling-Hammond, L. (2000). *Solving the dilemmas of teacher supply, demand, and standards: How we can ensure a competent, caring, and qualified teacher for every child.* (Report No. UD 034 850). Kutztown, PA: National Commission on Teaching and America's Future. Retrieved from http://www.nctaf.org/documents/supply-demand-standards.pdf

Darling-Hammond, L. (2003). Keeping good teachers: Why it matters, what leaders can do. *Educational Leadership, 60*(8), 6.

Darling-Hammond, L., & Berry, B. (n.d.). *Recruiting teachers for the 21st century: The foundation for educational equity.* Retrieved from http://www.teachingquality.org/pdfs/RecruitingTeachersforthe21stCentury.pdf

Darling-Hammond, L., Chung, R., & Frelow, F. (2002). Variation in teacher preparation: How well do different pathways prepare teachers to teach? *Journal of Teacher Education 53*(4) 286–302.

Feistritzer, C. E. (1999). *The making of a teacher: A report on teacher preparation in the United States.* Washington, DC: The Center for Education Information. Retrieved from http://www.ncei.com/MOT/MOT-5.htm

Feistritzer, C. E. (2011). *Profile of teachers in the U.S. 2011*. Washington, DC: The National Center for Education Information. Retrieved from http://www.ncei.com/Profile_Teachers_US_2011.pdf

Fisher, D. J. (2004) An investigation into the attitudes toward and participation in online instruction among higher education business education faculty at NABTE institutions. *NABTE Review*, (31), 36–43.

Gaytan, J. (2008). Teacher recruitment and retention: An essential step in the development of a system of quality teaching. *Career and Technical Education Research, 33*(2), 117–132.

Gillies, W., Hite, C. E., & Evans, L. (2003). It's not the kids! Advice for beginning teachers. *Florida Educational Leadership, 3*(2), 21–25.

Hagler, B. (2009). *Business education in the United States: 2006–2007 NABTE survey results*. Southern Illinois University–Carbondale, Carbondale, IL.

Ingersoll, R., & Kralik, J. M. (2004, February). *The impact of mentoring on teacher retention: What the research says*. Retrieved from http://www.ecs.org/clearinghouse/50/36/5036.htm

Kwiatkowski, M. (1999). Debating alternative teacher certification: A trial by achievement. In M. Kanstoroom & C. E. Finn, Jr. (Eds.), *Better teachers, better schools*, (pp. 215–238). Washington. DC: Thomas B. Fordham Foundation.

McLaurin, S. E., Smith, W., & Smillie, A. (2009). *Teacher retention: Problems and solutions*. Retrieved from http://www.eric.ed.gov/ERICWebPortal/detail?accno=ED507446

Morgan, M. M., & Kritsonis, W. A. (2008). A national focus: The recruitment, retention, and development of quality teachers in hard-to-staff schools. *National Journal for Publishing and Mentoring Doctoral Student Research, 5*(1), 1–7.

NBEA. (2007). *National standards for business education* (3rd ed.). Reston, VA: Author.

NBEA. (2010). *Business teacher education curriculum guide and program standards*. Reston, VA: Author.

National Center for Alternative Certification. (n.d.-a). *Introduction and overview*. Retrieved from http://www.teach-now.org/intro.cfm

National Center for Alternative Certification. (n.d.-b). *My Teach-Now!* Retrieved from http://www.teach-now.org/index.cfm

National Center for Education Information. (1999). *Alternate routes to teacher certification: An overview*. Retrieved from http://www.ncei.com/Alt-Teacher-Cert.htm#6

National Education Association. (n.d.). *Research spotlight on recruiting & retaining highly qualified teachers*. Retrieved from https://www.nea.org/tools/17054.htm

No Child Left Behind Act of 2001. H.R. 1, 107th Cong. Pub. L. No. 107-110, 115 Stat. 1426 (2002) (enacted).

Nye, B., Konstantopoulos, S., & Hedges, L. V. (2004). How large are teacher effects? *Educational Evaluation Policy Analysis, 26*(3), 237–257.

Policies Commission for Business and Economic Education. (2006). *Policy Statement 78: This we believe about business teacher education programs*. Reston, VA: National Business Education Association.

Roth, D., & Swail, W. S. (2000, November). *Certification and teacher preparation in the United States.* Pacific Resources for Education and Learning. Retrieved from http://www.educationalpolicy.org/pdf/PREL%20Certification.pdf

Ruhland, S. K. (2001). Factors influencing the retention of secondary business teachers. *Delta Pi Epsilon Journal, 43*(4), 215–228.

The Teacher Center. (n.d.). *Alternative certification for "career changers" and recent college graduates.* Retrieved from http://www.theteachercenter.org/NewTeacher/GeneralInfo/altern_cert.asp

Wikipedia. (2010). *Masters of arts in teaching.* Retrieved from http://en.wikipedia.org/wiki/Master_of_Arts_in_Teaching

Wilson, S. (Ed.). (2009). *Teacher quality* (Education Policy White Paper). Retrieved from National Academy of Education Web site: http://www.naeducation.org/Teacher_Quality_White_Paper.pdf

Wright, S. P., Horn, S. P., & Sanders, W. L. (1997). Teacher and classroom context effects on student achievement: Implications for teacher evaluation. *Journal of Personnel Evaluation in Education, 11,* 57–67.

Yohon, R. (2005). Investigation of the challenges, mentoring needs, and support for business and marketing teachers. *Delta Pi Epsilon Journal, 47*(2), 53–66.